IRISH DEMESNE LANDSCAPES, 1660–1740

This book charts the history and development of formal gardening in Ireland in the late seventeenth and early eighteenth centuries, and in particular the grand geometric style garden that was fashionable between 1660 and 1740. It examines the people who created these gardens, the influences that affected them, the materials that they employed and the uses of landscape interventions. Using a wide range of sources, including several previously unpublished, this is the most extensive survey of early Irish gardens to date.

VANDRA COSTELLO has taught courses on garden history at University College Dublin, Ulster University and University of Limerick. She is the garden editor of Image Interiors & Living magazine.

Irish Demesne Landscapes, 1660–1740

VANDRA COSTELLO

FOUR COURTS PRESS

Typeset in 10.5 pt on 13.5 pt CaslonPro by
Carrigboy Typesetting Services for
FOUR COURTS PRESS LTD
7 Malpas Street, Dublin 8, Ireland
www.fourcourtspress.ie
and in North America for
FOUR COURTS PRESS
c/o ISBS, 920 NE 58th Avenue, Suite 300, Portland, OR 97213.

A catalogue record for this title is available
from the British Library.

ISBN 978-1-84682-596-5 pbk

SPECIAL ACKNOWLEDGMENT

This publication has been made possible by financial assistance from the
Marc Fitch Fund for Research and Publication (established by Marcus Felix
Brudenell Fitch CBE DLitt HonFBA FSA in 1956).

MARC FITCH FUND

Printed in Ireland
by SPRINT-Print, Dublin.

Contents

Acknowledgments

THERE ARE A NUMBER of people to whom I owe a debt of gratitude for helping me along the long and tortuous path to completion of this book. It wouldn't even have begun without the support of Dr John Olley and Professor Loughlin Kealy of University College Dublin. Huge assistance was given to me by the ever-patient and knowledgeable library staff from the following (in no particular order) institutions: the British Library Manuscript's Room, the Irish Architectural Archive, the Royal Society of Antiquaries of Ireland, the Royal Irish Academy, the Duke Humfrey's library, the Bodleian Library Oxford, Archbishop Marsh's Library, the National Library of Ireland, Early Printed Books and Manuscript departments of Trinity College Dublin Library, the Royal Irish Academy, and, in particular, Maureen Comber of Clare County Library, Ian Montgomery of the Public Record Office of Northern Ireland and Gregory O'Connor of the National Archives of Ireland. To all the generous landowners and custodians of demesne lands who allowed me the freedom to wander up hill and down dale on their property or to rummage around their archives a great big thank you is due; these include Adrian Cosby, Norman Ievers, Thomas Pakenham, the Earl and Countess of Rosse, Julian Gaisford St Lawrence, the Earl of Meath and Lord Ardee. Great assistance and/or encouragement was also given to me by Peter Bland, David Bland, Professor Rolf Loeber, Professor Toby Barnard, Christopher Catling, Judith Gantly, Eliza Chisholm, Belinda Jupp, Kieran McLaughlin, Clodagh Hannon, William Laffan, Livia Hurley, Des Byrne and Jill O'Connell.

Financial support towards the production of the book was provided by the Marc Fitch Fund and the Royal Horticultural Society of Ireland. A wonderful place to work was given to me by the Ireland Fund of France, and the Princess Grace Irish Library of Monaco.

Four Courts Press demonstrated the patience of saints with me and corrected my rather seventeenth-century use of unnecessary capitalization and erratic spelling.

Finally, thank you to my husband Kevin and daughter Millie for being so full of love and enthusiasm.

Illustrations

PLATES
appear between pages 128 and 129.

Preface

MY INTRODUCTION TO SEVENTEENTH-CENTURY gardening came about when, in 2001, an interest in the diaries of Samuel Pepys led me to begin reading another seventeenth-century diarist, John Evelyn. What particularly fascinated me about Evelyn's diary were the many references to gardens in Ireland. Evelyn was a friend of Henry Hyde, the earl of Clarendon, who was, for a time, lord lieutenant of Ireland, and they corresponded about estate and horticultural matters. This topic led me to an article by Toby Barnard on Irish gardens in the Cromwellian period,[1] which compelled me to dig further into the history of gardening in Ireland. Serendipity had a part to play in encouraging me to pursue this line of study further, when visiting London I happened upon the Chelsea Physic Garden, founded by an Irish man, Sir Hans Sloane.

This book is an attempt to describe the demesne landscapes of Ireland in the late seventeenth and early eighteenth centuries. This was when the formal, symmetrical style of garden was fashionable, heavily influenced by French, Dutch and Italian garden design. The study begins at 1660, the date of the restoration of the crown to Charles II who spent his period of exile on the Continent where he and his court (in particular James Butler, later 1st duke of Ormond) developed a taste for the continental style of gardening. The study ends at around 1740 when the geometric or *grand siècle* style of garden became deeply unfashionable and most such landscapes were superseded by the advent of the English landscape garden as conceived by William Kent, Charles Bridgeman and Lancelot 'Capability' Brown.

This is not a theoretical study of garden design but is a descriptive study of the features and elements of demesne landscapes and the reasons behind those landscape interventions. Every element of the designed demesne landscape had an aesthetic and utilitarian element. The survey is based on existing physical features, archival sources, mapping and the literature, guide books and gardening manuals of the late seventeenth and early eighteenth centuries.

The survey begins by looking at the political and intellectual background to Ireland during the late-seventeenth century. Chapters 1 and 2 consider the changing appearance of the Irish landscape in the late seventeenth century and the response of English settlers to their new environment. In chapter 3 the concept of improvement and the garden is examined. Chapter 4 examines the pleasure garden and the various features within it. *Utile et dulce* were combined to the most aesthetically pleasing and economically sound effect. Subsequent chapters examine the advances made in horticulture, the use of trees and timber plantations, botanical studies and the physic garden, and the use and control of water and hydraulic improvements. The book concludes with a description of the role of parks for field sports and domestic animals.

For consistency, names have been spelled the same way throughout even though they appear in a number of forms in manuscript and other sources. Seventeenth-century spelling was rather erratic and use of capital letters quaint, so most anachronisms have been corrected for the modern reader.

CHAPTER I

The political, intellectual and economic background to landed estates

Those few Irish we have amongst us are very much reclaimed of their barbarous customs, the most of them speaking English and for agriculture they are little inferior to the English themselves; in a word the fertility of the soil the curious enclosures, the shady groves and delicate seats, that are everywhere dispersed over this barony doe all concur to make it a paradise of pleasures.[1]

WHEN THE FIRST PARLIAMENT convened in Ireland after Restoration in July 1661, the immediate task facing the administration was the re-distribution of land. This was an intractable problem with no satisfactory solution. There were so many diverse and conflicting claims for land in Ireland that it was impossible to satisfy everyone. In the late seventeenth-century land in Ireland was a valuable possession. Writing in 1910, Robert Pentland Mahaffy noted that 'Ireland was looked on in the period of the Restoration in much the same way as land in Canada is looked upon in England in the present day'.[2] Ireland's strategic value to ambitious Englishmen was high, the lord lieutenancy of Ireland 'being one of the greatest employments his Majesty has to give'.[3] Throughout the Cromwellian period some Royalists, such as the 1st duke of Ormond,[4] managed to hold on to some of their land for use of their wives and children[5] but most had forfeited their estates.

The Commissioners appointed to administer the Act of Settlement 1662 were constituted as a Court of Claims. Broadly speaking, it was proposed that Cromwellian supporters who were in possession of land granted for money or services given to the cause should have that land confiscated. Royalists who had supported Charles I or Charles II in Ireland and abroad should have lands that they had owned prior to 1641 restored. Preference was to be given to claimants who followed the King into exile (ahead of those who had chosen to stay, accepting lands in Connaught). The King was also keen to reward those loyal and hardworking officials who helped prosecute the settlement.[6]

Irish gentry, who in many cases were allied to the Anglo-Irish Royalists – more anti-Cromwell than anti-Crown – also sought to have their land restored.

Ireland's social elite at the close of the seventeenth century was composed principally of first-generation English settlers and the descendants of the Elizabethan and Jacobean settlements of the fifteenth and sixteenth centuries together with landowners of Anglo-Norman and Gaelic origin who successfully adopted English customs and manners. Alliances between these groups were secured by judicious marriages,[7] ensuring, as Jane Austen would later so minutely observe, that the right connections were made.[8] The elite became intricately and intimately connected to each other, the Court and even the Monarchy itself through familial relations. These connections ensured that nepotism prevailed in political appointments and offices, many of which generated substantial incomes and entitlements to lands for their holders. The shifting sands of political allegiance were reflected in land ownership. In the first half of the seventeenth century the great Kildare estates of Castletown and Carton[9] were owned respectively by the Dongans[10] and the Talbots, both Roman Catholic. By the end of the century, both estates were owned by Protestant families, the Conollys and the FitzGeralds. In both cases, the families were closely allied: William Dongan was married to Richard Talbot's sister, and the Conollys and FitzGeralds were famously united in marriage to two Lennox sisters, Caroline and Emily.

English impressions of Ireland and the Irish

In the years following the Restoration of Charles II in 1660, the wealth and prosperity of Ireland grew considerably. The lord lieutenant, Arthur Capel, earl of Essex,[11] remarked in 1673 that 'The city of Dublin is now very near if not altogether twice as big as it was at his Majesty's Restoration'.[12] A view which was confirmed by Sir William Petty,[13] who, having spent more than three decades in Ireland, wrote that 'In domestic wealth of which sort is building fine houses and gardens, orchards, groves … the improvement of Ireland has since the year 1642 [to] 1673 advanced from one to four, and I think to a better state than before 1641, that is, than perhaps ever it yet was'.[14]

The Restoration settlers retained the suspicion that the Irish were somehow feckless and in need of constant paternalistic supervision. Sir William Petty, who was genuinely sympathetic to the Irish and had a real interest in improving living standards, was of the view that English rule was good for the Irish and had generally improved the life of the Irish.[15] The established plantations – places where English customs and manners prevailed – were seen as models for the rest of the country for the redemption of the Irish population at large. Uncultivated land was regarded as symbolic of 'uncultivated men'.[16] Sir John Davies wrote in 1610 that the Irish, through their own naivety, had failed to exploit their land to its best advantage and was of the opinion that 'it stands neither with Christian policy nor conscience to suffer so good and fruitful country to lie waste like a wilderness'.[17]

Several English visitors and settlers expressed a less than enthusiastic view of the country with one commentator moved to say 'I find little or nothing that can be said of this country that may not be said indifferently of all'.[18] Another unidentified author, who accepted the popular wisdom that it was a badge of civility to have a well-run estate, was shocked by what he found in Ireland, laying the blame fairly and squarely at the door of the colonists and great landowners:

> It tastes of the savage to see an ancient estated family continue to live in the country on their lands, yet without a tolerable habitation: without the decorums of garden and pomaryes: without meadows and enclosed pastures; without the coverture and embellishment of quicks and trees: without in fin anything that may speak of a gentle and wise economy.[19]

The Jacobite War of 1689–91 had caused destruction throughout the countryside. Many great houses, including Burton and Castlemartyr, were laid waste by soldiers.[20] The billeting of soldiers on country estates was a frequent cause of complaint. Their encampments ruined crops and often woodlands.[21] This destruction of the landscape unravelled many of the advances made in the years prior to 1660 but it also left the great estates ripe for redevelopment and re-planning once the war was over.

The war, later billed the Glorious Revolution (1688–9), was a Protestant victory with William and Mary ascending the throne. Many Old English Catholic Jacobites, such as Nicholas Plunkett, found their lands forfeited again. To their dismay, they were permanently dispossessed and went into exile.[22] Others such as Thomas Dongan, the 3rd earl of Limerick, who was restored to his substantial estates at Castletown Kildrought in Kildare, sold the lands to the Conolly family who developed Castletown, which became a great eighteenth-century estate.[23] In 1687 Dongan obtained an estate of 25,000 acres on Staten Island in New York which he named 'Cassiltowne' in memory of his old Irish home; among other things the estate had a manor house, a grist mill and a hunting lodge.[24]

New towns

Many new towns were created post Restoration. Some were incorporated under royal charters[25] while others were established and grew up without the benefit of a charter.[26] These new towns were usually situated adjacent to a demesne with a great house at its centre. The towns housed industry and labourers who, directly or indirectly, contributed to the demesne economy. The main avenue to a great house was, in most cases, planned as a straight approach usually on an axis with a feature in the town such as a church, as at Blessington. The new towns were often heavily populated with English, Dutch and French Huguenot tenants, encouraged to move to Ireland in order to promote the agricultural, horticultural and linen industries.[27] The towns were intended to look like English or Dutch towns; for example, Robert Molesworth wanted Phillipstown in Offaly (now Daingean) to have trees planted along the street 'before the doors with a row on each side like a Dutch town; it is a Dutch situation already by reason of the bogs and rivers', and recommended planting of it with 'elm or oaks, or (if those cannot be had) with strong ash or abeles'.[28] Some fine planned towns were created and the layouts of many survive today. These include Sir William Petty's Kenmare in Kerry, George Lane, Viscount Lanesborough's Lanesborough in Longford, Henry Bennet, the earl of Arlington's Portarlington (designed for him by Sir George Rawdon), John Eyre's Eyrecourt in Galway, Archbishop Michael Boyle's Blessington in Wicklow and Roger Boyle, earl of Orrery's Charleville in Cork.

Each town had at least one Protestant church or meeting house; many had free schools, alms-houses and hospitals. With the possible exception of Charleville, most had a substantial 'native' Irish population, who tended to live in their own quarters in traditional thatched houses or mud cabins just outside the town boundaries, hence the frequently-seen placename 'Irishtown'.[29]

Infrastructural improvements were undertaken by local landowners in their areas of jurisdiction. Richard Dobbs,[30] writing in 1683, noted that the highways of Lambeg in Antrim were very good due to the efforts of Sir George Rawdon[31] on behalf of the Conway estate at Portmore.[32] The improved demesne landscape influenced the layout of estate towns and beauty and utility were combined to the best advantage. The placement of municipal buildings and public works were designed to enhance and add to the unified and ordered appearance of the demesne itself. Pole Cosby,[33] boasting of his improvements, recorded that in 1698 'the town of Stradbally was no town, no more even a village, for there were ... but two stone houses in it and those but about six feet height, and a few mud and wattled walled cabins'; he continued that his father was 'ever doing some improvement or other, for Stradbally when he came to it ... it was but a rough uncouth place'.[34] The earl of Burlington was pleased with the plans for a new bridge at Tallow, 'I like [it] very well, for it will be an advantage to the park as well as a public good'.[35]

What is particularly striking about Ireland in the late seventeenth and early eighteenth centuries, is just how cosmopolitan and multi-ethnic it was. Those living in coastal towns were continually exposed to foreigners and exotic produce as everything imported into the country was channelled through the ports. Cargo ships from the West Indies and Americas, and slave ships, regularly dropped anchor in the western seaboard ports.[36] Ships from Europe arrived in the southern and eastern ports. Thousands of English, Dutch and French Huguenot families settled in Ireland, encouraged by laws passed that welcomed them into Ireland, and by the offer of certain employment and housing on arrival.[37] This was an attractive proposition, especially to the French Huguenots, to whom Ireland offered a welcome refuge from the persecution they faced at home. The inns and a few new coffee and chocolate houses of Dublin were not merely recreational places; they were places where correspondence was distributed, and political and scientific discussion took place. This discourse had a direct effect on how people viewed the wider world and dealt with and managed their estates. The Dublin Philosophical Society met regularly and had a continuing discourse with fellow natural scientists and historians in England and the Continent. Most of its members were prominent landowners, and keen to discuss horticulture and botany. Others like Sir Richard Bulkeley of Old Bawn in Tallaght continued their scientific and agricultural endeavours at home.[38]

The combination, during the reign of Charles II, of relative political calm, general physical reconstruction and new wealth provided the environment in which a group of landowners established their seats in Ireland and transformed the appearance of the Irish landscape.

CHAPTER 2

The changing appearance of the Irish landscape in the seventeenth century

IT IS A COMMON ASSUMPTION that Ireland lay bereft and neglected during the seventeenth century while England, with numerous great houses and gardens, prospered.[1] The evidence available does not support this contention. In fact, England suffered greatly during the Civil War, was not bejewelled with sophisticated landscape projects, and lagged greatly behind France and Italy. As in Ireland, many seats in England (such as Althorp) were destroyed by Commonwealth forces during the Civil War.[2] John Evelyn's diary gives countless examples of post-Civil War improvements and repairs carried out on the great estates of England. Evelyn wrote in 1661 that Charles II 'discoursed to me of the improvement of gardens and buildings (now very rare in England, comparatively to other countries)'.[3] In June 1662 work was underway at Hampton Court gardens, 'formerly a flat, naked piece of ground'.[4] The English seats of Irish landowners, such as those of Lord Arlington and others, were rebuilt and improved at the same time as work was going on at their seats in Ireland.[5] In his essay on gardening, *Upon the gardens of Epicurus*, Sir William Temple[6] confirmed that gardening in England had only taken off and reached new heights since the Restoration, writing that gardens had been:

> Mightily improved in three or four and twenty years of his Majesty's reign, that perhaps few countries are before us, either in the elegance of our gardens, or in the number of our plants; and, I believe none equal us in the variety of fruits which may be justly called good; and from the earliest cherry and strawberry, to the last apples and pears, may furnish every day of the circling year.[7]

The burst of improvements seen in England after the Restoration also took place in Ireland. Gardening trends were brought to Ireland from the Continent. Just as the political power and wealth of France was reflected in its magnificent palace gardens,[8] English territorial ambitions and presence were expressed in the demesnes of Ireland. The superior taste, education and culture of the colonists were demonstrated by their improvements to buildings, gardens, model farms, agricultural innovations, plantations, statuary and hydraulic achievements.

It is accepted by most, if not by all, art and literary historians that landscape design and aesthetics reflect the political ideology and prevailing philosophy of the garden's owner and designer. In Britain especially, the division between Whig and Tory tastes is said to be reflected in architecture and landscape. In the late eighteenth century, neo-classical landscapes and Palladian villas came to be associated with Whiggish politics, while the old geometric-style gardens were thought to be indicative of Toryism. The rigid design of 'absolutist' gardens was seen as representing the Tory ideology – a reverence for the monarchy, logic, order and control, both of nature and man. A more commonplace explanation for a Tory adherence to the *grand siècle* style may be that conservative traditionalists liked to preserve old customs, habits and fashions, while those of a more liberal tendency embrace new fashions and styles more readily.

It has been suggested that arguments about the aesthetics of landscape were almost always arguments about politics.[9] The notion that a landscape can describe or express its owner's ideology is a complicated one. How do you demonstrate political and social ideas through landscape? Not all landowners were intellectuals or philosophers. Obviously the appearance of a garden will indicate its owners taste, and level of sophistication. An effort was made by all improving landowners to combine art and nature to the greatest extent, but discerning the political leanings of late seventeenth- and early eighteenth-century Irish landowners from their gardens is more complicated. The difference in gardening styles did not become explicit until the latter part of the eighteenth century. The impetus to show variety, productivity, scientific development and technology in the garden was not the exclusive preserve of those of a Whig political persuasion.[10] Equally, gardens owned by high Whigs such as Molesworth's Breckdenston conformed to the classical seventeenth-century layout with its hierarchy of avenues and dense forest planting.[11]

The Whig and Tory parties only appeared in Ireland during the reign of Queen Anne.[12] In Ireland the opposing political factions were more commonly labelled 'court' and 'county', with the county faction including both those with Whig and Tory sentiments. David Hayton points out that these factional divisions in Ireland never entirely conformed to the English pattern.[13] Most Irish Protestant landowners after the Williamite wars were Whiggish given that their status and fortunes were dependent on their support for William and Mary, which was the most important definition of a Whig. Some Irish landowners nominally espoused Whig principles in defence of liberty and the

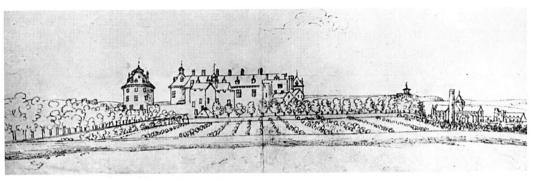

1 'The east side of the Castle of Kilkenny', 1669, by Francis Place. Taken from John Maher, 'Francis Place in Drogheda, Kilkenny and Waterford, etc'. *JRSAI*, 64 (1934).

reformed religion while maintaining conservative views on the preservation of the establishment in church and state. By the late seventeenth century only a few supporters of Charles I and veterans of the Royalist party of the 1640s survived on whom the term Tory could be grafted. The chief example was the duke of Ormond.[14]

The adoption of classicism and rejection of the baroque is regarded as the mark of Whig design. Prominent Whigs such as Joseph Addison described Virgil's *Georgics* as a 'collection of the most delightful landskips than can be made out of fields and wood, herds of cattle and swarms of bees',[15] but classical influences were not the preserve of eighteenth-century Whigs. Both Virgil and Pliny were hugely influential on seventeenth-century garden design and on landowners of every creed. It has been stated that 'Irish neo-classicism was free of Jacobite thought'.[16] However James Butler, the 1st duke of Ormond, who was both a Jacobite and a Tory, and a key figure in establishing taste in Ireland in the late seventeenth century,[17] introduced classicism to Ireland. Ormond classicized the medieval Kilkenny Castle (fig. 1), building a fine classical gateway and introduced classicism to Dublin when he commissioned William Robinson to build the Royal Hospital at Kilmainham. Thomas Burgh, surveyor general of Ireland and Tory MP for Naas built a magnificent early classical house in the Palladian style at Oldtown Demesne in Kildare *c.*1707, and later worked on the classical Dromoland House for Catherine O'Brien.[18]

In practice, the rigid geometric style of design lasted well into the eighteenth century, when the 'Whiggish', 'naturalistic' landscapes promoted by Addison, the earl of Shaftesbury, and Alexander Pope became the norm, and the two styles were often integrated. In fact, a close reading of Addison's *Spectator* articles of the early eighteenth century reveals that his 'new' ideas (a rejection of topiary and excessive ornamentation) were not so ground-breaking and varied little from what had gone before. They may have advocated a more 'naturalistic' style of gardening; however, as Williamson notes, 'square level lawns, straight walks flanked by topiary, wildernesses criss-crossed with allées, and avenues focused on the main façade of the house continued to be popular into the 1730s and 40s, and indeed beyond'. He continues that 'Addison's own garden' was laid out 'in straight lines, with long thick hedges of yew' organized around a single axis. Shaftesbury's garden was equally geometric, with walks, canals and hedges in profusion. The garden designer Batty Langley bemoaned the narrowness of walks, but did not suggest that they should be abandoned altogether.[19] Mary Delany, a central character in early eighteenth-century Irish Whig society and a friend of Jonathan Swift, created a garden at Delville in Dublin that had a bowling green, terrace walk, parterre, orangery, a green oval lawn edged with double rows of elm and little grass walks.[20] This describes a typical old-fashioned garden despite Joseph Cooper Walker's assertion that Delville was the first demesne to abandon 'the obdurate and straight line of the Dutch'[21] Brewer in his *Beauties of Ireland* noted that Delville 'retained the stiffness of the old garden; walks in right lines terminating in little parterres'.[22]

As David Leatherbarrow has commented, Shaftesbury's only departure from the style of gardening prevalent during the early part of the eighteenth century was his apparent rejection of outlandish topiary. Instead he favoured the pruning of trees and shrubs along their 'natural' form, to tidy up and improve on what nature intended. For instance, yew lent itself naturally to be cut into pyramids, holly into globes.[23] The allegedly 'Whiggish' landscapes of Breckdenston and other estates nonetheless contained many, if not all, the features of the 'absolutist' landscapes seen at Killruddery, Antrim and Portmore. Breckdenston in particular conforms far more readily to the seventeenth-century style, of formal alleys, symmetry, wilderness and canals. A cogent argument has been made that the fashion for neo-Palladian architecture and landscape was in fact apolitical, and foremost an aesthetic style adopted equally by both Whig and Tory and that 40 per cent of subscribers to Colen Campbell's *Vitruvius Britannicus*[24] were Tories 'if not hardened Jacobites'.[25]

Changing philosophical ideas were an important factor in the development of garden design, but as the garden historian Tom Williamson points out, letters and diaries from the period make it clear that in the seventeenth and eighteenth centuries abstract moral philosophy was of little or no concern to the great majority of people. The evidence from seventeenth-century Ireland indicates that the parks and gardens of Whigs and Tories were not strikingly different until the period between 1760 and 1820, and that prior to the mid-eighteenth century the Tory/Whig dichotomy is of little use as an analytical device.

Utility and experimentation in the garden

The post-Restoration period saw Irish landowners, like their English counterparts, begin to expand and develop their gardens and demesnes. The demesne was the part of the estate which was attached to the great house itself. It generally comprised of the ornamental and vegetable gardens, the park, woodlands and farm buildings connected to the house. During the upheaval of the Civil War and Cromwellian period, some of those landowners who managed to remain in possession of their estates retreated to their gardens.[26] Improvements and experimentation in gardening and agricultural techniques certainly took place in Ireland prior to 1660, but the Restoration saw these developments and the exchange of ideas proceed at a far greater and more ambitious pace. The utilitarian landscape as a whole could be managed in such a way as to be aesthetically pleasing as well as productive.

In the latter half of the seventeenth century the plantations and ornamental pleasure gardens of the ruling elite were the physical embodiments of the colonial endeavour. They were a showcase for the prevailing scientific, aesthetic and 'improving' ideals of the period and were arranged so as to mimic the great gardens of England and act as a template for how an ordered society should be run. Utility and productivity, order and fecundity were displayed within the estates of improving landowners and were disseminated to all areas of the estate. This idealized landscape was the standard to which all other gardeners should aspire. Colonization presented an opportunity to create a new Eden or Utopia. Technological developments were utilized in the garden and advances in engineering and hydraulics drove many interventions on the demesne landscape.[27]

The garden also created an opportunity for scientific empiricism in the fields of botany, pomology, arboriculture and agriculture. There was a sense of camaraderie and partnership among landowners which was evidenced by the continual exchange of plants and knowledge (examined in further detail below). In this study, the term 'garden' is used, as it was by the seventeenth-century writers, to refer to the pleasure grounds of the demesne, its ornamental gardens, woodlands, parks and game reserves. A spatial hierarchy of elements was common to all gardens of the period: from the pleasure gardens close to the house, along with the kitchen garden, and woodlands and parkland further away.

2 A Persian waterwheel from Worlidge's *Systema agriculturae* (1668). Doneraile in
Co. Cork had a similar wheel.

The idealistic demesne was centred on the authority of the great house,
while the fecundity of the demesne was demonstrated by the multiplicity of
sources of food: the kitchen gardens, the presence of wall-fruit on the brick-
faced walls of the enclosures, orchards, the palisaded deer park, the warren,
pigeon houses, wildfowl in decoys, cattle in the pastures and fishponds well
stocked with perch. Rivers were channelled and controlled with weirs and
damns to fill the basins with their jets d'eaux and to turn waterwheels to power
mills. At Doneraile, water was supplied to the fishponds by a novel device, a
wooden Persian waterwheel (fig. 2).[28] The waterwheel was described in 1777
by Arthur Young as 'working constantly and regularly without trouble or
expense'.[29]

Nature was further utilized and bent to the landowners' will by the creation
of plantations and groves of trees. Superiority and taste were expressed by the
ornamental clipped shrubs, imported exotic tree species and ornamental layout

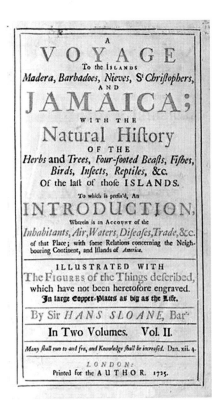

3 Title page of Hans Sloane's
Voyage to Jamaica (1725).

of the gardens. Jacques Boyceau, the French garden writer and supervisor of
the gardens of Louis XIII, discussed in detail the idea of *utile dulci*, the
combination of utility and pleasure in the garden. Boyceau, however, distin-
guished between the *jardin de plaisir* and the *jardin utile*, the former being
strictly for *le plaisir and la beauté*, the other for agricultural purposes.[30] In
Ireland the distinctions between *utile* and *dulci* became blurred and the entire
demesne contained elements of both, all driven by the necessity to be
productive and self-sufficient.

Botanical interest had become so advanced in Ireland, that by the 1690s
Arthur Rawdon of Moira in Co. Down had one of the best botanical
collections in Europe. On his estate were cultivated plants from all over the
known world. Many of these were obtained from friends and colleagues, and
others from exploratory trips he commissioned.[31] In 1690/1 he sponsored
James Harlow on a voyage to the West Indies.[32] This expedition was a
tremendous success and Harlow had a cargo of about 1,000 new plants when
he landed in Carrickfergus in April 1692 to the delight of both Rawdon and
Sir Hans Sloane of the Chelsea Physic Garden.[33] The fruits of the West Indies

expedition were propagated and distributed to other European gardens, primarily to Chelsea, while surplus seeds were sent to the botanic gardens of Leiden university and to Jacob Bobart, superintendent of the physic garden of Oxford university.[34]

House building

Until the Restoration, owing to the unsettled and dangerous political situation, 'gentlemen' still tended to live in houses that were defensive, fortified and insular looking.[35] A number of these houses were large and rather grand, but retained their bawns and fortifications; for example, Glinsk Castle in Galway, built in the early part of the seventeenth century, and Loughmoe in Tipperary, Leamaneh in Clare and Burncourt Castle in Tipperary. One of the first great manor houses of the seventeenth century was Jigginstown House in Naas in Kildare, built for Thomas Wentworth, the earl of Strafford, lord deputy of Ireland during the reign of Charles I. The house, one of the first to be built in red brick, was said to have had a planned formal pleasure ground with terraces and fishponds.

New houses were a departure from the Norman-style tower houses still common in Ireland up until the late seventeenth century. Construction of unfortified manor houses began in the early part of the century, but building was halted by the rebellion and the establishment of the Commonwealth under Cromwell. These new houses were frequently built or finished in fashionable red brick and often incorporated the earlier tower houses. The English antiquary Thomas Dineley's illustrations of 1681, depicting older houses such as Mount Ievers and Ballicar (fig. 4), show them as rather bleak and formidable fortresses, but his illustrations of more modern houses indicate gardens on a more formal and sophisticated level. They show enclosures surrounded by the necessary strong stone wall, inside which gardens were laid out, for example, Ballynunnery (fig. 5), situated 'upon a rising hill among good gardens, orchard, meadows, and other profitable lands. At the foot of this hill, by the side of gardenage, near the castle, runneth a pleasant river abounding with trouts'.[36]

In the early part of the seventeenth century, the pleasure gardens of the landed gentry in Ireland were, for the most part, comparatively small spaces. Gardens were usually separated from the surrounding countryside by high hedges, fences or walls. Many contemporary (and possibly biased) accounts of the Irish countryside during the seventeenth century confirm the countess of Clarendon's observation that Ireland was 'not cultivated' and bereft of trees and shrubs.[37] Based on the evidence available this criticism was overly harsh. One

4 Ballicar Castle by Thomas Dineley taken from Evelyn Philip Shirley and James Graves (eds), 'Dineley's journal', *JKSIAS*, 6:1 (1867).

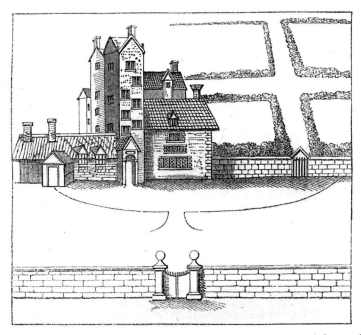

5 Ballynunnery House by Thomas Dineley taken from Shirley and Graves (eds), 'Dineley's journal', *JKSIAS*, 4:1 (1862), p. 47.

of the earliest illustrations of a formal ornamental garden in Ireland is a picture of Thomas Phillips's house in Limavady dating from the early seventeenth century in which knot gardens are clearly visible (fig. 6).[38] Brereton, describing

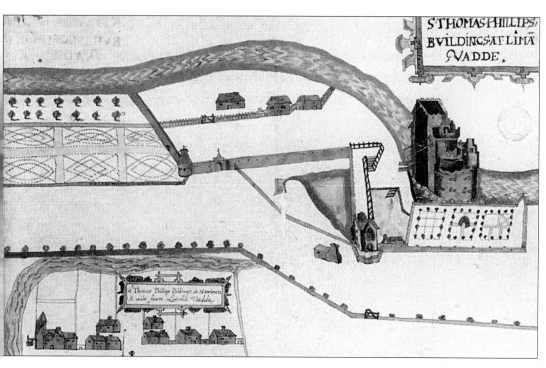

6 Thomas Phillips's house at Limavady by Thomas Raven, 1622 (courtesy of the Deputy Keeper of the Records, Public Record Office of Northern Ireland, PRONI (T510/1/15) and the Lambeth Palace Library). An arbour can be seen in the centre of the garden on the right-hand side of the picture.

Lord Chichester's gardens on the site of an old monastic settlement at Carrickfergus in 1635, reported it as having 'a graceful terrace … a fine garden and mighty spacious orchards'.[39] After 1660, modern house building, and the creation of open pleasure gardens, commenced in earnest. Defensive moats and walls were often retained; these protected the gardens from thieves and political rivals, but gardens could be opened up into the surrounding countryside and related axially to the main house by trees, avenues and waterworks.

Many other notable houses were built or renovated during the seventeenth century. Turvey House in north Co. Dublin was completed c.1690 and survived until 1987 when in an incredible act of vandalism it was demolished and the grounds made into a golf course. Thomastown Castle, built in Tipperary by George Mathew, half-brother of the 1st duke of Ormond, was a magnificent manor house with extensive and elaborate gardens.[40] Old Bawn in Tallaght near Dublin (figs. 7 & 8) (also demolished in the late twentieth century), was built by Sir Richard Bulkeley and was described as:

7 Harold Leask, 'The House at Old Bawn, Co. Dublin', *JRSAI*, 43 (1913), p. 320.

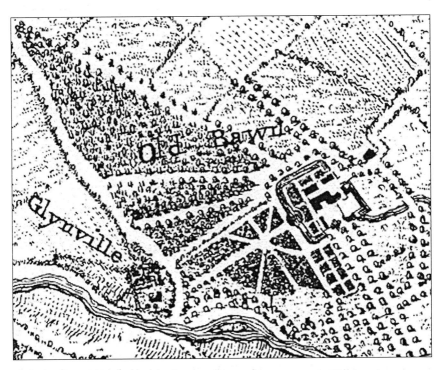

8 Old Bawn, detail from *Map of the county of Dublin* by John Rocque (1760), showing the moat or fosse around the house.

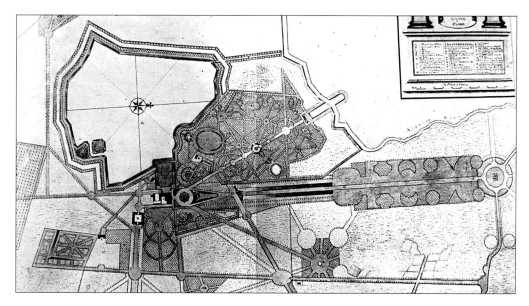

9 *Ichnographia Dromolan* (1720) (courtesy of the National Library of Ireland). The plan shows the Dromoland gardens, which had a grand avenue with a triumphal arch, a great gravel walk leading to a temple, a canal cut through the Asssulas river, numerous basins, rides, a bowling green, an obelisk and decorative woodland.

a quaint specimen of early seventeenth-century domestic architecture, such as is frequent in England, but seldom met with in this country, for at that period the principal dwellings in Ireland were mostly castles or fortified houses. The house is built in the form of the letter H, and has no fewer than fifteen gables. It was erected about the year 1635, and is said to have cost £3,000.[41]

From 1685 the house was occupied by Bulkeley's grandson, his charming namesake Richard Bulkeley, whose letters are a wonderful source of garden and scientific history.[42] Rathfarnham Castle, which still stands, though with a greatly depleted parkland, was described by one observer in 1699 as 'the greatest house I saw in Ireland all free stone surrounded with woods in abundance'.[43]

By the early eighteenth century, most new houses were built in the contemporary style, completely without fortification, a fine example being the great house at Dromoland, built in the early part of the eighteenth century and commissioned by Sir Donat O'Brien.[44] The project was continued after his death by Lucius O'Brien's widow Catherine who worked with 'Browne the

10 Beaulieu House, view of north side (courtesy of Cara Konig-Brock).

Contriver' on the design of what was probably the greatest baroque garden in Ireland which was designed in tandem with the house to create an entirely unified and inseparable whole (fig. 9). Other notable early eighteenth-century houses built around Dublin were Santry Court, built of red brick *c.*1708 by the Barry family, Westown House in Naul *c.*1710 and Rathbeale Hall *c.*1710. Most of these great houses have been lost completely, or are now in ruins, but often traces of the landscape remain in the form of tree-lined avenues, parklands and water features. The only complete and unmodified example of a house built prior to 1715 that survives intact is Beaulieu in Co. Louth, seat of the Tichbourne family, and childhood home of Robert Molesworth (fig. 10).[45] Older houses such as Leamaneh and Ormond Castle, which had been renovated in a grander style, had new gardens laid out to enhance their new grandeur. The Dromoland Album of plans for the construction of the house and gardens at Dromoland Castle contains an elaborate plan, assumed to be for the gardens of another O'Brien house, Leamaneh, which was terraced and laid out with a long canal and walks (fig. 11).[46]

11 Leamaneh Castle. The old tower house, which was incorporated into the new building, is clearly visible to the right of the picture.

Pleasure gardens, parkland and the surrounding landscape began to be designed in tandem with the house and planned as a unified scheme, with features laid out on axis with the house. Older features were adapted and made more in keeping with fashion. Dramatic avenues were fashioned from old approach roads and lanes leading to the demesne; today many such avenues are now roads and parks often follow earlier field patterns. Tower houses were regularly incorporated into the structure of new houses and many are still visible.[47] As well as being a practical solution, the adaptation of existing features such as ruins, mounds and woodlands made economic sense. This fiscal pragmatism dictated that nothing should be wasted and often ensured the survival of features that would, with greater financial resources, have been obliterated.

A constantly recurring theme of manuscript letters relating to Irish garden design is the desire to equal, or if possible better, the great parks and gardens of England, even those of the Monarch.[48] This ambition was to be achieved by means of conscientious stewardship, intensive cultivation and grand landscape interventions under the general heading of 'improvement' – the subject of the following chapter.

CHAPTER 3

Improvement and the culture of improvement

THE 'IMPROVEMENT OF GARDENS AND BUILDINGS' became a pre-occupation of landowners, and of the King himself.[1] The definition of the word 'improve' is first to make or become better in quality; its secondary meaning is to make (buildings, land, etc.) more valuable by additions or betterment. When the writers of the seventeenth century refer to improvements, they intended to 'improve' land in both its meanings but perhaps most tellingly, they used the word with reference to its sixteenth-century root, which was from the Anglo-French *emprouer*, 'to turn to profit'. The term 'improvement' generally applied to land as much, if not more, than to the great house itself.[2] Travel writers like Loveday also referred to the aesthetics of landscape and garden design as improvement.[3]

Charles Smith applauded the improvements carried out by George Rye at Ryecourt in Cork: 'besides good gardens and orchards, Colonel Rye raised and planted many thousands of oaks, and other forest trees, and was a great improver in several branches of agriculture'.[4] Many still saw making a profit out of Ireland as a way of making money to establish a seat in England as evidenced by a letter from Sir Robert Southwell to his grandson Sir Phillip Perceval of Burton in Cork:

> I am glad that English tenants are so plentiful with you, and particularly that you are so intent upon the method of taking fines, for that does not only tie the tenant fast and encourage him to all improvements of advance of and beautifying the estate, but by this method of raising stock you will be enabled to get a footing here in England.[5]

Irish estates were transformed in the decades following the Restoration. In 1635 Sir William Brereton journeyed to Ireland where he wrote of Ormond's house at Carrick-on-Suir on which he commented: 'if his land were improved and well planted, it would yield him greater revenue'.[6] In 1686, Paul Rycaut was able to report that Carrick had 'the most pleasant park that ever I did see'.[7]

Clarendon himself also thought Carrick 'one of the prettiest places' he had ever seen'.[8]

William Waring is an example of a landowner who recognized that improvement was both beneficial to himself and the country as a whole. Waring came into possession of land in Donaghcloney, Co. Down, that had been confiscated from the Magenis family. He built a seat, Waringstown House, in 1667 and set about his improvements:

> I do assure you I will not spare [money] to lay out my own to improve the land and if I can … plant it so as to secure your rent and make myself but a saver, I will not complain and though I say it I think I am not behind any of my neighbours improving where I am concerned.[9]

During the Civil War and Commonwealth, sections of the nobility who remained in Ireland and England retreated to the sanctuary of their demesnes and directed their minds towards the improvement of their gardens. Gardens were romanticized and there was an increase in the number of poems celebrating rural life and the garden.[10] This interest in gardens continued into the Restoration period and beyond. Improvement was seen as a morally superior pursuit. It was sought to achieve the perfect balance of utility, beauty and retirement as advanced by John Evelyn.[11] In Ireland the superiority of the new English settlers was expressed by their attention to gardens and good husbandry. 'Improvement' was also seen to justify the colonization of Ireland by planting it with English settlers.[12] In his account, c.1682, of the barony of 'Onealland' in Portadown, William Brooke wrote approvingly of the good influence the English had had on the native Irish agricultural practices.[13]

Garden writers and books

Many gardening books appeared in the latter half of the seventeenth century with chapters devoted to pleasure gardens. Earlier gardening books tended to be more concerned with husbandry and agriculture rather than purely or predominantly ornamental matters. Many were available for consultation in Ireland. Private collections such as Marsh's Library (though not a lending library) held a substantial range of gardening books. At the forefront of the English language books was John Worlidge's *Systema horticulturae, or the art of gardening* (London, 1677) (fig. 12).[14] This set out the mechanics of creating a visually pleasing garden. Paradoxically for such a labour-intensive method of

12 & 13 Title page and a design for a garden from John Worlidge, *Systema horticulturae*.

gardening that involved extreme contortions of the natural form, Worlidge professed that in planting a garden 'one ought to have more regard to nature than art'. He piously affected disapproval of too many things done 'by dint of money; such as high walks to terraces, great stairs of stone; like so many quarries, fountains cluttered with ornaments, and abundance of arbours, cabinets, and porticos of lattice work filled with figures, vases etc.' He rather diluted his avowed hatred of the unnatural garden when he stated what he thought were the elements of a successful garden with regard to nature, such as the 'noble simplicity we see in steps, slopes, and banks of turf, natural arbours, and plain hedges without lattice-work, set off and heightened here and there with figures and other ornaments of sculpture' (fig. 13).[15]

From the mid-seventeenth century, English landscape was heavily influenced by classical texts and the concept of arcadia, the most influential work being Virgil's book on agriculture, animal husbandry and cultivation – the *Georgics*.[16] William Petty's wife, Elizabeth, recorded how her son 'Charles is now learning Virgil's *Georgics* in pure Latin, an excellent poem, and the best rules for the most honest trade of husbandry'.[17] In the *Georgics* Virgil discusses crop rotation, irrigation, times for sowing,[18] arboriculture, viticulture and methods of propagation.[19] Literary representations of the landscape appeared in the work of poets such as Andrew Marvell and John Donne. The horticulturists approached garden design as a serious philosophic exercise.[20] Books such as Evelyn's *Aceteria* and *Silva* and Moses Cooke's *The manner of raising, ordering, and improving forest and fruit trees* (London, 1679) were instruction manuals for gardeners and arboriculturalists in the same way that the *Georgics* was.

Worlidge, in his *Systema horticulturae*, wrote that '[t]he original of gardens was from [the] divine hand'.[21] A sense of the divine purpose to be served by rendering the earth more fertile, more productive and more beautiful pervades much of the writing on husbandry throughout the Interregnum.[22] Protestant sentiments relating to the notion of personal salvation through good works also led to the idea that good husbandry was a duty.[23] The French Huguenot writer Olivier de Serres thought of gardening as a form of public good. He argued that ownership of land should contribute more to the wealth of France and not just provide a basis for determining social rank.[24] In his introduction to the *Elysium Britannicum*, Evelyn described the garden as that 'delicious place' called 'paradise', from which our forefathers had been exiled. He defined the garden as a place 'of all terrestrial enjoyments the most resembling heaven'.[25] The emphasis had shifted to the pleasure and benefits to be obtained by man in the garden, rather than the more onerous duty of Christian stewardship. Man was free to manipulate nature and shape it to his own ends. Dennis Cosgrove has argued that this shift in view also had the effect of placing a moral authority on landowners to manage their estates in such a way as to maintain a peaceful and harmonious kingdom.[26]

The second half of the seventeenth century was a period of great advances in the understanding of the universe and a period of great scientific curiosity.[27] Landowners and estate managers began to take a more scientific approach to plant cultivation, under the general heading of 'improvement'. Settlers such as Sir George Rawdon[28] were presciently progressive in their farming methods and infrastructural interventions, whether by making roads, planting orchards or improving the sporting amenities on his own or Lord Conway's demesnes.[29] The work of these men and women in collecting data on the physical landscape, native and newly introduced plant materials, experiments with propagation methods, and ways to improve agricultural practices was often carried out under the auspices of the Dublin Philosophical Society.[30] The spirit of empirical enquiry in matters horticultural was pursued by garden writers of the latter half of the century when there was a huge increase in the number of gardening books published.[31] Many new books were published dealing specifically with the kitchen garden, beekeeping, wall-fruit and cider making.[32]

In the early part of the century Samuel Hartlib (1600–62) led the field in his facilitation and encouragement of agricultural research and writing.[33] Books published prior to 1660, especially during the period of the Commonwealth, tended to concentrate less on practical tips and more on religious proselytizing. Ralph Austen, author of *A treatise of fruit-trees* published in 1653,[34] was concerned with the 'spiritual use of an orchard' and his book is full of references to scripture, so much so that the English antiquary Anthony Wood was moved to write in 1691 that 'being all divinity and nothing therein of the practice part of gardening, many therefore did refuse to buy it'. This was thought unfortunate by Wood who referred to Austen as 'a very useful man' who spent all his time in planting gardens and raising fruit-trees.[35]

The rapid development of fruit and vegetable cultivation at this time represents one of the clearest expressions of the utilitarian impetus behind seventeenth-century improvements. Whereas early garden books related almost exclusively to agricultural concerns and improvements, writers of the latter half of the century addressed the importance of beauty and utility in the garden, paying particular attention to the aesthetics of design and the pleasure garden. In Evelyn's opinion gardening was 'one of the noblest and most refined parts of agriculture'.[36] According to his view, 'people would frame a type of heaven, because there is nothing in nature more worthy and illustrious they describe a garden'.[37] Despite the reverence shown to the classical gardeners, it was hoped to recreate the classical style garden with a new English character, creating a hybrid of the two to include modern advances in horticulture.[38] That serious gardening was viewed as the exclusive pursuit of the educated and wealthy can be in no doubt, Evelyn had no qualms about who he was addressing: '[I] pretend not here to write to cabbage-planters; but to the best refined of our nation who delight in gardens, and aspire to the perfections of the arte (and for institution)'.[39]

Richard Lawrence, in his book *The interest of Ireland* (1682) 'being the experiment of many approved applications by a well-wisher to Ireland's prosperity', tried to analyse the reasons for Ireland's poverty and poor agricultural husbandry compared with that of England. He concluded that it was because 'rather than imitating the English in their improvements, and the English jealous of disturbance from the Irish, discourageth their industry in improving'. Lawrence was deeply concerned with imparting his suggested methods of improving land and stock, which he thought vital to Ireland's prosperity. He suggested the planting and propagating of new crops such as rose madder,[40] liquorice, hops and saffron.[41]

The first book or manual on farming printed in England was John Fitzherbert's *Boke of husbandrye* in 1523, which paved the way for several similar publications over the century. The first time 'improvement' appears in the title of a treatise was in 1649 when Walter Blith published *The English improver; or a new survey of husbandry* (London, 1649). The second edition, *The English improver improved* (1652),[42] published three years later, included a discussion of ways to drain land for agricultural purposes. This was followed shortly by Sir Richard Weston's, *A discourse of husbandry used in Brabant and Flanders, showing wonderful improvement of land there* (London, 1649).

Various almanacs were used as planting guides. English ones, such as *The gardener's almanack* by Samuel Gilbert (London, 1683) and John Evelyn's *Kalendarium hortense* (London, 1684), were consulted, and new ones were written and produced for the Irish market: only three Irish almanacs survive from the period 1601–60, yet twenty-one were published during the last forty years of the century. This indicates the considerable growth of interest in science and gardening during the post-Restoration period.[43] These included Dominic Russel's *New almanack for the year of our Lord 1690* (Dublin, 1690) and Ambrose White's *Almanack and prognostication for the year of our lord God 1665* (Dublin, 1665), which prescribed how and when gardens should be planted, seeds sown and digging and manuring undertaken. In his book *Considerations on the agriculture and employment of the poor*, Robert Molesworth suggested that Thomas Tusser's *Five hundred points of good husbandry* should be taught to young boys, as 'the very best English book of good husbandry and housewifery that ever was published, fitted for the use of humble men and farmers, and ordinary families'.[44]

Many landowners had great libraries. The library of Peter Plunkett, earl of Fingall, at Somerset House,[45] contained a wide selection of books on agriculture and husbandry including, inter alia, Worlidge's *Systema agriculturae*, John Houghton's *Collections for the improvement of husbandry* (1681), John Smith's *England's improver revis'd*, and Walter Blith's *The English improver improv'd*. As a response to the dearth of books dedicated specifically to husbandry in Ireland, George Rye of Ryecourt in Cork published his own book on agriculture and husbandry, *Considerations on agriculture*, in 1730,[46] stating that the 'general books of husbandry writ by English authors will not serve for Ireland, the culture of beet barley is scarce known to them' and that 'every labourer would laugh, if he could read how they mention the manner of setting potatoes'.

It has often been argued that the late seventeenth century saw the arrival of the pleasure garden as an art form freed from utility.[47] It has also been suggested that treatises such as Evelyn's *Elysium Britannicum* were concerned essentially with the ornamental pleasure garden, as opposed to the productive garden and that the missing chapters on the orchard and kitchen garden were conceived only in relation to the 'garden of pleasure'.[48] However, in the *Elysium Britannicum* Evelyn dealt with the 'philopsophico-medical garden', which he regarded as 'an ornamental … addition [to] these royal gardens', and also with orangeries, and conservatories of rare plants and fruits, both of which were primarily utilitarian in nature. Evelyn also noted in his diary that his translation of *The French gardener* was 'the first and best of that kind that introduced the use of the olitorie garden to any purpose'.[49] It seems to me that it is impossible to separate the productive garden from the decorative garden during the period under discussion. Both were inextricably linked, and each intervention on the landscape had a practical purpose. The survival of the demesne was dependent on the economic and material benefits conferred by the utilitarian aspects of the garden. The creation of the great pleasure garden, with its practical and decorative elements, was as we shall see, a direct consequence and a physical manifestation of the wider cult of improvement.

CHAPTER 4

Pleasure gardens

THE SEVENTEENTH-CENTURY DEMESNE contained a complex hierarchy of elements; almost all of the various pieces in the garden had a productive or utilitarian purpose, and all were seen as having an aesthetic value of their own and within the wider scheme. By design, the gardens close to the mansion house were well manicured and un-naturalistic; however, as they moved further from the house their style loosened and became less prim and manicured in appearance. Outside the highly artificial and structured walled gardens were sited the deer parks, which were large tracts of land fenced in by walls or palisades. The following chapter will examine each of the elements of the garden in roughly the sequence that would be observed from the house, out to the boundaries of the demesne, and beyond.

Gardens did not only pay for their own upkeep, the money made from their produce also supported the lifestyles of the gentry. In 1704, Robert Molesworth wrote of how the gardens at Breckdenston would not only 'pay for their keeping', but would also cover 'the repairs of the house and tax'.[1] Sometimes work on the gardens commenced prior to the rebuilding or remodelling of the house itself. In the early 1660s, Sir John Perceval employed the architect Captain William Kenn, who was not formally contracted to rebuild the house itself until 1670,[2] to work on the gardens at Burton House in Churchtown, Co. Cork. Work continued on the gardens at Burton over the following decades with a 'herbhouse' and 'turfhouse' being built within it.[3] Leamaneh Castle was described in 1593 as a 'castle or stone fort ... with ¾ of land adjacent, now waste and uncultivated'.[4] By end of the seventeenth century, the tower house had been incorporated into an open manor house, with an elaborate pleasure garden.

The literary critic Tom Turner suggests that in order to resolve this contradiction between metropolitan sophistication and agriculture, the rural element of the gentleman's life was elevated to that of an exceptional experience, 'a *villeggiatura* or rustic episode in which the business of life is left behind'.[5] This requirement was fulfilled by the creation of the great pleasure gardens, which, to a certain extent, masked the utilitarian purpose of the garden with an aesthetic veneer. In this way the garden, as well as fulfilling its productive role, became a sophisticated sensory experience in itself. In his essay *Upon the gardens of Epicurus*, William Temple summed up the sensory benefits of the Restoration garden:

> The most exquisite delights of sense are pursued, in the contrivance and plantation of gardens; which, with fruits, flowers, shades, fountains, and the music of birds that frequent such happy places, seem to furnish all the pleasures of the several senses, and with the greatest, or at least the most natural perfections.[6]

The extent to which new houses and gardens were established in the post-Restoration period in Ireland can be assessed from the descriptions found in manuscripts and in the few surviving paintings and drawings. A contemporary description of Sir Robert Colville's new house in Newtown in Co. Down (the original building house had burnt down in 1664) reveals the level of sophistication Irish gardens had reached twenty-three years after the Restoration:

> [Colville] hath in a few years from the foundation built up a large double roofed house, stables coach-houses, and all other necessary or convenient edifices with inner, outward and back courts and spacious well planted olitory[7] fruit, and pleasure gardens, which have fish ponds, spring wells, long and broad sanded walks, and bowling green – all thereof walled about and reared (with diverse curious hewn stone gates uniformly regarding one another in a regular and comely manner, the whole considered, there is few such, and so much work to be seen [in] any one dwelling in Ireland, nor any so great done by a gentleman at his own expense.[8]

And in 1686 the earl of Clarendon wrote of Thomastown in Tipperary:

> This is a very fine place, and the most improved of any situation I have seen since I came into this kingdom, especially considering that it is but fifteen years since he first sat down upon it, when there was not a house upon it.[9]

Much has been written about the various different 'styles' of gardening prevalent in the seventeenth century; the Italian, Dutch and French variously being credited with being the major influence on gardening in England and in Ireland. It is arguable that these distinctions are over-dogmatic. Rather than being discrete styles, the gardens in each country had more elements in common than opposition, there was a continual and complex interchange of ideas,[10] and where the styles diverged, the modifications were often dictated by topographical, political, economic or climatic factors rather than any ideological or aesthetic preference. This was observed by William Temple in 1685, who wrote:

> In our north-west climates, our gardens are very different from what they were in Greece and Italy, and from what they are now in those regions in Spain or the southern parts of France. And as most general customs in countries grow from the different nature of climate, soils, or situations, and from the necessities or industry they impose, so do these.[11]

The gardens of the Medici villas in Tuscany are regarded in the popular consciousness as the typical gardens of the Italian Renaissance. That these tended to be composed on a series of terraces, and were generally much smaller in scale than the *grand siècle* French gardens of Mollet and Le Nôtre was due, in the main, to the hilly nature of the northern Italian countryside and the myriad tiny principalities and city-states into which the country was divided. The topography lent itself to the creation of several different levels linked by steps. However, 'atypical' Italian Renaissance gardens were developed on the flat plains of the Po valley that were not terraced and which do not conform so readily to the received image. It has been noted that in the three centuries during which the Italian garden flourished, the Italian peninsula consisted of independent states in shifting alliances, many occupied by foreign rulers – French, Spanish and Austrian – who intermarried with their subjects, making the very possibility of a discrete Italian garden tradition questionable.[12] The great gardens of the Loire valley and northern France were possible because of the great wealth of the ruling class who owned vast tracts of land and the political structures that they upheld. The scale and extent of the gardens was facilitated by the flat terrain and a high water table. From the Renaissance onwards, there was steady infiltration of Italian influence on the French garden. By the seventeenth century, however, French gardening had found its own expression and equalled, if not surpassed, the scale and complexity of Italian gardens, and these ideas were in turn transmitted back to Italy. In 1600, Olivier de Serres (1539–1619) felt confident enough to state that 'one need not travel to Italy or elsewhere to see gardens finely set out, since our own France has won the prize from all other nations'.[13]

In the Netherlands and the Low Countries gardens were, of necessity, smaller. The Netherlands was densely populated and generally wealthier. The spatial restrictions imposed by land shortage meant that Dutch gardens rarely, apart from those of royal palaces such as Het Loo, contained features such as deer parks or forests. The Dutch garden tended to be smaller, was contained and did not spill out over landscape. The characteristic canals were a *sine qua non* for reclaiming land without which the garden could not exist. Within the garden were parterres displaying topiary and rare flowers. The only distinguishing factor of the parterres within the Dutch garden was their shape. Le Nôtre liked to emphasize the scale of his gardens and create further depth by using oblong parterres. In Dutch gardens such as Het Loo and Honselaarsdijk, square parterres were used to accentuate width rather than length, as they were in Italy.

The gardens of France, Holland and later, England, were all strongly influenced by the technical innovations of the Italian Renaissance garden. From the description by Pliny of his garden Laurentum, many of the features we associate traditionally with the Italian Renaissance garden (and, by analogy, seventeenth-century French gardens) were present in antiquity: allées, box parterres, walks, grass terraces, topiary and flower gardens.[14] What all gardens had in common were features that were necessary to exploit their commercial and practical potential to the full. Technological developments were copied and adapted for use in vastly differing physical environments and ideas were continually being transferred from one country to another. Earthworks such as terracing made economic sense: the creation of terraces provided a greater surface area of flat, productive ground on which to grow trees and crops; intensive planting prevented soil erosion; the terraces themselves created a series of vertical structures which gave shelter and support for plants, creating a series of microclimates. Terracing was found in all areas of the Continent where attempts were made to create gardens on sloping ground for logistical rather than aesthetic reasons. A garden described as 'Dutch' in style was often given this label due to the presence of canals, while statuary and balustrading may have been held to impart an 'Italianate' theme. An excessively abstracted and stylistic analysis obscures the greater similarities between the gardens of Britain and Ireland and the rest of the Continent in the late seventeenth and early eighteenth centuries.

Designers, practitioners and inspiration

In the seventeenth century, master gardeners such as the Frenchmen Le Nôtre and Mollet were the exception rather than the norm. Two interesting memorials survive in the British Library between Sir John Perceval of Burton and John Barbor of Cork, who was recorded here as being a 'gardener'. In fact, it appears that Barbor was a consultant, which made him the first recorded landscape professional working in Ireland at this period.[15] A later landscape architect was 'Browne the contriver', who was instructed in 1720 by Catherine O'Brien in landscaping the gardens at Dromoland.[16] 'Browne the Contriver' was also recommended by Madame Catherine Da Cunha to her nephew Valentine Browne, 3rd Viscount Kenmare, who said that he had 'been for several years employed by most of the people of quality of Ireland, who has a greater genius for laying out new ground than anybody of this time'.[17]

The gardeners

Becoming a professional gardener was quite a good career option for a working man of small means; in return for his toil he generally received a salary, as much fresh produce as he could eat (and in some cases sell) and a decent house to live in.[18] The duties of the 'gardener' were delineated in a sixteenth-century manuscript book in Trinity College. These included:

> To look well to my lord's gardens and orchard, that the garden be well and in due time digged … and wooded, and the kitchen garden well stored with roots and herbs for my lords kitchen, he not to sell any fruit, but to dispose the same as the steward shall appoint, or lord or lady commands, and to provide roses for rose water and rose cakes, and the same to deliver to my lady for such uses as shall thought convenient. And that he use not himself nor suffer any other to play at cards or tables in his chamber or any other part of his office.[19]

Each demesne had a head gardener and several under-gardeners. These would be supplemented seasonally by casual labour acting as jobbing gardeners. Gardeners were afforded some status if they were full-time employees. It appears that one of the perks of the job was that head gardeners could sell some of their master's crops for their own profit.[20] Excess produce was sold on, sometimes illegally.[21] Thomas Flower's gardener 'proved a great rogue' and his servant Edmond Doyne was of the opinion that all gardeners were thieves.[22] This theory was borne out by one of the Molesworth's gardeners who was 'discarded' for selling cauliflower plants. When the gardener was confronted with the 'cheat', he argued that all gardeners did the same.[23] In some cases, the fruits of his labour were all the gardener received in pay, and selling excess fruit was their only source of income. The countess of Orrery clearly saw nothing unfair about this scheme:

> You say the gardener complains he has a hard bargain having only the fruit of the gardens for looking after them. In the first place you never say whether he keeps the gardens well and clean as he ought to do, for if he does not that in having the fruit I am sure he has a great deal too much.[24]

Happily, not all gardeners were treated in such a cavalier fashion, but Irish gardeners appear to have been paid substantially less than their English counterparts; the 2nd earl of Burlington's gardener, James Ronan, who was paid about £4 a year in 1687,[25] compares very unfavourably with Lord Chesterfield's gardener who was reputed to receive a salary £12 per annum four years later, in 1671.[26] And John Gregory employed as gardener at Carton, 'the house of the late Lord Tyrconnell', was paid £10 'on account of his allowance for looking after the house and gardens'.[27]

Finding and keeping a good and trustworthy gardener was difficult. It is likely that those with an interest in botany would try to recruit gardeners from the Huguenot immigrant community. The earl of Orrery's gardener at Charleville, who also worked for the Perceval family, was called Anthony Tilleman, indicating that his origins may have been Huguenot.[28] Others brought gardeners over from their English estates. In the 1670s John Worlidge spent a short period in the service of the earl of Cork at Lismore.[29] Most of the gardeners working on large properties appear, judging by their names, to have been English or of English extraction: for instance, at Burton the gardeners were called William Hickman and Peregrine Bradstone, Bishop King's gardener was a Mr Phillips.[30] A Val Savage of Chester wrote to Sir John Perceval that he could send 'a very good gardener, who would be satisfied with the little house of two rooms in the corner of the garden, and the benefit of the garden beyond what is needed for the house'.[31] Sir John Temple, brother of the more famous Sir William, had a gardener called Thomas Simpson at Palmerstown who was a brother of John Evelyn's gardener at Sayes Court. Each autumn, Simpson wrote to England to order new trees and 'any seeds extraordinary of salad or flowers'.[32] Sometimes the English gardeners found living in Ireland too difficult to bear: in June 1727 a row broke out between Lord Kenmare's English gardener, John Henshaw, and Andrew Bridges, a nursery owner from Mallow in Cork, about whether a yew hedge would do better if planted from cuttings or seed.[33] The row culminated with Henshaw's resignation when he stated 'it is impossible for an Englishman to live in your lordship's family if he was a saint'.[34] Sir George Rawdon felt the need for specialist help with the orchards at Lisburn saying 'we want a gardener here, for the young trees are not thriving so well as I have seen them do in other places'.[35] Rawdon eventually found a gardener called Francis who appears to have been both loyal and competent and stayed with him and Conway for several years, despite the occasional spat.[36] Sir George's son, Arthur Rawdon, engaged a gardener from London called Thomas Harrison on the recommendation of the botanist William Sherrard.[37] It would be interesting to know whether Richard Bulkeley's gardener at Old Bawn, a Mr Harrison 'bred up under Bobart' was Thomas Harrison. Curiously the gardener at the Royal Hospital in 1694 was also called Thomas Harrison; it is possible that Harrison worked at all three places consecutively.[38]

In Britain and Ireland, the great demesne landscapes of the seventeenth century seem to have resulted from a pooling of ideas between the landowner, his architects, agents, jobbing gardeners and tradesmen. The sense of empirical inquiry applied to arts and science by the virtuosi of the period was equally evidenced in gardens.

The garden at Killruddery, Co. Wicklow, is regarded as the most complete surviving example of the classic geometric Restoration garden in Ireland.[39] It is now part of garden history orthodoxy that Killruddery was created for Edward Brabazon, 4th earl of Meath (1638–1707), by a French gardener called Bonnet, possibly a pupil of Le Nôtre himself.[40] It would indeed be highly significant if a landscaper who was apprenticed to the greatest of *grand siècle* gardeners – the creator of both Vaux le Vicomte and Versailles – had worked in Ireland: unfortunately, it seems that this long-held assertion may be the result of a simple misunderstanding.

Killruddery, which lies south of Bray in Co. Wicklow, has been the seat of the earls of Meath since 1618. The formal garden was laid out in the 1680s. A description of the gardens survives from 1711:

> Killruddery … being a large house with four flankers and terraces, and a new summer-house built by the said earl … with pleasure garden, cherry garden, kitchen garden, new garden, wilderness, gravel walks, and a bowling-green, all walled about and well planted with fruit trees, with several canals or fish-ponds, well stored with carp and tench … with a deer-park.[41]

The garden was later lauded as an Irish version of a great seventeenth-century French landscape by the nineteenth-century travel writer James Brewer:

From the natural grandeur of the surrounding county, the formality of
the mode stands revealed with peculiar distinctiveness. The enclosing
mountains rise boldly and at once, with all their brilliance of purple and
brown colours, above the long avenues of stately elms, the close cut ewe
hedges, the regular terraces of this St Cloud.[42]

The gardens were certainly designed in the grand manner made fashionable
by Louis XIV, but the evidence concerning its supposed French gardener and,
more particularly, his association with the renowned Le Nôtre is problematic.
The prevailing orthodoxy appears to have its origin in some confusion concerning
a reference among the papers of Sir William Petty. In 1684 Petty referred to a
gardener called Bonel or Bonet (the writing is difficult to decipher) working
at his town garden in George's Lane, Dublin.[43] It has been stated that, in 1686
Petty wrote 'ruefully in his diary' that he had 'lost his gardener of twelve years
standing', a Mr Bonnet, 'to the earl of Meath'.[44] In fact, no diary exists among
Petty's manuscripts. By 1685, Petty was an absentee landlord, having made his
permanent home in London. In any case, the house in George's Lane, now
George's Street, would not have had a significantly large garden, being in the
heart of an already congested city. The document referred to as a diary appears
to be a letter from Petty's agent Thomas Dance, dated 28 August 1686, which
states that 'Bonel' 'goes to live with my lord of Meath'.[45]

Even if the letter does refer to Petty's gardener, it is unlikely that he was
the instigating designer of the formal garden at Killruddery; the landscaping
of the estate being well underway by 1682. The 3rd earl's land agent, Oliver
Cheyney, described the progress of the work:

> I went on Friday last to receive you remainders of rents in the county of
> Wicklow and lay at Killruddery two nights ... Capt. Ed Brabazon has
> and will make new great improvements there, the park for his colts is
> long time since finished and he is making also a deer park and decoy.
> The decoy will be the finest in the kingdom or I believe in the 3
> kingdoms. The pond is already made and the reed wall is making, round
> about which he will build a wall at so great a distance that the fowl shall
> not be frightened thereat, the south and north ends of which wall shall
> be of lime and stone the other two ... a dry wall. Against the south wall
> without and against the north wall within he will plant fruit of all sorts
> and will make a treble ditch without the south wall and quickset the fen
> to the end that the deer may not get to the fruit and that the park may
> be completed.[46]

From this we can see that the essential elements of the seventeenth-century layout – its walls, the decoy, the fruit garden and deer park – were already present at Killruddery by 1682, four years prior to Dance's letter announcing Bonel's departure from Dublin.

Cheney states that 'Captain Brabazon' was responsible for creating the garden.[47] Brabazon already had some experience of managing great landscapes; he was appointed Ranger of the Phoenix Park in 1665, a time when Charles II was walling and developing the park as a large pleasure ground for the nobility of Dublin. Later, in 1693, in his capacity as Master of the Royal Hospital at Kilmainham, he was charged with preparing 'an account of what is necessary to be done in the garden'.[48] From this it may be presumed that the earl was cognisant of continental ideas, and there is no reason why he may not be given full credit for the formal design at Killruddery. It was commonplace for landowners to act as designers, often drawing on their experiences of visiting France and the Low Countries. Unfortunately we do not know whether Edward Brabazon travelled abroad, although he may have done during his period serving in the army. 'Bonel', then, remains something of a mystery. If he had been a driving force behind the creation of Killruddery, it is curious that his name does not appear in any other letters or related literature for the period. The gardener Bonel or Bonet referred to by Petty's agent was possibly a jobbing gardener, albeit one that was evidently respected by his employer. If such a man existed and was employed by the earl of Meath, it is likely that he would merely have realized plans drawn up the earl himself.

Landowners

Landscape interventions were often created by trial and error with landowners making garden plans themselves. Most of the great landowners in Ireland had travelled to Europe, going into exile with the Court, on State business, or on a Grand Tour, which became an established part of a young person's education in the seventeenth century.[49] Foreign travel was educational and young men were encouraged to learn French and Italian and develop an appreciation of European architecture, fashion, history and culture. In 1649 the young earl of Ossory enrolled at Monsieur de Camp's Academy in Paris and later hoped that his heir might take lessons at Monsieur Faubert's Academy.[50] The young earl of Orrery took a tour in 1685,[51] Lord Inchiquin's sons and the earls of Roscommon and Antrim spent long periods in France.[52] The tour took members of the aristocracy to the major cultural centres of the Continent – Paris, Rome, Venice, Florence and Naples. Here they were exposed to the grand French garden and the more compact Italian gardens, and, perhaps most importantly, to classicism which they had been tutored in prior to embarking on the tour. These sights and tastes would have been absorbed and inspiration taken from them. Other influences came from friends and colleagues. The 4th earl of Clanricard, Richard Burke (1572–1635), who laid out the early elaborate formal gardens at Portumna Castle in Galway, may have been influenced by Sir John Danvers' (c.1585–1655) garden at Chelsea.[53] Some gardeners took great interest in what their neighbours were doing, sometimes coordinating their landscape interventions. However, Robert Molesworth, who kept a keen eye on what landscape modifications and planting were taking place on adjoining demesnes, declared that 'the beauties of Breckdenston' were not dependent on what changes were being wrought at the neighbouring Brazeel estate (although he was keen to know what his other neighbour, 'cousin Forster', was doing).[54] Molesworth relied heavily on his wife Lettice to ensure that his ideas for the garden were executed. He also appears to have used his nephew John, or Jack, Tichbourne to oversee much of the work in the garden.[55]

The most salient feature of the design of gardens is the intense interest taken in them by their owners, even when abroad, on business or generally absent. This shows the high priority that was placed on the garden's design and its productiveness. While away from Kilkenny on State business, the duke of Ormond continued to oversee modernization and improvements to the Castle. He must have taken some of his inspiration from many gardens he had seen during his exile in France and the Low Countries and through the Court progress in England. At Kilkenny, where the medieval castle was being modernized to resemble a French chateau, the earl of Longford was deputized to consult with the greatest architects of the day who worked on the royal palaces. Sir Hugh May (1622–84)[56] was engaged to design a new classical gateway and said he would immediately consult Sir Christopher Wren about its design.[57] During Edward Viscount Conway's lifetime, most of his energies were spent in his Irish seats at Portmore and Conway Castle in Lisburn rather than at his English estate.[58]

Military technology and garden design

The military technology involved in the great earthworks and terracing to build Charlesfort in Kinsale was applied to garden works – levelling planting areas, removing stones and controlling water, cutting down trees, erecting retaining walls, holding back hillsides and raising terraces, diverting rivers and

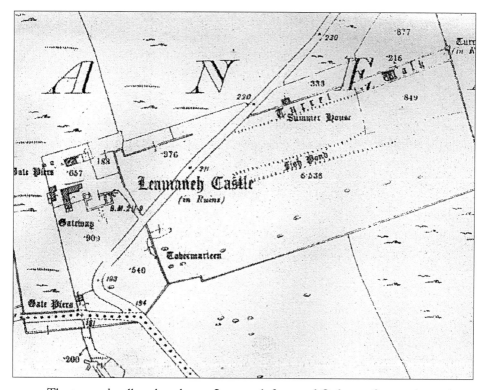

14 The terraced walk and gardens at Leamaneh from 2nd Ordnance Survey, sheet 16 (1897) (courtesy of the Trustees of Trinity College Dublin Library).

15 The remains of terracing at Leamaneh, with the terraced walk surrounding the gardens.

streams, cutting canals and draining potential arable land. The descriptions of the earthworks and engineering carried out at the fort are reminiscent of those carried out during the creation of the gardens at Burton in Cork. The workmen were instructed to level the garden with twenty men and two horses:

> To raise a wall against the terrace walk at the east end of the said garden four foot higher than the level thereof and two other walks of the same height each of those two walks such distance from the north and south walls of the said garden or as designated an advantage, drain thereof and all those three walks of the breadth designed in the said draught which said walls there to be [and the] level of the garden to be given suitable slopes on three sides and what earth is now within the bounds of the said garden more than will be disposed of in levelling it and raising the aforesaid three walks

The terraces were to be shored up by 'ramming' the sides so that they would not 'hereafter settle and thereby the garden become unlevel'.[59]

Hydraulic interventions were carried out by plumbers who were employed to lay pipes for waterworks, and engineers who designed reservoirs and channels to create an adequate water supply before planting began in earnest.[60] Brick- and stone-laying skills used in fortifications were modified for use in garden enclosures.[61] The benefit of strong garden walls was that they rebuffed cold winds and, equally importantly, thieves. They were built of brick or stone, or stone faced with brick, the latter material being more useful as it held the sun's warmth for longer, keeping the plants warm at night.[62] The vocabulary of martial architecture was used in gardening discourse, with references to 'flankers', 'turrets' and 'plats' becoming commonplace.[63] Fortifications generally consisted of a complex set of raised flat terraces, interspersed with deep ditches or canals; walls were constructed of back-filled stone or brick. These techniques were paralleled in a modified form in gardens engineered to manage vision as well as physical access. Terraces, ditches and canals were central features of Le Nôtre's gardening idiom with battlements used in the *jardin potager* at Versailles.[64] Though of far smaller scale, Leamaneh Castle in Clare too had a walled garden with stone reinforced banks of earth, turreted at each corner.[65] The strong walls were used to make a terrace walk, and within the walls was a terraced garden. Similar turret walks can be seen at the ruins of Rathcline (figs. 16 & 17) in Longford and Lismore Castle in Waterford.

16 The turret walk at Rathcline (courtesy of Ordnance Survey Ireland, permit ID 158).

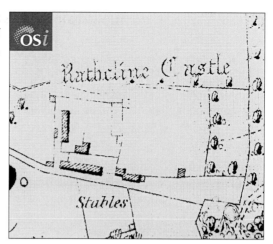

17 The turret walk at Rathcline today.

18 The Leamaneh gate now at Dromoland (courtesy of Dromoland Castle Hotel & Golf Country Club).

The elements of the pleasure garden

PARTERRES AND KNOTS

Medieval knot gardens evolved in the seventeenth century, growing larger and more elaborate – reaching their peak in the 1680s, and declining in intricacy until the Queen Anne period when simple grass plats became the norm. On Rocque's map of Dublin, the once-elaborate Viceregal Lodge, Chapelizod House, is depicted as having four plain grass plats in an almost square garden to the rear of the house.

The nomenclature is confusing and terms such as knot and parterre are used interchangeably. For instance, John Evelyn was never explicit about the distinction between the knot and the parterre. The decorative and practical purpose of the knots is clear from a 1638 lease from the benchers of the King's Inns, which instructed a tenant to plant a garden 'with knots and borders of sweet herbs, pot herbs, flowers, roses and fruit' for the kitchen and for 'strewing' and 'dressing' the chambers of the judges and barristers resident in the Inns. The sweet herbs would go some way to combating the foul smells emanating from the nearby river Liffey.[66]

Perhaps the most familiar and ornate type of parterre was the *parterre de broderie*, consisting of box or other evergreens planted in the style of embroidery, the ground between the box being covered in with a decorative material such as 'smith's dust', which was composed of iron filings and dust created in forges, 'black earth' or soot, fine gravel, sand or other loose chippings.

Antoine Dézallier d'Argenville (1680–1765) discussed the complexities of parterres in his book *The theory and practice of gardening* (1712) and explained how '*compartimenti*' differed from that of the *parterre de broderie*, in that the design was repeated and symmetrical and included 'shrubs and other grass-works, knots and borders of flowers' (fig. 19).[67] The simpler *parterres à l'Angloise*, English parterres (described by Dézallier d'Argenville as the 'plainest and meanest of all'), consisted of large grass plots encompassed within borders of flowers surrounded by a sanded path.[68] Despite their 'plain and mean appearance', grass plats would have been expensive and difficult to maintain. Their growing popularity in England and Ireland during the reign of Queen Anne may have reflected a desire for a more calm simplicity in style, but were deceptive in appearance as they were extremely labour intensive, requiring constant cutting, weeding, re-seeding, mowing and rolling, in contrast to hedges, which could be clipped once or twice a season to maintain a neat and tidy appearance. Bishop William King's accounts for 1700 show regular payments being made to an Elias Roberts for 'rowling' his lawns and 'keeping the garden clean'.[69]

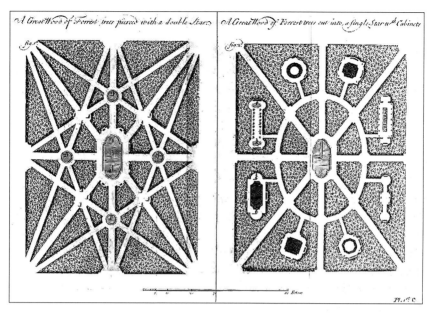

19 Designs for parterres from Dézallier d'Argenville, *The theory and practice of gardening* (1712).

By 1720, the upper garden at Breckdenston was composed of fashionable 'grass plats' with a fountain and a basin at its centre. This garden was designed to be visible 'from the parlour door'[70] and obeyed William Temple's diktat that the pleasure gardens 'ought to lie to the best parts of the house, or to those of the master's commonest use, so as to be but like one of the rooms out of which you step into another'.[71] The proportions of the parterres and enclosures close to the house were reminiscent of those within the house, and this attention to the scale of the various compartments combined with the canopy provided by 'close' walks blurred the division between house and garden indicating that the house and garden were conceived as a single entity. The designs of the parterres were sometimes reflected within the house itself and vice versa. This created a seamless progression from house to garden. The sixteenth-century Italian architect Sebastiano Serlio pioneered the idea of combining motifs for the house and garden in his designs for plasterwork ceilings and garden parterres, an idea used at Het Loo Palace in Holland.

It was suggested that planting within the parterres be low and flat in contrast to the woods surrounding the house. 'Fine openings should be preserved about the building, and in other places where the prospect of the country can be seen to advantage; for which reason we never set anything

20 A garden 'devoted to Flora' divided into 'several lesser squares'. John Worlidge's plan for a garden from *Systema horticulturae* (1677).

upon parterres, terraces, bowling greens, slopes etc., but small yews and flowering shrubs'.[72] These 'fine openings' could take the form of gaps in hedges, views beneath standard trees and hedges, arches, colonnades, and vistas along walks and avenues.

The coronary or flower garden also lay close to the house and was usually accommodated within the parterres.[73] This presented an opportunity to delight both the visual and olfactory senses. John Worlidge, as a lover of 'flora', was dismissive of the fashion for planting gentlemen's country seats with architectural plants alone. In 1677, he wrote contemptuously:

> The new mode of gravel walks and grass-plots, is fit only for such houses or palaces that are situated in cities and great towns, although they are now become precedents for many stately country residences, where they have banished out of their garden flowers, the miracles of nature, and the best ornaments that ever were discovered to make a seat pleasant. But it is hoped that this new, useless, and unpleasant mode, will like many other vanities grow out of fashion.[74]

A garden 'devoted to Flora' should be divided into 'several lesser squares' and grass parterres edged with flower beds which could be viewed closely when walking through the surrounding paths (fig. 20).[75] The model described by Worlidge was followed at Burton in Cork, which had four large grass plots surrounded by raised flower beds on all sides,[76] and also at Breckdenston where the 'large grass plots all of a piece, or cut a little' were surrounded by flower borders full of carnation pinks planted along 'the edge of all the borders as thick as they can stand'.[77] Far fewer plants were available for use in the flower garden than the thousands of species, varieties and hybrids existing today (excepting perhaps the tulip, which Dutch breeders had already successfully produced in a wide range of colours and formations).

Without the range of constantly changing and developing cultivars available to today's gardeners, the seventeenth-century garden's hectic clutter of topiary, pots and garden ornaments was offset by a more restricted palate.[78]

Nevertheless, many hundreds of plants, both native and exotic, were available to the seventeenth-century gardener. Named varieties were being established and Versailles was already famous in Ireland for its plant collection.[79] Tender plants could be grown in pots and taken out in the daytime,[80] new introductions such as *Pelargoniums*, imported to Britain by the Tradescants in 1631, were useful colourful additions to the flower garden. Such were their popularity that John Evelyn felt it necessary to write instructions for the care of tender pot plants such as 'setting the pot under a south wall and covering it with moss, and a bell glass, or better in the conservatory'.[81] Other popular flowers were tulips, anemones, ranunculus, crocuses, polyanthus, iris, narcissi and 'pinks' (various carnations and other *Dianthus*) and auriculas.

Both cutwork and *parterre de broderie* were observed in Boyle's survey of Lord Massereene's[82] gardens at Antrim Castle, described as 'one of the pleasantest seats in the kingdom'.[83] The survey mentions 'a curious little parterre' to the western side of the wilderness, which is still visible today. This was 'surrounded by a beautiful lime hedge 20 feet high and laid out in the most fantastic manner. Some of the beds contain flowers but numberless little ones laid out in every variety of shape, enclosed by boxwood edging contain only gravel, each containing a different colour. In the centre of the parterre is a yew tree fourteen feet high in the form of an obelisk'.[84] This description is consistent with Worlidge's suggestion that obelisks be placed in the centre of squares and parterres.[85] Obelisks were, and continued to be until the nineteenth century, a popular feature of gardens and landscapes in Ireland.[86] Early obelisks tended to be small and made of wood, vegetation or stone, and were often used as supports for climbers.

STATUARY AND GARDEN ORNAMENTS

Statuary proliferated towards the latter part of the seventeenth century. Gardens were decorated with statues brought from the Grand Tour of the Continent or cheaper copies made by local artisans. The discerning William Temple noted haughtily that 'good statues are in the reach of few men, and common ones are generally and justly despised or neglected'.[87] John Molesworth showed a distinct lack of refinement and disregard for antiquity when he wrote to his father Robert that 'good copies are better than scurvy originals'.[88] Those who could afford it commissioned works by renowned artists. The duke of Tyrconnell is said to have commissioned statues for the gardens of Carton House from the Dutch sculptor Artus Quellinus II[89] whose father, Quellinus the Elder, created statuary for the palace gardens of the Stadholders of Holland.[90] Statuary usually took the form of characters from classical history and legend. Sculptures were often used as eye catchers at the end of vistas or displayed in niches as at Breckdenston.[91] William Chetwood wrote that the cascade at Burtonhall in Carlow was 'adorned with elegant statues, some of which are originals brought from Italy' and at the end of a vista a statue of a gladiator, 'a good copy of that finished original now in Hampton Court Gardens'.[92]

Garden writers recommended that the centres of squares should be ornamented with statues, or, where water was available, with fountains.[93] A painting of the seventeenth-century Stradbally Hall[94] in Laois shows statues placed at the centre of wooded walks in the pleasure gardens.

Statuary depicting figures from classical texts indicated that the owner was a man of education and sophistication. Exclusivity was added by the fact that the statuary could only be fully appreciated by those of similar education and discernment. At Doneraile, a pedestal with a 'statue of a gladiator, with other lesser figures' stood in the front court.[95] The statues at Breckdenston were placed in centre of grass plats. Molesworth's son John suggested that these should be 'Fauns and satyrs, or at least some of those pastoral figures of shepherds and shepherdesses seen on the road to Hyde Park', continuing that 'Venus, or any other graceful statue' would be suitable for the 'middle of the grass plots'.[96] The duke of Ormond commissioned 'the casting and making of four large statues and sixteen smaller' to be executed 'in hard metal or hardened lead'. The large figures of Diana, the Sabine women, Hercules, Commodus and Antoninus were to be 'full as large as those figures so called in his Majesty's privy garden upon which figures John Bonnier shall take off his mould'. The 16 small statues were to express the 12 signs of the zodiac and the 4 seasons.[97]

The duke's half-brother, George Mathew, was said to have had 'statues thick as trees'[98] and terraces 'thickly studded with busts and statues' at his garden in Thomastown in Co. Tipperary.[99] Sometimes less famous and therefore probably cheaper artists could be found to create garden statuary; Lord Donegall engaged two 'Polanders' to make 'statues and many fine things of alabaster'.[100]

It was fashionable to display flowerpots and urns around the garden, at the corners of beds and parterres and on terraces. Pots were necessary for tender plants such as citrus fruits, which had to be taken out during warm weather and sheltered during the cold and at night. The grandest gardens used antique urns collected on the Grand Tour or good modern imitations. These pots were as decorative and often more valuable than the plants themselves. Worlidge suggested that if such luxurious containers were not available, lead pots were the best sort of substitute. He added that they should be placed near the house, presumably to preserve them from theft as much as to ensure their visibility from the main salons.[101] The flowerpots used for beds and parterres needed to be large enough to be visible and to articulate the corners of the parterres. Lord Conway's gardener Francis complained about a consignment of pots for Portmore; he did 'not like the fashions' of the pots as they were 'too low', in other words they did not stand sufficiently proud to counterpoint the level of the planting within the beds.[102] In 1695 Bishop King paid 9s. for 37 pots for the garden at his palace in Derry, which he appears to have developed considerably during his tenure.[103] Lord Shannon writing to Sir John Perceval in 1682, referred him to a good potter he knew who 'serves all Cork and the county about it', who had made pipes for him 'as also flower pots for garden'.[104]

SUNDIALS

John Evelyn urged his readers to reject the more 'obscene' classical statuary such as priapus, suggesting that in its place one should insert features more consistent with modern thinking and sensibilities, such as sundials, which achieved 'a modern elegancy'.[105] The dials could take any of several forms, simple small stone dials on pedestals or columns, wall-mounted dials, and, most interestingly, those made of plant materials.

Sundials were frequently mentioned in both contemporary gardening literature and descriptions by visitors to gardens.[106] Dials would have been placed in the pleasure garden close to the house, perhaps in a parterre or as a piece of statuary. In Thomas Fale's *Horeologiographia, the art of dialling* (London, 1593), the author hoped his book would be 'of special use and delight not only for students of the arts mathematical, but also for diverse

artificers, architects, surveyors of buildings, free-masons, sailors, and others'.[107]
Dials were found in centres of learning; John Dunton observed two sundials
in the gardens at Trinity College in Dublin, one placed on the top of a stone
representing a pile of books, and the other, more unusually, 'set in box'.[108] The
reference to the dial being set in box is reminiscent of those at Pembroke
College Cambridge and New College Oxford, the latter designed by Sir
Christopher Wren in 1658.

A sundial was also installed in the garden of the old King's Inns in
Dublin.[109] Lord Conway had a sundial sent by ship from England to put in
the gardens at Conway Castle in Lisburn.[110] In 1686 Clarendon wrote to
Evelyn sending him 'a little pamphlet of a new contrived dial', designed and
dedicated to him by Gerard Boate who had presented him with a model of the
dial itself.[111]

BOWLING GREENS

Lawn bowling, a popular sport since the sixteenth century, was, like pell mell,
played by all classes and sexes. Bowls was frequently played for money at the
public alleys and greens.[112] The demand for public bowling greens must have
been strong, as they appear to have reached the point of ubiquity in towns and
cities by the 1660s. The duke of Ormond's set in particular had a fondness for
gambling on play. For the gentry and aristocracy, the bowling green was a place
where people could meet and parade in their finery. Good sport was had,
introductions were made and deals struck on the green.[113] The duke of
Ormond used Oxmantown Green on the north side of the Liffey frequently,
which, to the dismay of some, allowed women to play 'kettlepins' (skittles).
Oxmantown also had a banqueting house which could be hired for parties.[114]

Though surviving manuscripts make frequent references to bowling greens,
private bowling greens were the preserve of the very rich such as Lord
Conway.[115] John Dunton, a keen bowler, noted that private greens were the
exception rather than the norm:

> The bowling green above all has charms for me: I think it no improper
> recreation for ladies; and where men, who are desirous to civilize
> themselves in ladies' companies, might partake with them there. The
> only difficulty is that there are very few bowling greens in private
> families, they are so chargeable to keep.[116]

Keeping the green velvety smooth in the days before mechanical lawnmowers
was both difficult and expensive; the grass would have to be cut slowly and

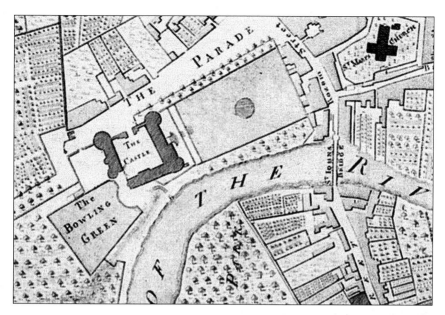

21 Kilkenny Castle with its large bowling green from John Roque's *Map of the County of Dublin* (1760).

laboriously by hand scythe and then compressed by a heavy roller. It was also difficult to find gardeners with the necessary expertise to manage the greens. The duchess of Ormond bemoaned the fact that money saved by discharging a good but dishonest gardener '… may soon be lost' by 'his ignorance or negligence of the bowling green'.[117] In his *Account of my conversation in Ireland* John Dunton wrote that the garden next to the Kilkenny bowling green had gone to seed but was in the process of being repaired by 'a young gardener from England, and will in a few years, be as pleasant as the Spring Gardens near Vauxhall'.[118] By the mid-eighteenth century, Kilkenny Castle's bowling green was opened to the public, probably to offset the immense cost of maintaining the castle and gardens (fig. 21). Chetwood, visiting in 1748, wrote that 'the noble large gardens are in much the same state as the place; and the bowling-green is now common for any gentleman that pays for his pleasure'.[119]

Private greens were usually situated within the pleasure garden, a short distance from the house. The green at Killruddery was to the east of the house, surrounded by trees. Similarly, a sunken area lies adjacent to the house at Eyrecourt before the start of the canal which it is reasonable to suppose was the bowling green. The green itself was usually rectangular in shape (though John Evelyn's green at Sayes Court was semi-circular). Greens were surrounded by trees, usually yew or other evergreen, to deflect light and to frame and shelter the green. Evelyn's green was edged with holly and a variety of fruit trees interspersed with gooseberries, currants and strawberries.[120]

As bowling greens became less fashionable, or became too costly to manage, they were often replaced by other features. At Castlemartyr, the bowling green was used for growing timber, being planted with sycamore in 1728,[121] and Killruddery green, prone to flooding, was planted with a matrix of birch.

WALKS AND ALLÉES

Gardens were given their characteristic geometry and vertical structure by the creation of straight walks and allées bordered by trees and shrubs. Gardens were places where a measure of privacy and calm could be achieved which was impossible elsewhere. Walks often lead to ornamental garden buildings. In the section of his book called 'Walks, arbours, and places of repose in gardens' Worlidge explained:

> [I]t is not the least part of the pleasures of a garden, to walk and refresh yourself either with your friends or acquaintances, or else alone retired from the cares of the world, or apart from company that sometimes may prove burthensome to you … [122]

Walks were 'places of divertissement after a sedentary repast. The aromatic odours they yield, pleasant refreshments after a gross diet'.[123] After a bout of illness, Sir William Petty wrote to his wife of how he longed to get back to his garden and to create some new walks – 'the first piece of my new care for my own health is the fitting our garden for my exercise and diversion [with walks] 1,000 foot'.[124]

Petty lived in George's Lane in Dublin at this time, which shows us that fashionable gardening was not confined to large country estates. In 1637 and 1638, the benchers of the King's Inns in Dublin (which at the time was situated on the north bank of the river Liffey, approximately where the Four Courts now stands) leased part of their property to a Randall Beckett, imposing conditions that he was also required to lay out walks around the plot and generally to keep it in 'good and decent order'.[125] Garden writers devoted sections of their work to the layout of the garden and its walks. Walks in gardens were laid out on the same principles as 'streets in a town, serving to communicate between place and place'.[126] The ambulatory groves and walks invited the user to go from one part of the garden to another. This was achieved by the placement of objects such as statuary, or the exploitation of existing features, to create interest and stimulate the impulse to explore the garden further. Sometimes walks extended the view from the garden by means of a gate or *claire-voie* piercing the enclosing wall. This feature was an opening, usually circular, cut out of the wall through which to view the countryside beyond. *Claire-voies* can be seen at Thomastown in Tipperary.[127] At Thomastown the walls are still pierced with large round oriels, which are, like so many features of the lost gardens in Ireland, partly bricked up and overgrown.

Garden writers differentiated between walks in the various parts of the garden, some were more important than others within the hierarchy. Worlidge directed that the 'principal walk should extend itself as far as you can in length directly from your choicest plants for beauty and scent, and that there may be a succession of them through the year not without flower pots which grace the best of gardens'.[128] There were many conventions to be followed with a different style of walk for each situation: 'the close and the open, the single and the double'. Principal walks, or 'those that face a building, pavilion, cascade, or the like' should be of the open type, wider than other walks to allow a view and preferably with 'close' counter walks either side to provide shade like colonnades.

> The two middle rows should be planted with trees detached, that is to say not shut up with a palisade, but free, that you may go round them; and the two other rows should be filled up and edged with palisades. As double walks are the most esteemed, so they are generally made to possess the finest parts of a garden.[129]

'Close' walks were those formed by trees or hedges, which were trained to meet at the top to form a canopy. These walks tended to be narrower than open walks to enable the branches to meet sooner.[130] Close walks allowed the garden to be enjoyed even in inclement weather. The new Viceregal Lodge at Chapelizod was laid out in close walks by the duchess of Ormond, which were later dismissed disparagingly by the countess of Clarendon who felt they compared very unfavourably to the walks in her garden and John Evelyn's in England.[131]

Again there is some confusion over the term 'palisade', which could be used in one sense as a reference to fencing or walls, or in another sense to intertwined trees used to make boundaries for walks. For instance, Lucius O'Brien of Corofin House wrote to his wife Catherine requesting that she order the gardener to 'get the foundation for the upper terraces cleared of the rocks he tells me are there with all speed but let not the foundation be laid or the palisades be set up till I return which I protest to you (my Dr Cate) I long to do as much as you can conceive'.[132] In this context, it is clear that O'Brien was using the term 'palisade' to indicate some kind of paling. Living palisades were created to provide shade or windbreaks for walks. By pruning and manipulation of young branches the palisade could take on any form desired. Dézallier d'Argenville instructed his readers that there 'is no difficulty in executing such forms ... but there has to be much work and devotion in order to train them and make them grow in their appropriate form ... which they only acquire with time', and continued: 'this is a prime example of how art surpasses nature which is ordered and subjected to the genius of the gardener'.[133]

Palisades were used to make grand statement walks and entrances to avenues. For instance, at Breckdenston, Molesworth's son-in-law suggested that the canal should be extended to reach 'the lower end of the cherry garden and make fine palisades with a great gate opening to it which would look very grand and magnificent to the country for some miles and you may make the walks in the cherry garden parallel to those on either side your canal'.[134] Whether or not this work was actually undertaken is not known, but it is consistent with what is known of the rest of the gardens at Breckdenston.

Gardens situated on sloping ground were generally terraced to make them workable; the declining sides planted either with grass alone or fruit.[135] An example of such a garden can be seen at Castletown in Kildare on the 1760 John Rocque map. The gardens were laid out on a series of three terraces gradually declining towards the river's edge. Leamaneh Castle in Clare was also terraced and the north-west facing terrace is still clearly visible within the walls of the turret walk. Pakenham Hall in Westmeath was built on a hill which was terraced in order to lead gently down to a series of water gardens below.[136]

Open walks referred to either of three types, those between allées or parterres, walks planted with high hedges or tall trees that opened at the top or to the principal walks.[137] William Cobett described the garden designed by Evelyn for the duke of Norfolk as having yew trees grown as standards: 'a row of small yew trees, the trunks of which are bare for about eight or ten feet high, while the bottom branches come out on each side of the row about eight feet horizontally'. The trees were planted close together so their canopies melded together, creating a 'hedge on stilts', which surrounded a walk covered in hard gravel or a very fine grade of sandy gravel.[138] By growing trees as standards, the trunks could be utilized as supports for climbers such as honeysuckle, rose or clematis, all of which added to the sensory experience of the garden.

As with the spaces between parterres, walks were surfaced in turf, gravel, sand or ashes, which were plentiful and inexpensive. At Kilkenny Castle the garden walks were described as being surfaced in black gravel by Loveday.[139] A later visitor described how 'ashes' were used in the 'fourfold walks'.[140] Loveday's version is almost certainly the correct one. Kilkenny is famous for its black marble, and chippings were probably used in the walks which could have been mistaken for ashes at a distance. Excavations reveal that the garden paths at Blessington House were composed of red brick, pebbles, limestone and mortar,[141] while the walks at the Viceregal Lodge at Chapelizod were surfaced with ash.[142] In either event the dark coloured surface would serve to warm the surrounding soil and benefit the plants. Gravel surfaces were particularly suitable for fruit walks as they reflected the rays of the sun better than grass;[143] William Temple wrote that 'peaches and grapes will have no taste but upon a sand or gravel'.[144] Such walks had to be carefully managed to stop them becoming weed infested or waterlogged. For gravel walks 'fine screened' gravel was used. This was mixed with clay or loam or the 'refuse of brick kilns' or sea shells 'to make it bind better'.[145] The gravel used on the 'low walks' at Burton was described as a combination of 'good gravel and lime well-tempered and mixed together'.[146]

At Conway Castle in Lisburn the walks were 'finely gravelled' [147] Huge quantities of gravel were used in creating walks, and was 'tedious work' for the unfortunate gardeners.[148] William King paid for 142 loads of 'fine gravel for the pleasure garden' at the Bishop's palace.[149] Depending on where one lived, 'good gravel' in large amounts could prove difficult to come by. Locally obtained materials were commonly used. At Portmore, Rawdon worried that he would 'be at a loss for gravel next spring for that new way (which is surprising given that Portmore was situated between Loughs Beg and Neagh and one would imagine that there would be no shortage of gravel).[150] Molesworth complained that his gardener had been rather over-enthusiastic about grading; he 'screens our stuff so fine that little besides the earth came home to our walks, the large binding gravel was left behind ... about a thousand load of that gross sort of gravel [not stones] now at and about the sand pit mixed with what we have would make all our gravel walks good again'.[151] In summer the gravel could become uncomfortably hot to walk upon so it was suggested that a narrow walk of turf each side of the main walk should be provided for use in warm weather. Worlidge suggested that, ideally, gravel walks should have a central path paved with stone five or six feet broad. Grass walks usually had a gutter channel running along either side which 'not only receives the waste water but preserves the grass or weeds from mixing with your borders'.[152]

Dézallier d'Argenville, believing that turf walks in the garden were a 'constant charge to keep', and too bothersome, recommended that instead of grass, planting two double lines of box and filling it with red sand.[153] Despite the cost, Rathbeale in Swords had terraced 'broad grass walks' from one end to the other', which were 'sprucely kept and at least twelve score yards long with a descent of 10 or 12 steps every 30 or 40 yards'.[154]

The levelling, excavating, surfacing, planting and maintenance of the more ornamental walks could be very expensive. Sir Donat O'Brien was continually exasperated by his son Lucius's extravagant ways with money. He found it impossible to understand how someone so continually short of money could spend so much on his garden at Corofin House,[155] which he felt was detrimental to the ancestral home at Leamaneh. He wrote in anger to his daughter-in-law Catherine in March 1713/14, berating Lucius for his obsession with creating walks in his garden:

> To continue still the expense of an unnecessary improvement … for gardens and walks at a place that will never make any suitable returns for it, and where my posterity cannot be presumed to make it the place of that residence, nor that any tenant … will pay for the land they take and not for walks and gardens. But perhaps you may think it reasonable that your husband ought to be allowed to do these things for his amusement and diversion though never so expensive and unnecessary, unless it be intended that place [Corofin] shall demolish and destroy Leamaneh.[156]

The duke of Ormond bought Moore Park in Hertfordshire in 1663 for £2000 for use when attending Court or other business in England.[157] He renovated the house and undertook extensive tree planting, stocking the park with deer and laying out the gardens, which were later eulogized by Sir William Temple in his *Gardens of Epicurus*.[158] The earl of Anglesey wrote of a visit to Moore Park in the autumn of 1663 and conveyed his delight at what he saw in the way of avenues and walks:

> I was last week to new Moor [Moore] Park, which I find to be still the same sweet and pleasant seat I knew it before … The gardens are extraordinary, full of delightful walks and fountains and terraces with covered walks for rainy weather … The park is set out into walks shaded with trees set in rows, and there is a fair brick lodge, that hath the prospect of most of the park and country, and may be seen at the end of a long walk out of your dining room window.[159]

ORNAMENTAL GARDEN BUILDINGS

A range of buildings made of various materials were been erected and placed in appropriate positions throughout the garden for differing purposes. Arbours made from trees and shrubs or climbers trained on trellis had been popular in Elizabethan gardens. Worlidge rejected these on the grounds that they were too high maintenance, for, in his opinion, in creating 'a garden of pleasure you ought to be frugal of cost and pains'. Worlidge suggested 'boxes to seclude you from the too cold breezes'. Additionally, he was of the opinion that arbours were injurious to health as their seats were 'apt to be moist', which of course in those days was thought to cause all sorts of terrible ailments.

A 'healthier', that is, less damp, alternative to arbours were seats set in niches and 'pleasure houses'. All were common features in gardens both grand and modest. These were sometimes glazed (with glass windows), which would allow the garden to be enjoyed even during inclement weather. Grottoes were the precursor to some of the more elaborate garden follies that followed in the eighteenth century. Worlidge devoted a chapter of his book to them[160] and in the unpublished *Elysium Britannicum*, Evelyn listed the minerals that could be used to create them.[161] Grottoes could take the form of small rustic stone buildings or rather grand classical follies built primarily for decoration. The large walled garden at Howth Castle in Co. Dublin had a very smart pitched roofed garden building at its centre (fig. 22).[162] Worlidge suggested that in gardens where water was unavailable, a garden house for dining called a 'banqueting house or house of pleasure', placed somewhere central to the garden, would be an adequate alternative as a showpiece.[163] In Dublin city a 'banquetting house' was constructed on the 'high ground', a raised terrace, to the west of the walled garden at the King's Inns.[164] Here the benchers of the Inns could dine in style with views of the river and Phoenix Park beyond. Bishop King had a 'garden house' constructed by a Mr Ellis at his palace in Derry; it is unfortunate that no further details remain about its form.[165] At Kilkenny Castle, the duke of Ormond commissioned a grotto or banqueting house (figs. 23, 23a), now sadly gone, which appears to have been very fine indeed. It was reported that:

> The court will look much better than when your grace was here when the new pavement is finished which will be done in a fortnight of fair weather. On Monday and Tuesday next the marble piers by the grotto will be got up, which could not be carried through the bowling green until this dry weather came in. I believe the like were not seen in this kingdom heretofore.[166]

22 Detail from the overmantel painting at Howth Castle showing a garden building at the centre of the walled garden. Straw bee skeps can also be seen in the garden to the left of the building (courtesy of Mr and Mrs Julian Gaisford St Lawrence).

The grotto at Kilkenny may have been inspired by that at Moore Park, which Sir William Temple described as being 'covered with lead, and flat' and 'embellished with figures of shell-rock-work, fountains, and water works'.[167] Shell houses appear to have become much in vogue from the end of the seventeenth century. There was a shell house in the gardens of the Elizabethan Turvey House in Meath, and at Mount Merrion an octagonal shaped shell house (probably early to mid-eighteenth century), described as being supported by eight pillars of stone, stood in the centre of the huge scotch fir grove.[168] A spectacular obelisk erected on four rustic arches survives in Stillorgan, which once stood in the parkland of Stillorgan House. The obelisk was designed in 1727 by Sir Edward Lovett Pearce for the 2nd Viscount Allen (fig. 24). Dromoland Ccastle had an early example of a circular garden temple

23 Francis Place's sketch of 'Ormond's house at Kilkenny taken from the bridge' *c.*1669. The open space to the left of the picture is the bowling green and the circular building is the banqueting house. Taken from John Maher, 'Francis Place in Drogheda, Kilkenny and Waterford, etc.', *JRSAI* 64 (1934), pp 41–53.
23a (Detail taken from fig. 23, showing the banqueting house at Kilkenny Castle.

24 The obelisk at Stillorgan House.

25 The temple of Mercury at Dromoland (courtesy of Dromoland Castle Hotel &
Golf Country Club).

26 The gazebo at
Dromoland (courtesy
of Dromoland Castle
Hotel & Golf Country
Club).

of six columns that stood on a mount (fig. 25). This was possibly influenced by that at Oldtown Demesne in Kildare, which also had a temple on a mount, which was destroyed in 1881.[169] A further garden building was added to Dromoland in 1730 by Sir Edward O'Brien who built an octagonal gazebo (fig. 26), designed by architect John Aheron, on top of an artificial mound in order to watch horse racing in comfort.[170]

Often machinery and other engines necessary for the workings of the garden such as fountains, water cisterns and wheels were disguised in small follies and outbuildings. Worlidge suggested that cisterns be made of lead and concealed in a 'lodge or grot'.[171] Molesworth's cistern at Breckdenston, which was designed 'to hold 50 or 60 ton', was 'set a top of a water house'. What is presumed to be the remains of the water house still survives within a farmyard adjacent to a housing development at Knocksedan Demesne.

BEEHIVES

Beehives, usually associated with orchards and kitchen gardens, were also situated in pleasure gardens. Sometimes the hives were contained in alcoves in brick or stone walls (called bee boles) for protection from the elements, and thieves.[172] Woven straw beehives, called skeps, can be seen in the orchard in the overmantel painting of Howth Castle in the early eighteenth century. Bees were admired by the improvers of the Commonwealth and Restoration, who saw the industry, order and hierarchy of the hive as a model for society as a whole.

Robert Child wrote to Samuel Hartlib about the potential profits to be made from honey and wax, bemoaning the deficiencies of beekeeping in England, arguing that there were too few bees and that English techniques for managing them were poor; '[t]he husbandry of bees is an excellent way of enriching and would bring in to the kingdom of England yearly above a hundred thousand lb'.[173] In addition to their wax and honey, bees were also useful aids to plant fertilization and propagation, flitting from bloom to bloom within the fruit and flower gardens. Hartlib had incorporated the bulk of Child's letter into his *Legacie of husbandry* (London, 1651) but his material on bees grew too substantial for inclusion in the second and third edition of the *Legacie* and was eventually published in a separate tract in 1655, *The reformed commonwealth of bees*. It has been argued that Hartlib's beekeeping project was a serious economic proposition, an important feature of his agricultural programme and a direct product of the Commonwealth government's stimulation of economic and social reform.[174] Richard Lawrence proposed to include a chapter on 'good huswifry in the right ordering of butter and cheese,

27 A bee shelter, 'where the bees lye' from William Lawson's *Country housewife's garden* (1635).

bacon, wax and honey for foreign markets' in his unwritten second volume of *The interest of Ireland*.[175]

Hives were considered important enough to merit frequent mentions in correspondence and sometimes bees or honey were moved from one estate to another.[176] Rawdon established beehives in the orchard at Portmore, judging it a 'place fitter' for them.[177] And Richard Cox, reporting for the Dublin Philosophical Society in the 1680s, noted the abundance of honey and wax in Co. Cork.[178]

Sometimes hives were created in a 'bee shelter' (fig. 27), described by Worlidge thus:

A frame standing on posts with one floor (if you would have it hold more hives, two floors) boarded, laid on bearers, and pack posts, covered over with boards, flat wise. Let the floors be without holds or clefts, lest in casting time the bees lie out and loiter. And though your hives stand within a handbreadth the one of another, yet will bees know their home. In this frame may your bees stand dry and warm, especially if you make doors like doors of windows to shroud them in winter, as in a house, provided you leave the hives mouth open. I myself have devised such an house, and I find that it strengthens my bees much, and my hives will last six to one.[179]

Occasionally hives were kept near the house for scientific purposes. John Evelyn had an 'observational beehive', described by Samuel Pepys in his 1665 Diary, as 'a hive of bees, so as being hived in glass, you may see the bees making their honey and combs mighty pleasantly'.[180] Richard Bulkeley of Old Bawn, Tallaght, was not so lucky with his glass hive, which he had set up by his 'parlour window', explaining that observing the bees was difficult because 'their breath does so much obfuscate the glass'.[181]

ICE HOUSES

In Britain and Ireland the practice of storing ice and snow in specially constructed chambers began in the seventeenth century[182] and ice or snow houses were built within the demesne landscape of Ireland at the same time. They were frequently, though not necessarily, situated near to water, as at Stradbally Hall, for the obvious reason that ice would be easily accessible. However, snow was often used in place of or in addition to ice and was stored in either straw-thatched ice-houses or snow-pits, dug deep into the ground.[183] The snow or ice was stacked in the chamber of the ice house, insulated by straw to ensure it remained frozen. The ice was used throughout the year in the kitchens for cooling and preservation.[184] The recipe book compiled by Dorothy Parsons of Birr Castle in 1666 includes a recipe for an early form of ice-cream – 'cream with snow' – which would indicate the presence of a snow house at Birr at that date.[185] Today the remains of an ice house are situated on the high walk between the pond and the house. This would be convenient for both the collection of ice and transport to the kitchen. Most domestic ice houses were comparatively small with a single sunken circular chamber 2½–3m (8ft–10ft) in diameter and about 3m (10ft) deep, with a domed roof. Loading was normally through a hatch in the roof and the ice was removed through a horizontal tunnel with double doors. Melt water was discharged through a drain from the lowest part of the base.[186] In general, ice houses were built below ground or into the side of a bank and covered with earth to increase insulation. The bank would often be planted with trees to provide further shade for the ice house and to improve drainage. At Breckdenston the ice house was situated 'on the hill side over the tuckmill and to a decoy'.[187] Ice houses were usually composed of brick but other local materials were also used.[188] It may seem inconceivable today that such quantities of snow and ice could be saved as to fill an ice house, but it appears that snow was quite plentiful. Winters were hard, and references to cold weather appear quite often in letters.[189]

DOVECOTES AND PIGEON HOUSES

Carefully designed dovecotes (or pigeon houses) were ubiquitous features on the demesne landscape. These frequently elaborate and complex structures had been existence since medieval times, and remained popular until the mid-nineteenth century. In the seventeenth-century garden dovecotes were built to house pigeons for food, not merely for the ornamental value a flock of billing and cooing white doves gave to the garden.[190] Pigeon, a useful source of meat, was valuable and was therefore subject to poaching. The lease of land did not automatically confer a right to take its game,[191] and pigeon houses appear frequently in conveyances and assignments of land.[192] The dovecote had the added advantage of providing manure from droppings (an excellent soil enricher), which is why they were often situated within or close to the pleasure garden and were often ornamental as well as practical. With characteristic precision, Molesworth directed every element of the design of his pigeon house at Breckdenston, specifying that it should be 'roughcast' and painted white and boasting that he thought 'the pigeon house is placed as handsomely as anything of that sort in Ireland it makes a fine show yet it stands not in the way of any of the avenues'.[193] The pigeon house probably stood in the pigeon park which was just south of the great avenue at Breckdenston.[194] A pigeon house also stood in the park at Rathcoffey in Kildare and at Portmore in Co. Antrim, designed by Lord Conway himself.[195] Aviaries were also kept in order to show off more exotic species. These were occasionally situated under terraces or mounts but were sometimes made as attractive free-standing buildings. Lord Conway directed that 'an arched vault' was to run along under the walk without the foregate'.

MOUNTS AND TERRACED WALKS

Mounts were a feature of the seventeenth-century garden, but had been in existence since medieval times. The positioning of mounts within parterres

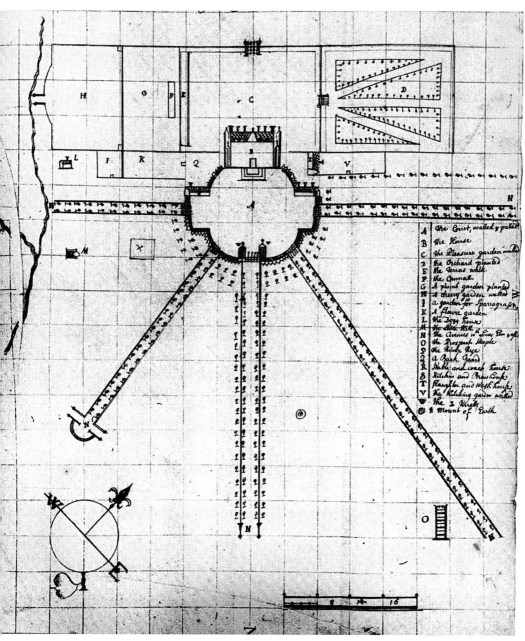

KEY:
A   the court, walled
B   the House
C   the Pleasure Garden, walled
D   the Orchard planted
E   the Terras walk
F   the Cannall

28 Detail from 'A Draught of Carton, The Duke of Tyrconnell's House; 'A resemblance of the Improvements of Carretowne', anon., c.1680s, showing the great patte d'oie to the front of the house (courtesy of Viscount Coke and the Trustees of the Holkham Estate and Trinity Images).

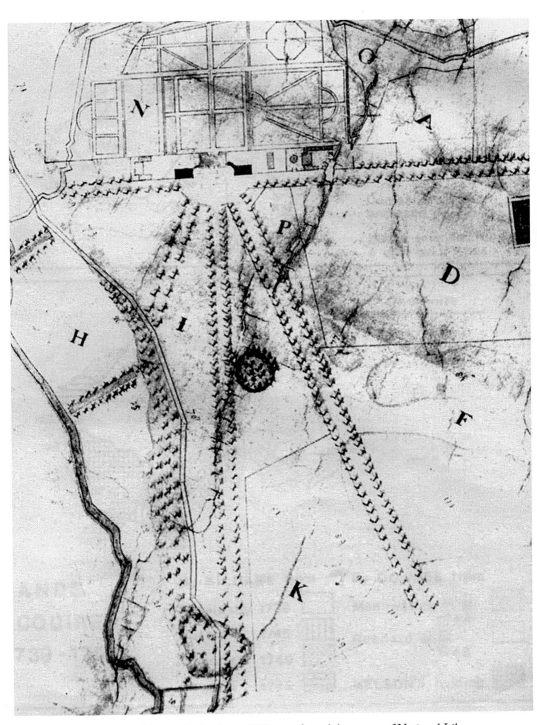

29 A survey of Carton by Baylie and Mooney (1744) (courtesy of National Library
of Ireland).

was an early sixteenth-century development, when mounts were placed to one side of the garden to allow oblique views across intricately planted parterres.[196] Ancient mounts could be utilized and drawn into the wider scheme of the garden. The Talbot house at Carton had what is thought, due to its shape and apparently random position within the greater garden scheme, to have been an ancient mount. This 'mount of earth' was about thirty feet high and is keyed in the anonymous plan of Carton (fig. 28) and clear visible in both Baylie and Mooney's map of 1744 (fig. 29), an eighteenth-century plan and van der Hagen's painting (see plate 2).[197]

The mount is still at Carton in John Rocque's map of 1760, although by this time the great *patte d'oie* had been raised to make way for the landscape park. When William Duncan mapped the estate in 1821, all traces of the mount were gone. Dineley's drawing of the Turrets at Staplestown in Carlow shows a mount outside the walled gardens overlooking the woodland beyond (fig. 30).[198] The mount overlooked the wilderness and views of the entire demesne could be taken from it. At Gaulstown the original house was sited within view of a medieval mount (fig. 31).

New mounts were also created as a way of using the spoil or earth or rubbish from excavations for ponds or sunken terraces.[199] Apart from the traditional circular 'mound' shape, mounts were composed in various forms. Some were very elaborate, made of a series of square, rectangular or circular tiers, sometimes hedged. Most mounts had sloping grass sides, more unusually, although some had masonry walls.[200] The space under mounts and terraces could be supported by stone walls and was often used for grottoes, orangeries,[201] or other useful features. A mount, or volary was created at Lisburn Castle in 1667.[202] George Rawdon was disturbed that 'neither William Hoole nor I heard anything about this before and it will have to be covered in with lead to keep off the drops – an expensive work, and I should like to know your Lordship's will before setting about it'.[203]

As with many aspects of historical garden design, some confusion can arise as to the exact meaning of the terminology used. A mount would normally be held to refer to a circular mound of earth, usually with a spiral path or steps to its summit. However the term mount can also be used to describe the turret at the end of a raised or terraced walk or even the walk itself. For instance, at p. 13 of *The country house-wife's garden* (London, 1618), William Lawson lays out a garden plan, which includes features described as mounts. These are raised walks along the central terraced gardens from which the various compartments can be viewed. Stairs or steps lead down to each section of the garden. At each corner sits a turreted house used variously as a still-house or bee shelter. A

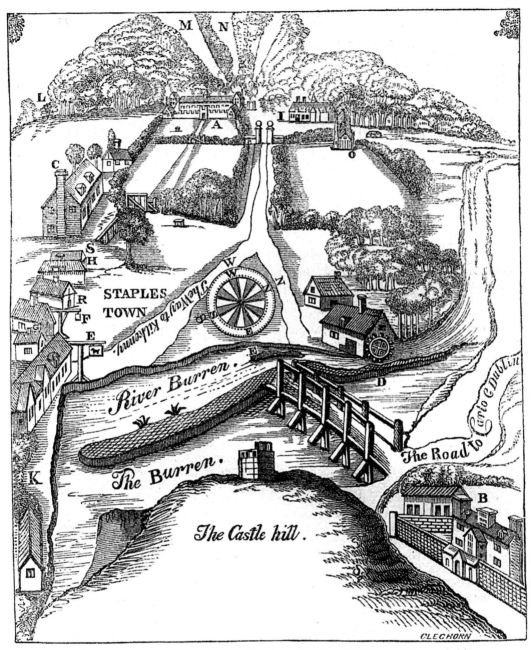

30 Staplestown House by Thomas Dineley taken from Shirley and Graves (eds), 'Dineley's journal', *JKSIAS*, 4:1 (1862), p. 44.

KEY:

A   The Turrets belonging to John Tench Esq.
B   Bennekerry belonging to William Ewers Esq.
C   Worthy Mr James Moor, ye Minister
D   Robert Lackey, Miller
E   Thomas Harris, at the Crowne, Saddler and Innkeeper
F   Thomas Glaseby Taylor and Victualler
G   Thomas Gould, Farrier
H   Joseph Davis, Gardiner

I   Ye stable of ye Turrets
K   Nicholas Langford, Carpenter
L   The Mount
M   Glades in the wood
N   Glades in the wood
O   the Barnes
R   Hugh Brookshaw, Mason
S   ? Shoomasker; all Protestants

31 The mount at Gaulstown today.

similar layout can be seen at Lismore Castle in Co. Waterford, which has been remodelled over the centuries but retains its original overall plan and fabric as laid out in the seventeenth century.[204]

The garden at the King's Inns had what was referred to as a 'mound walk', which may or may not have been the 'high green walk' referred to in a map of 1728.[205] The King's Inns mount may date from its days as a monastery garden. Certainly a similar walled 'mount garden' existed at Audley End in Essex which dates from at least the early seventeenth century and can be seen on a plan of *c.*1676.

As with mounts, 'terrace walks' were usually to be found where excavations had taken place in the garden and some use had to be found for the spoil.[206] The southern wall of the bowling green in Dublin (perhaps the one at Oxmantown) had a 'handsome terrace walk its whole length',[207] which was probably created from the spoil left over from excavating and levelling the green. At Gaulstown the earth excavated to make a huge canal was used to create islands within the canal and terrace walks along each bank which were

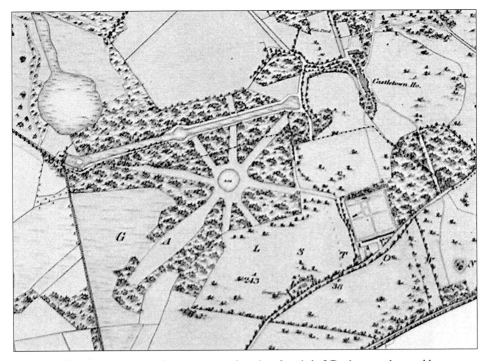

32 The 'curious groves, fine avenues and enclosed paths' of Gaulstown observed by
Isaac Butler in 1744 (Itinerary of a Journey 1744, Armagh Public Library P00180987x).
Dean Jonathan Swift, Dr Patrick Delany and Thomas Sheridan spent time boating
on the canal.

planted with lime trees (fig. 32).[208] At Leamaneh Castle in Clare, seat of Sir
Donat O'Brien, the turret walk survives, though broken in places where a road
runs through it. The turret walk had a summer house set in its middle
overlooking the long canal in the centre of the garden to one side and the wild
Clare countryside to the other. Although the gardens at Leamaneh were not
axially linked to the house, the elements in the garden were all sympathetically
placed to maximize enjoyment of the garden and its surrounding landscape.

At Burton in Cork the gardens to the east of the house were 'sunk' and
surrounded by three raised walks, each terminating with a mount. These
terraced walks were huge in scale, running the 'full length of the garden from
north to south and 24 foot of assize compleat broad' and were six feet in
height.[209] The large grass plat to the east of the house was to be dug in order
'to move easily and less discernibly towards the west side adjoining the house'.
In other words, the ground was to be levelled, making the slope of the lawn

'less discernible'. The spoil from this work was to be used 'at a piece of ground near or adjoining onto the said east mount and marked out and intended for a terraces walk and other wise make good the said mount'. A further terrace walk, a 'full six foot of a size higher than the east mount', was created using 'the earth and rubbish which shall as aforesaid be brought thither out of the plane of the side garden and with such other earth and rubbish contiguous and thereunto'.[210]

A copy of one of John Evelyn's plans for a garden he made for the duke of Norfolk at his house at Albury in Surrey exists, dating from about 1685.[211] This is a useful guide to garden design at this period. The plan shows a canal, sixty feet wide, trees planted concentrically around a grassy centre circle, and randomly planted to one side, an octagonal pool with a fountain jet, terraces, a 'vineyard of twelve acres, of the same length with the canal, upon the ascent of a hill, which faceth the south'.[212] An Irish garden, Newtown in Co. Down, described earlier, compares most favourably with the improvements carried out by the duke of Norfolk in their extent and complexity, with its olitary, fruit and pleasure gardens, fishponds, walks and bowling green.[213]

The accumulated evidence suggests that the layout and structures in the Irish pleasure gardens of the late seventeenth and early eighteenth centuries, with their ordered walks, parterres, ponds and garden buildings, were comparable to those of England. It is also clear that many of these features had a practical importance and were of economic benefit to the demesne as a whole.

CHAPTER 5

Horticultural improvement

THROUGHOUT THE LATTER PART of the seventeenth century, English and Irish landowners began to explore and exploit the commercial possibilities of better agricultural and forest management. Land was levelled and drained and some arable fields were converted into orchards. Ornamental, yet productive, vegetable gardens were established. Ornamental fruit and vegetable gardens became an integral part of large pleasure gardens. Nicholas Fouquet employed Jean de la Quintinye, one of the best gardeners in Paris, to set up his potager at Vaux le Vicomte, to ensure that he would be supplied with the earliest and most exotic fruit and vegetables.[1] Developments in Irish gardens took a similar course, with the English settlers and aristocracy expressing their ascendancy through a more sophisticated and varied cultivation of the land. Growing edible crops within the confines of the enclosed garden had always been necessary, and was traditionally carried out in a decorative and aesthetically pleasing manner. In Ireland some monastic gardens had survived the destruction of ecclesiastical establishments that took place during the sixteenth century; for example George Holmes observed that at Inisfallen, the Abbey of St Finian had 'fruit-trees, plums, pears etc.' that had 'outlived the wreck of this abbey'.[2] After the Restoration the reestablishment of orchards and the expansion and refinement of varieties of fruit and vegetables exercised the imagination of the improvers. Kitchen gardens were enlarged and crops diversified.

The scientific virtuosi saw improving crop production as an important part of their remit. In 1694 the Dublin Philosophical Society sent to Holland for market gardeners to teach its members new advanced techniques of growing fruit and vegetables.[3] New species were introduced and breeding programmes were undertaken by enthusiasts such as Sir John Temple to improve varieties of produce.

In order to grow crops successfully it was necessary that the soil be fertile and friable, whether for food crops or industrial ones, such as madder (which was used to dye cotton red and said to be 'of value to apothecaries for medicines').[4] Bog and scrub were reclaimed and made productive to maximize land available for crop growing. At Castle Forbes in Co. Longford, Arthur

Forbes successfully converted bog lands into 'firm and good land', enabling him to plant orchards and groves.[5] Obtaining enough good manure sometimes proved difficult. This led to some innovative improvisation on the part of gardeners, especially the rural labourers; Rawson noted the custom of cottagers in Kildare of growing cabbages in the poorest soil, by collecting sheep dung on the Curragh, dissolving it in water and making a good liquid fertiliser to steep the cabbage roots in prior to planting.[6] Bishop William King related that the inhabitants of land around the Strangford river manured their land with seaweed, 'by them called tangle which being spread on it and ploughed down makes winter grain and summer barley grow in abundance'.[7] King took an interest in the various methods of 'rendering boggy, acid land workable and productive'. On another occasion he observed how turf was burned and scattered on the soil, although he felt this was unsuitable:

> The inconvenies are first that such burning defiles the air, causeth rain and wind, is not practical in a wet summer and by destroying the sap of the earth and roots of grafts and other vegetables renders it useless for several years after three in which it is ploughed.[8]

In areas of acid soil, flocculants such as lime were added, but King noted that this was both expensive and difficult to purchase. He regarded as 'a far better method' the manuring of land by seashells, which he observed in Londonderry and Donegal. The shells, composed mainly of calcium carbonate, were collected and left in heaps until dry then burnt and scattered adding lime to the soil. King testified to the efficacy of this method of soil improvement:

> I made my gardener use the shells in my flower garden and never saw better carnation or flowers fairer or larger than in that cold climate and it contributes to destroy weeds at least.[9]

In addition to the more prosaic soft fruits such as gooseberries and currants, root vegetables, apples and pears, the kitchen garden sheltered exotics and fruit newly introduced to the country. Walled gardens were useful for the creation of microclimates suitable for growing tender and ornamental fruit from the Continent. Joseph Cooper Walker described how a house in Cork, probably Palace Anne, had a walled enclosure of two acres appropriated to a 'nut grove'.[10]

It became a preoccupation among seventeenth-century gardeners, especially the English improvers, to grow as many and varied types of fruit and vegetables as possible. The kitchen garden became a sort of laboratory where new techniques of growing, training, grafting and propagation took place. Henry Bathurste writing to Roger Boyle, the earl of Orrery, articulated this juxtaposition of science and horticulture found in the garden when he referred to the constant changes in the heavens and in the plants of his garden, remarking how 'the long studied for perpetual motion is found out' in his garden.[11] When the benchers of the King's Inns leased part of their property they required that their tenant plant it either with fruit trees or 'any garden stuff (cabbage only excepted)'. The tenant was permitted to keep the profits made from the sale of any produce from the vegetable plot or orchard.[12]

The potato had already gained prominence as the chief crop of choice for the Irish poor.[13] In the 1690s John Dunton, a traveller and commentator, observed their gardens:

> Behind one of their cabins lies the garden, a piece of ground sometimes of half an acre, and in this is the turf stack, their corn, perhaps two or three hundred sheaves of oats and as much peas. The rest of the ground is full of their dearly beloved potatoes, and a few cabbages.[14]

Thomas Dineley also remarked that the 'diet generally of the vulgar Irish are potatoes, milk … besides potatoes roasted in the embers, they feed on parsnips, carrots and watercreses'.[15] However, the general standard of diet among the Irish appears to have been rather better prior to the complete monopoly of the potato. Vegetables and green herbs such as lettuce, watercress and sorrel were the staple diet of the rural labourers in the early part of the century. Small crops of vegetables were grown around the cottages of the wealthier agrarian class. Fynes Moryson had observed that 'the air of Ireland is inapt to ripen seeds, yet the earth is luxurious in yielding fair and sweet herbs'.[16] Herbs and salads were widely grown and eaten by the Irish. This coincided with the cult of 'saladism', which became a popular fad among the elite in the Restoration period. As one would expect, John Evelyn, ever the influential trend-setter, was a pioneer of this movement; he wrote in his book *Acetaria* of the many virtues of lettuce:

> It is indeed of nature more cold and moist than any [other vegetable]; yet less astringent, and so harmless that it may safely be eaten raw in fevers; for it allays heat, bridles choler, extinguished thirst, excites appetite, kindly nourishes, and above all, represses vapours, conciliates sleep, mitigates pain; besides the effect it has upon morals, temperance and chastity.[17]

The earl of Clarendon, lord lieutenant of Ireland and a disciple of Evelyn, was a known saladist.[18] In 1686 he wrote to Evelyn extolling the virtues of Irish crops:

> People have begun to grow curious in kitchen gardens: the salads are very good, and the roots generally much better than ours in England. Asparagus here are very good, large and green: but they do not (pardon the expression) make the urine smell at all, of which I would be glad to know the reason.[19]

Between January 1684 and 28 August 1685 a Nicholas Shepard supplied the Fellows of Trinity College Dublin with seeds of beans, peas, lettuce, spinach, parsley, garden cresses, cucumbers, cauliflowers, turnip, radish, sweet marjoram, curled endive, corn salad, clary bugloss, purslane and 4,000 cabbage plants.[20] Menus found among the Orrery, papers include several references to such other vegetarian delights as 'Harty Choakes', beans, salad and buttered parsnips.[21] Exotics such as artichokes were introduced as fashionable additions to the salad crops popular in Ireland. Irish farmers were encouraged to diversify their crops, to plant peas, beans, wheat and hops[22] – perhaps under the influence of the Huguenots who grew hops, peas and vetches with apparent success in Ireland.[23] Rape or 'coleseed' was introduced to Ireland, apparently by Dutch settlers, sometime after 1660.[24] Bulkeley who alleged that he had 'succeeded well enough' in his experiment to grow Indian wheat, tried to grow kidney beans.[25] He later boasted 'I believe I am the first that ever in Ireland had a crop of Virginia wheat, which I have great probability of, as also of other southern plants by, is thought hitherto uncultivateable'.[26]

A well-tended and productive fruit garden was regarded as one of the most important improvements that could be made to the demesne. Produce that was surplus to requirements was sold at market.[27] The commingling of beauty and utility in the fruit garden was praised by Switzer who saw it as being close to heaven:

> A well contrived fruit-garden is an epitome of paradise itself, where the mind of man is in its highest raptures, and where the souls of the virtuous enjoy the utmost pleasure they are susceptive of in this sublunary state for a fruit-and kitchen-garden that has a proper extend, may be as beautiful as useful.[28]

In 1683, Richard Dobbs of Castle Dobbs in Co. Down had high hopes for his gardens, writing ambitiously, if not modestly, that the house 'in a few years may

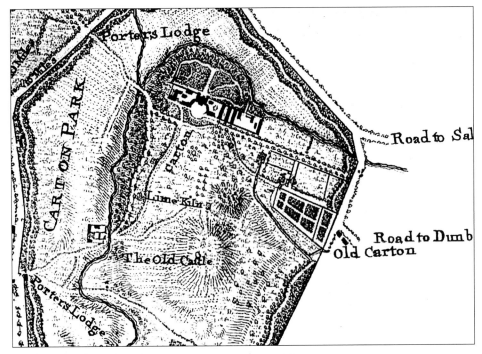

33 Detail from *Map of the county of Dublin* by John Rocque (1760) showing the walled garden at Carton House, part of the original garden's layout.

be remarkable for the orchards and gardening about it'.[29] The early Carton House, built at some time prior to 1685, and thought to have been on the same site as the present house, was owned by Richard Talbot, later earl of Tyrconnell.[30] There was an earlier settlement on the site, mentioned in the Civil Survey of 1654, 'upon the lands of Cartowne aforesaid one chapel of ease, one ruined stone house, with a garden and orchard thereunto belonging one decayed water mill, and one decayed dovehouse'. This appears to refer to the area called Old Carton, visible on John Rocque's map of 1760, on which a walled garden laid out in regular plots is adjacent to the site of old Carton House (fig. 33).[31] By the time of the first Ordnance Survey map in 1839 the garden's orderly seventeenth-century style plots had disappeared.

A late seventeenth-century map shows that the locus of productive gardening had shifted to an area to the rear of the new house on either side of the main pleasure garden. To one side a 'plumb garden' and a walled cherry garden, both of which were overlooked by a terraced walk. To the other side were a large formal orchard and a walled kitchen garden.

The important role that fruit trees played in the garden is illustrated by William Temple's instructions for planting a garden:

> The part [of the garden] next to the house should be open, and no other fruit but upon the walls. If this take up one half of the garden, the other should be fruit-trees, unless some grove for shade lie in the middle. If it take up a third part only, then the next third may be dwarf-trees, and the last standard-fruit; or else, the second part fruit-trees and the third all sorts of winter greens, [evergreen shrubs] which provide for all seasons of the year.[32]

In the gardens of great houses, kitchen gardens were given prominence and were regarded as part of the overall decorative scheme.[33] It was recommended that the sections of garden either side of the main pleasure garden should be used for orchards and kitchen gardens because of the ornamental value they would give as well as for convenience.[34] There were many instances in which decorative kitchen gardens are reported as being located in a prime position, where they could be viewed and admired, for instance at Burton Hall in Dublin, where the 'kitchen garden and fruitery' were 'to the front of the house',[35] or Carton and Eyrecourt where they were sited at either side of the pleasure garden, where they were visible from the main salons, which were generally on the first floor of houses. De Serres suggested putting the more ornamental and intensively cultivated areas like flower and vegetable gardens close to the house where their 'beauty and sweet smells' could provide pleasure to its owner.[36]

Even the most modest of country houses had walled kitchen gardens constructed of brick or stone,[37] sometimes used in combination when stone walls were faced with brick. This feature can be seen in the remains of many early Irish gardens and their kitchen gardens such as those at Stradbally Hall; such walls are also known to have existed at Charleville in the 1660s,[38] and Luttrellstown's date from the late seventeenth to early eighteenth century. The walled garden at Ballybegg in Co. Wicklow was described as being composed of 'stone and clay'.[39]

These secure enclosures sheltered crops and also served to protect the nurseries from theft.[40] The more unusual and difficult the fruit was to grow, the greater the premium that was attached to it, which meant that many fruits, regarded as commonplace today, were very valuable and therefore subject to theft.[41] Sweet chestnuts at Ormond's Moore Park were planted 'for their preservation by the lodge where they bear' and 'the walnuts planted in the view of the house' in order to spare them from thieves.[42] Many people were drawn to thieving through severe poverty.[43] George Rawdon wrote that 'the very night the Bishop [of Down?] died the orchard was broken into and the fruit all stolen'.[44] Bulkeley, during the upheavals of 1686, made sure that his valuable fruit and other plants were transferred to a secure orchard, which with his house was 'within a very large and deep mote for their future security'.[45] By 1688 the political situation had become so unstable that the Burlington estate paid a mason to work on the walls for eight days to secure the orchard.[46] Thieves would exploit conveniently placed raised walks to their advantage as a means of gaining access to the garden; as George Rawdon explained:

> People here think that the banks cast against the walls in the low square next the river of no use, except to have it robbed. A ladder on the outside takes the knave to the top on the outside of the wall and then he needs no help to get up or down within.[47]

The greatest innovation of the seventeenth-century fruit garden in Ireland was the introduction of the espalier method of growing fruit trees. Fruit had been grown against walls for centuries to exploit their protection and heat. Early Italian gardens of the fifteenth and sixteenth centuries had fruit growing close against their walls, with niches protecting lemon trees. The French had developed the espalier technique for training fruit trees to increase their production. Espaliers were formed when the branches of fruit trees were trained horizontally against walls and pruned so as to send out vertical shoots, which were attached to the wall in a fan or similar shape. Erasmus Burrowes, writing in the nineteenth century, quotes the seventeenth-century French writer, Robert Arnauld d'Andilly, explaining the benefits of the espalier to northern French gardens and describes how innovative this method of fruit production was:

> The advantage of the new plan of espaliers was soon established by its success. By it one sees a wonderful abundance of fruits in districts where they were previously rare, and to which it was necessary to bring them from remote provinces. By this process they now have in France, fruits which require a warmer climate than ours to ripen, and they can collect on one wall the different productions of various climates.[48]

Making the trees two dimensional, and keeping them flat and snug against the wall, ensured that the whole plant gained heat, which had been soaked up by the brick or stone during the day, and protected the plant from harsh weather.

Light infiltrated all the branches of the tree, ripening the fruit before the dangers of the first frosts, and thinning out the shoots ensured heavy fruit production on the remaining stems. By this method fruits such as fig, quince, apricot and peach were grown successfully in Irish gardens.[49]

The espalier technique was widely used in Ireland by the 1690s. Loveday wrote that there was 'a very great quantity of wall-fruit' at Belan in Kildare.[50] Fruit, which needed heat in order to ripen, or that was tender in the Irish climate, could be trained against the warm south facing walls of the kitchen garden or any other available vertical surface. At Castle Durrow, a specialist called Derby came to maintain the wall-fruit[51] and Molesworth's cousin 'Forster had an old Scotch gardener who understood pruning of his wall trees' and who helped with the fruit in Breckdenston.[52] William Temple sent a gift of several fruit trees to Sir Robert Colville, along with instructions on where to plant them:

> I send you some grafts of the best sorts of fruits that I have, and hope
> you are not unprovided of stocks for them. I have ordered my gardener,
> to make labels of the several kinds, and to set down which of the pears
> and plumbs must be set against walls, there being some of them that
> will not bear upon standards, yet be good upon any, but a south wall. I
> wish they may succeed with you, and that I may have the good fortune,
> to eat some of the fruits of them with you.[53]

Temple enjoined a gardener not to plant any tree 'unless dwarf' within forty feet of walls, in order to give the fruit as much sun and air as possible.[54] Fruit trees were not confined to the walled kitchen garden. A perusal of manuscripts, documents and illustrations of seventeenth and early eighteenth-century gardens shows that wall-fruit was grown on every available sheltered wall or palisade and was present in the pleasure garden as much as the kitchen garden and orchard. A good example of this can be seen in Charles Brooking's 1728 survey of Dublin which shows fruit trees growing against walls in the garden of the Royal Hospital in Kilmainham.

Sir William Petty intended to cover the walls about his walks 'with the best walled fruit that Ireland affords'.[55] At Breckdenston, fruit trees covered the walls around the parterre garden, and the bowling green, and were also planted against the house itself.[56] However in 1699, one observer noted caustically that the fruit gardens at Breckdenston did not produce any decent fruit, saying 'I never eat nor saw scarce any fruit that was tolerable either for bigness or taste though; it was the best year that had been of 7 years past'.[57]

Wall-fruit was grown in the close walks at Lisburn Castle causing some concern as to whether the trees would fruit or not.[58] Fruit trees were also planted in towns around municipal recreational spaces. For instance, Dunton wrote that the bowling green in Dublin (at Oxmantown) was 'well walled in' and that the walls were 'covered with fruit-trees'.[59] A 1684/5 plan by Evelyn contains a 'table of fruit planted in the east and west triangular grounds' of his bowling green.[60] Evelyn also specified that wall-fruit be grown along the retaining walls of raised terraces.[61] A note about the progress of the gardens at Killruddery demonstrates how the walls of the gardens were utilized to best effect:

> Against the south wall without and against the north wall within he will plant fruit of all sorts and will make a treble ditch without the south wall and quickset the fen to the end that the deer may not get to the fruit and that the park may be completed.[62]

Growing wall-fruit became the norm in the centuries that followed. In 1702, the Committee of the Royal Hospital requested that 'fruit trees for supplying the wants in the garden' be planted.[63] On the same date 64 apple trees, 64 pear trees, 64 plum trees and 64 cherry trees were ordered for the garden. Similarly, in November 1683 Sir John Perceval placed an order for 36 peaches and nectarines, 18 figs, 30 apricots, 15 pears, 37 plums and 40 cherries[64] for his garden at Burton.

At Dunmanway in Cork, Francis Hodder planted in his new garden 6 different varieties of peach, 16 of plum, 13 of cherry, pears as well as apricots, figs, vines, Bellegarde, May duke, Morello and Archduke cherries.[65] In 1719, the Dublin nurseryman Peter Landrè delivered, in one consignment alone, 3 dwarf varieties of apples, 3 varieties of peach, nectarines, apricots, 3 varieties of pears and 6 varieties of plum. All these were intended to be grown against a wall and, helpfully, he specified on which walls each variety should be planted.[66] In the mid-eighteenth century William Chetwood described the seventeenth-century kitchen garden at Low Grange near Gowran in glowing terms, its 'orchard is planted with wall-fruit trees of the best sort that can be purchased in Europe'.[67]

Orchards and cider making

At a time when water could be dangerous to drink, with frequent outbreaks of cholera and plague, wine, cider and 'small beer' were drunk as an accompaniment to food. Cider was also a profitable cash commodity. In late Elizabethan and early Jacobean Ireland, particularly in the eastern counties,[68] there was a revival of the monastic tradition of orchard management. However, many orchards fell into neglect or were destroyed during the Civil War period in both England and Ireland. Orchards had been of tremendous importance since the Middle Ages, the principal purpose being to grow apples for cider making and pears for perry making. Among the 'native Irish' the creation of orchards was less common. Sir John Davies (1569–1626), possibly correctly, identified the reason for this as being 'that inheritance in Ireland was so uncertain' and the fear of political upheaval was so great that they thought it hardly worth their while.[69] During the Commonwealth period there was a move to improve orchards in both Britain and Ireland.[70] Many thousands of orchards were planted throughout the seventeenth century, especially the latter half. Early in the century Lord Chichester planted walks around his 'dainty orchard gardens' and his apparently equally 'dainty stately house' Joymount in Carrickfergus.[71] There are few recorded instances of perry production in Ireland, although pears were widely grown and many varieties introduced, from which it is possible to infer that it was made. Perry had been produced in England for many years using 'choke' pears, which were too sour to eat.[72] Throughout the latter part of the seventeenth century, many agricultural writers promoted the planting of more orchards across Ireland.[73] In *Vinetum Britannicum*,[74] Worlidge advocated the production of cider over attempts at viticulture in Britain, arguing that it was more suitable to the English climate. In 1665, George Rawdon was pleased to relate that 'whenever the trees come we shall be ready for them. I have the late book set forth by the virtuosi of planting and making cider'.[75] The book in question was possibly John Evelyn's *Pomona: a discourse concerning cider* (London, 1664), or perhaps his *Silva* which contained a tract written by John Beale, a fellow of the Royal Society, called 'Aphorisms concerning cider' which appeared in the 1664 edition.[76] A way of ensuring the proliferation of orchards and fruit gardens was by requiring tenants to plant as a condition of the rental of lands: the Fitzpatrick papers relating to estates in Co. Laois contain many covenants requiring tenants to plant orchards or fruit trees.[77]

The cultivation of named varieties of fruit trees began in the late seventeenth century. Attempts were made to grow as many winter varieties of fruit as possible to maximize the growing season. By planting trees on south facing walls they could be forced to fruit early, whereas fruiting could be delayed by planting on the cooler north facing walls. At the start of the seventeenth century new varieties of fruit were continually introduced from

Europe. Parkinson described 65 varieties, most of which seem to have been recent introductions. Few of the varieties he mentions are grown today.[78] In 1691, Worlidge listed 129 varieties of pear for the table. By the close of the seventeenth-century orchards became the norm, not only on grand estates, but also within the gardens of 'middling classes'.

Large quantities of cider were fermented, bottled and sold on many demesnes. It appears to have been made in large amounts at Conway's estates in Lisburn.[79] In 1664, Sir George Rawdon was, as ever, busy working for his brother-in-law, Conway, planning a new orchard specifically to grow apples for cider, which, like pear 'chokes', were otherwise inedible. He requested that Conway try to source some suitable trees 'of that naughty apple only fit for that use. I have forgot its name'. He also arranged a clever barter with Lord Massereene for 'bricks in return for good cider apples'.[80] However, as appears to be the case so often in Ireland, obtaining the equipment necessary to produce and bottle the cider sometimes proved difficult. In 1691, Edmond Doyne informed Thomas Flower that he had 'made 4 hogsheads[81] of cider this season out of your orchard and gardens at Finglas'[82] – but, by the time the cider was ready for sale, there was a shortage of containers for bottling the cider:

> Your honour wrote to me about bottling of one of the hogsheads of cider. Lieutenant Flower and I tried them the other day so that there is one of them that is tolerable but the other two are not worth much; neither can Dublin afford as many bottles as would contain a hogshead, for I have been in all parts of it looking to buy but could not get any except it be a dozen here and there and to pay 4 shillings ... per dozen so that I have left the cider much as I found it until I have further orders.[83]

Rawdon, who had ambitions to produce a high-quality drink that would appeal to the most sophisticated of palates, was rather disappointed by some of his early efforts.[84] He was, however, pleased to relate that he had 'made two hogshead of good cider this year besides all our bottles full, of Brookhill and Moyra apples'.[85] Cider production continued on estates in Ireland up until the nineteenth century at least: in 1874 Smith observed that Sir Maurice Crosbie's seat at Ardfert still had 'large plantations of cider fruit, and other apple trees, which thrive extremely well'.[86]

Melon cultivation

Cultivation of members of the cucumber or squash family increased greatly towards the end of the seventeenth century. Although Lord Donegall was recorded as growing melons in the 1650s in Co. Down,[87] melon cultivation only became common in Ireland during the last decades of the century.[88] A level of kudos was attached to growing these crops as they were difficult to grow in Ireland. They required lots of manure, and protection with cloches, 'glasses' (Bishop William King paid for several glasses for his garden in Derry),[89] or the creation of special melon-frames, like those the earl of Orrery had built in his garden at Charleville.[90] The cosseting involved in growing melons meant that only the rich could afford the time and attention necessarily lavished on the fruit. Richard Thornhill wrote of the necessity of growing plain pompion (melon) seedlings in a rich dungy bed.[91] The kitchen garden would contain 'hot beds' full of dung and organic matter to raise soil temperature to promote growth. Worlidge devoted a chapter to 'melons, cucumbers etc.' with the instructions that melons should be sown at full moon in a hot bed in February.[92] These principles – of what are now referred to as biodynamics – were first propounded by Virgil in the *Georgics* who advised that the waxing and waning of the moon should be used as guide for planting.[93]

Gardeners became very competitive about their melons, almost to the point of obsession. John Evelyn had been instructed by de le Quintinye himself, whom he had met on the latter's visit to England; Evelyn included these instructions in his English translation of *The compleat gard'ner*.[94] Robert Molesworth boasted 'that about Dublin they should not as yet have attained among all the gardeners the art of raising melons [which] we did at Breckdenston with great success years ago'.[95] However, there were sorry consequences of eating too much melon as mentioned by Sir George Rawdon in a letter to Lord Conway:

> I thank you for asking about my health on which I have had advice here. I do hope that distemper was not appoplexical but rather an accident of eating melon too freely that day before dinner.[96]

Viticulture

There was a surge of interest in growing grape vines from 1660 onwards – perhaps due to the fact that many of those exiled to the Continent during the interregnum had developed a taste for fine wines and wished to develop their own vineyards at home in England and Ireland. In 1665 and 1666, two books were published on viticulture. The first, *The compleat vineyard*, by William Hughes,[97] gave information on the planting and care of vines, harvesting grapes and manufacture of wine. The second, *The English vineyard vindicated*, was by 'John Rose gard'ner to His Majesty, at his Royal garden in St James's', but was ghosted by Evelyn, based on information conveyed to him by Rose, who may have been illiterate.[98] Many attempts at viticulture were made in Ireland. It seems though that the vines could not survive the Irish climate, although William Temple mentioned grapes suitable for growing in England and alleged that they ripened well.[99] Richard Bulkeley, ever the optimist, intended to establish a vineyard in the unlikely setting of Tallaght at the foot of the Dublin Mountains. He cited John Evelyn as being the inspiration for this project because 'the French gardener does attribute the want of vineyards in England, merely to the neglect of our ancestors in continuing it and give instances'.[100] In 1693, he planted 900 grape vines. In this endeavour, as with others, he sought advice from his friend Martin Lister who furnished him with the information he needed for his new venture.[101] Bulkeley employed a Swiss 'master vigneron' to aid him in this project, displaying a touching naivety and ignorance of climate when he claimed that he would prove useful as the Swiss 'climate is nearer akin to England than either Italy or France'. He was encouraged by the careless assurance of the Swiss man that he 'should not fail of having ripe grapes'.[102] The following year, Bulkeley wrote, with inevitable disappointment, that he was 'discouraged as to making a vineyard, because the great rains of this country make the grape to burst'.[103] The Molesworths were supplied with vines from no less a source than the earl of Shaftesbury.[104] Molesworth advised his wife, in his absence, to consult 'Bradley and Lawrence' for the 'right dressing and pruning' of their vines and to ensure that they were planted in the 'right places'.[105] Francis Hodder of Dunmanway, Cork, also attempted to grow vines although the success of his venture is not reported.[106]

Mulberry trees

Mulberry (*Morus*) is an attractive architectural tree with edible fruit. White mulberry, *Morus alba*, was a less common plant in gardens in Ireland, although the black mulberry, *Morus nigra*, had been grown for its fruit in Britain for many years. The Mulberry may have been brought from Virginia by Sir Walter Raleigh where the black Mulberry grows wild. Raleigh also introduced the cherry and planted myrtles at his park in Youghal.[107] In the early seventeenth century, James I had encouraged the planting of black mulberry in the mistaken belief that silk worms could be established in the trees in England. However, silk worms prefer the white mulberry, *Morus alba*, a native of China that does not grow well in the British Isles.[108] Despite this serious obstacle, the author of the pamphlet *The improvement of Ireland* still hoped that the silk trade would take off in Ireland.[109] Perhaps encouraged by this pamphlet, and by Olivier de Serres, who had included a chapter in his book on silkworm breeding in *Théâtre d'agriculture*,[110] the intrepid Richard Bulkeley hoped to breed silkworms in order to manufacture silk. Bulkeley yet again engaged the ever-patient Lister to send him some white mulberry seeds.[111] Despite Lister's view that the project was doomed to failure, and indeed must have failed, Bulkeley ordered more seeds five years later, justifying his folly by saying that he had nothing to lose as it would 'make as much moment to philosophy though it do not succeed, as it will be to trade if it do'.[112] Despite the now well-documented failure of silk-worm breeding in Ireland, Robert Molesworth requested his son John, who was in Italy, to send him 'some seed of the white mulberry tree so common in all the hedges in Piedmont for their silkworms'.[113]

Citrus fruit

Only the wealthy could afford to buy citrus fruit, which were generally imported from Spain.[114] Sometime during the seventeenth century, Irish landowners began to turn their attentions towards growing oranges and lemons at home. Glasshouses, orangeries and cold frames were built to shelter the trees from frost and cold winds, from whence they were wheeled out during the hours of sunshine in summer.

The Dutch writer Jan Commelijn's *Nederlantze hesperides* was published in English in 1683 as *The Belgick, or Netherlandish hesperides. That is: The management, ordering, and use of the lemon and orange trees, fitted to the … climate of the Netherlands*.[115] Towards the end of the century attempts – some apparently successful – were made to grow citrus fruit in Ireland, either from small imported plants or from seed.[116] Huguenot refugees were alleged to have imported citrus trees to Ireland in the 1690s, and records show that orange trees were grown in Ireland, which fruited successfully, though how abundant they were is not known. While in England, William Temple boasted that his 'orange-trees are as large as any I saw when I was young in France [or] the Low-countries, except some very old ones of the Prince of Orange's'.[117] Richard Bulkeley related how Temple's brother John[118] had grown tender fruits such as apricots, figs, grapes, nectarines, peaches and strawberries and oranges at Palmerstown in west Dublin.[119] In 1695, Robert Molesworth promised his wife that he would send her orange trees in Spring. The oranges were again mentioned by him in June 1703, when he reported that they were 'in good condition'.[120] In order to fruit, the citrus trees had to be carefully guarded against frosts or cold winds. In early Italian gardens this was done by planting them in niches. In Evelyn's 'directions for the gardener at Sayes-Court' he ordered the gardener 'never expose your oranges lemons, and like tender trees, whatever season flatter; 'til the mulberry puts-forth its leaf, then bring them boldly out of the green-house; but for a fortnight, let them stand in the shade of an hedge; where the sun may glimmer only upon them'.[121] By 1750, Richard Uniack of Cork was reputed to have orange trees which bore fruit, though this may have been due to more sophisticated greenhouses being in place.[122]

The extraordinary variety of fruits, many exotic, grown in gardens within the security of the enclosed demesnes was in stark contrast to the agricultural lands without. This intensity of cultivation served to emphasize the new order provided by the colonists and, as Toby Barnard has written, 'announced [the owner's] membership of the quality'.[123]

CHAPTER 6

Trees, woodlands and plantations

A T THE BEGINNING OF THE SEVENTEENTH century much of Ireland's ancient woodlands remained. It is a commonly accepted view that the loss of Ireland's native woodland cover was almost entirely due to irresponsible exploitation during the period between the seventeenth and early eighteenth centuries.[1] Yet landowners were concerned about the loss of woodland. Sir Robert Molesworth said that 'the cutting down of our trees displeases me much more than if they had burnt all our houses'[2] and the owners of estates were keen to make up for any depletion in Ireland's native ancient woodlands by pursuing a vigorous campaign of planting. In 1682, Sir Henry Pierse commented on the lack of timber, hedges and fences in Co. Westmeath, but noted that it was 'well stocked with coppice or underwood'.[3] In 1665 Sir George Rawdon noted that good building timber was so scarce that in Dublin it commanded 45s. a ton. This shortage necessitated importing timber from as far afield as Norway[4] and, where possible, wood was recycled.[5] Another observer noted that timber was so 'deficient' at an English colony in Wexford that dwelling houses there were roofed with gorse. In other respects this colony was praised for its good husbandry and stewardship of the land, which indicates that wood was naturally scarce.[6] On her arrival in Dublin in 1685–6 the vicereine, the countess of Clarendon, was moved to write to John Evelyn, 'I am come into a country that is not cultivated, not a tree nor shrub is here!'[7] When he visited Youghal in 1809 the writer Dillwyn commented, 'as in all the rest of the country there is a sad deficiency of wood in the landscape'.[8]

It was suggested by some observers in the sixteenth and seventeenth centuries that trees be cut 'to deprive thieves and rogues, who used to lurk in the woods in great numbers, of their refuge and storing-holes, and partly to gain the greater scope of profitable lands'.[9] Wild woodland was traditionally thought of as a sinister place; Thomas Phillips wrote:

> the woods and bogs are a great hindrance to us and a help to the rebel, who can, with a few men, kill many of ours in a wood through which they can pass only at certain paces [passes]. The rebels can then remain in the woods till they recruit their strength. In the bogs the old soldiers

who know them, can fight at no great loss, and can see the enemy's strength; but in the woods they may fall into an ambushcado.

However, Phillips continued his letter by offering a solution to the perceived dangers of woodlands as a refuge to rebels, not by suggesting destruction of the woods altogether, but by creating clearings and highways, while leaving enough trees to ensure a timber supply and cutting away shrubby underwood on a regular basis – a sensible method of good woodland management:

> If the country is quieted by cutting off the principal rebels much good could be done to the bogs by our labour and by Irish churls felling, dressing and burning the trees in heaps. This could be done while leaving sufficient timber for the use of the country, if a tree is left every twenty yards and shrubs either stocked up at the first or continually cut up.[10]

The production of timber requires the creation of sustainable plantations, with trees planted strategically in cycles. To this end, trees that were unprofitable were removed and oaks and other hardwoods were planted in their place as cash crops and managed as such. Timber was treated as a valuable resource and recycled when possible. Even ornamental trees in the pleasure garden were saved for use as timber when they had to be felled.[11]

An attempt to counter the depletion of woodland was made by landowners and massive planting schemes were undertaken between the late seventeenth and eighteenth centuries. Landowners sought to compensate for the loss of native woodland by increasing plantings of decorative woodlands and commercial plantations. The deceptively wooded appearance of the Irish countryside in accounts given during the later eighteenth and early nineteenth centuries is probably due to the large amount of trees on estates and demesnes and within hedgerows planted as a result of legislative initiatives introduced from the late seventeenth century onwards.[12]

To replenish Ireland's depleted woodland, Petty recommended planting 'three millions of timber trees upon the bounds and mears of every denomination of land in the country'.[13] The planting of hedgerow trees probably accounts for the number of large deciduous timber trees found in many field boundaries on Irish demesnes today. This also added to the impression that the country was 'well wooded'.

Worries about depredations on woodland were the impetus for several attempts to bolster Ireland's tree cover by enacting laws variously to criminalize certain activities, impose duties on owners to plant, and to provide financial and other incentives to encourage woodland regeneration. Laws for the preservation of woods had been in existence in England since Edward IV and similar laws were extended to Ireland. Both landowners and Government began to give serious attention to the importance of restoring and maintaining tree cover, the emphasis being on ensuring a sustainable stock of trees for future cropping.

In 1634, an Act was passed to protect gardens from theft, criminalizing inter alia 'robbing orchards or gardens, or breaking fences, pulling up fruit trees, barking trees, spoiling woods etc.'[14] This measure met with limited success at least in relation to tree barking as it was felt necessary to enact several more statutory provisions in order to address the problem. In 1654 a regular forestry service was established in the counties of Wexford and Wicklow where a head wood-reeve was appointed with four assistants and a clerk. This scheme was extended subsequently to Carlow and Kildare. This could explain why Wicklow and parts of Wexford today retain some of the country's remaining ancient woodland.[15]

Destruction of woodland was considered so serious that it was brought to the attention of the King when it took place on Crown lands. Having been 'informed that diverse persons' had entered woods belonging to the Irish Society in Derry and 'committed great waste, cutting down our timber and destroying the woods to our great damage and displeasure', the King ordered that 'no man do presume (under pain of our highest displeasure) to fell, cut or carry away, any timber trees ... unless licensed' to do so. Licences were only to be granted for timber for: 'plough boote, fire boote, hedge boote, cart boote and buildings in the tenement of those that are inhabitants on land where trees grow'.[16] 'Boote' and 'botes' referred to wood which it was permissible to use for the making of tools and instruments. In 1661 directions were given for the preservation of the King's woods in Ireland, and for the regulation of all felling of timber therein; permission to fell trees in the 'King's woods' could only be given under the licence of the ranger general.[17] Other mandatory orders were made against individuals who exploited woodland of value to the exchequer[18] and felling was not to be allowed for merchandizing or export.[19] Leaseholders were subject to stringent conditions in relation to woodland management. Almost all leases of the period contain conditions requiring the tenants to plant trees; these include fruit, hedgerow, softwood and hardwood species.[20] One required the tenant 'to preserve the timber on the premises, to cut, carry away and dispose of' the underwood of hazels 'at a seasonable time'. Another contained a condition that the tenant 'plant 500 ash trees'.[21] Leases frequently included similar covenants not to permit waste and destruction of woodland, granting liberty only to the lessee to use wood for specified purposes or 'bootes'.[22] During the Williamite War, much land, including woodland, was laid waste by warring factions, or simply by the destructive effects of military encampments. Primate Boyle was relieved that his demesne remained largely intact despite the billeting of French troops on his land:

> The present condition of Blessington seems not altogether so desperate as appeared unto me when I last wrote to you … the general has assured me that he … would absolutely forbid his troopers from going into the park or from doing any disturbance to the deer or any stock upon the place.[23]

Rathfarnham Castle's 'woods in abundance' survived the war because it was said that the earl of Tyrconnell 'had an eye upon this place to make it in due time his home'.[24]

In 1698, the author of the pamphlet *The improvement of Ireland* suggested that landowners be required by law to plant trees proportionate to their landholding. In particular he suggested oak plantations which 'should be fenced for sixty years without using it for timber'.[25] This suggestion was incorporated into law in 1698.[26] The Act ordered that certain freeholders and tenants were to plant 'from 25th March 1705 ten plants yearly for thirty one years of oak etc. and preserve them'. Those who had more than 500 acres were to enclose and plant one acre and keep it fenced (to preserve it from grazing and theft) for twenty years. It was aimed to plant 260,000 trees of oak, elm and fir for thirty one years from 1703 and restrictions were placed on tanning pits and the use of bark for dyes.[27] The Act of 1703 also removed the duty on imports of iron, staves and material for cooperage and additional duty was added to timber exports to places other than England to try and prevent exportation. These duties were designed to discourage the exportation of wood from Ireland in the hope of allowing the recovery of native woodland.[28] The drive to plant met with some considerable success. William Chetwood, writing about Burtonhall in 1748, described 'a wood not forty years old, cut into a variety of vistas', indicating that it was planted shortly after the 1705 Act.[29]

Cutting down ornamental trees was regarded as particularly heinous, perhaps in part because of their symbolic value as expressions of the alleged culture and civilizing influence of the landowner. Correspondence between Lord Thomas Coningsby, lord justice of Ireland, and Judge John Hely survives relating to the cutting down of a wood at Feltrim in Co. Meath. In the letters Hely, who suffered forfeitures for his offence, expressed his regret that he had ordered the demolition of the wood,[30] but protested, as in mitigation, that he did not cut down any ornamental trees.[31] Sir Donat O'Brien complained to his cousin, Inchiquin, about a tenant who 'abused' his licence to cut '200 sticks to 477 and cut down the trees of ornament planted by your grandfather and his brother'.[32] While allowing the commissioners of revenue at Dublin to cut and fell trees 'as shall be necessary for several buildings at the Phoenix [Park] near Dublin', the Commonwealth insisted that 'no woods that are an ornament to the said seat' were to be removed.[33] The value of wood as a precious resource is also indicated by the prevalence of thieving from parks and plantations, the stolen wood often being used for fuel and building.[34] Fines were included in leases, penalizing tenants for laying waste; one landowner provided that his tenant should pay '40s. for every oak or ash tree or sapling, and 10s. for every birch, alder, willow, or sally tree or sapling cut down'.[35]

Landowners showed great concern for the preservation of their plantations. After the crisis of 1689, Thomas Bligh[36] wrote to his agent 'I fear [for] nothing but my trees'.[37] When the Ormonds returned to Ireland, the duchess was most concerned that her steward 'use the best endeavour you can the meantime to prevent the place from being left waste, or the woods from destruction, both there and elsewhere',[38] while the duke asked his agent, Edward Cooke, to 'consider what trees are fit to be cut down for fuel or any otherwise, and to cause them to be marked, and that none other be felled upon any pretence whatsoever'.[39] The earl of Burlington was much angered when he discovered that one of his men had 'cut 16 oak trees in Ballyrafter, when I don't allow one stick to be cut upon my estate without my order or the approbation of my commissioners'.[40]

A combination of politics, bad or absentee landlords, unscrupulous traders, lack of enclosure and the destitute condition of the majority of the native population militated against preservation. Despite this, there is considerable evidence of efforts to properly manage woods. Ireland had a long coppicing tradition dating from the Viking and medieval period. Coppiced timber was used for building and a range of species were utilized, mostly willow alder, hazel and ash and holly for uprights, and hazel for horizontal rods. The Civil Survey of 1654–6 refers to pasturable wood, woody pasture, underwood and copps, all features associated with managed woodland.[41]

The pipe and stave industry was an important part of Ireland's domestic and export economy and a valuable part of her trade with Britain and continental Europe. Sir William Petty detailed the large quantities of 'staves, hoops, rafters, laths, plough-timber' and bark for tanning taken over a two-year period from Borlin woods in Bantry, Co. Cork. Stave making was carried out chiefly in three areas: the Bann valley, Wexford and parts of the south west. By 1625 it was said that France and Spain casked all their wine in Irish wood, but wood was also used to make the barrels in which goods were exported abroad, a vital part of the country's economy on which many a livelihood depended. Several efforts were made to regulate the pipe and stave industry; in 1613 Lord Deputy Chichester was censured for permitting woods in Cork to be cut and worked into staves and directed to take steps to preserve woods and prevent export of staves.[42]

Although Rackham argues that cooperage was not responsible for the loss of woodland, evidence from contemporary observers suggests that because of poor regulation and illegal felling, the industry did contribute to destruction of much timber.[43] The Civil Survey of 1659 recorded that woods in Co. Carlow had been 'very much wasted and spoiled by that plague of all good timber (to wit) pipe staves and barrel staves' and that the country would 'lament the loss thereof which might be employed to more honourable uses', concluding humorously that if this was 'not timely prevented, it may be conjectured that the inhabitants of this nation must with Diogenes live in tubs for the choicest timber is employed to that use'.[44]

Forges and foundries appear to have been the primary source of damage to woodlands.[45] The greatest damage caused to oak woods was done by tanners who used bark in processing hides. Much of the wood in Cork and Kerry had been destroyed by tanners who stripped off bark for 3 or 4 feet above the ground, leaving the trees only fit for use as staves. Petty's woods in Kerry only survived destruction by tanners because Kenmare was so thinly populated.[46]

Interruptions in ownership and management of woodlands caused by rebellion, civil war and changes in administration were a constant theme throughout the seventeenth century. The preamble to a statute of 1698 blamed military manoeuvres and ironworks together for damaging tree cover.[47] It is reasonable to assume that during the years of turbulence and war, management of woodland was a secondary consideration to the more pressing and urgent need for iron to supply military hardware. Timber would also have been in demand for use in weaponry.

> Forasmuch as by the late rebellion in this kingdom, and the several iron works formerly here, the timber is utterly destroyed, such that at present there is not sufficient for the repairing of the houses destroyed, much less a prospect of building and improving in after times, unless some means be used for the planting and increase of timber trees.[48]

In 1698 the earl of Burlington who owned both large tracts of woodland and ironworks in Cork and Waterford wrote to his agent William Congreve:[49]

> I desire great care may be taken that no trees be cut down there nor in any other part of my estate without my direction, though I am afraid it is almost too late to preserve them, there having been a great destruction made, but do your endeavours to preserve the remainder.[50]

The reduction of broadleaved woodland in Ireland can in part be traced to the growing popularity of conifers. New introductions such as Scots pine, Norway spruce and *Picea abies* reached maturity far faster than broadleaved species, and so turned a faster profit when grown as timber. Despite this broadleaved species continued to be associated with landed estates and were attributed patrician qualities, with frequent references made to their 'noble' appearance.[51]

The planting of tracts of woodland on demesnes symbolized the civilizing influence of landowners who created landscapes where productivity, amenity and delight were interwoven, overlapped and mutually supportive. The presence of trees planted in a regular, geometric fashion on the landscape, like a disciplined army, gives an immediate visual indication of cultivation and habitation. In Ireland it conveyed an unambiguous message that the land in question had been colonized. Where once there had been a perceived barren disorder, there was now, in its place fruitfulness and order. The imposition of values such as discipline, control and an iron will that would overcome the untidy vicissitudes of nature would, by analogy, tame the native inhabitants of Ireland. It was sought to transform demesnes in the Irish landscape into replicas of English country estates. In 1677, Lord Ranelagh described Lord Conway's estate s 'the best and most absolute English like plantation in the kingdom'.[52] Loveday remarked approvingly of Eyrecourt in Galway that its 'fine woods and improvements' made it look 'very English'.[53]

Avenues

Probably the most distinctive feature of the late seventeenth- and early eighteenth-century garden was its proliferation of avenues, which were fairly uncommon prior to the Restoration and re-settlement. Long, straight, tree-lined avenues made the most powerful aesthetic statement and even otherwise unremarkable parks were given an impressive sheen and grand first impression by their presence. When reading the descriptive material about gardens in Ireland, it can sometimes be difficult to distinguish between an avenue as we

understand it today, and a walk, or simply a road. For example, a description of
Dunmore House in Kilkenny makes it unclear whether the writer is referring
to a public road or a private avenue:

> the avenues that lead to it are shaded by rows of regular lofty trees,
> which called to our memories those walks from Petersham to Ham in
> Surrey, but these have the advantage in our opinion. The spacious
> garden is like a wilderness, and the park with very few deer. In short
> such a place, formed by nature for grandeur or pleasure, is not often
> found in England.[54]

Avenue is also often used to refer to the rides cut through forests for hunting.
Rides and avenues often took the form of a *patte d'oie*, or goosefoot, having
three prongs radiating from the area of the main dwelling house. This is one
of the most characteristic features of seventeenth-century avenues, seen from
the grandest of estates such as Versailles, to the smaller, more intimately
proportioned, gardens of Ireland such as at Breckdenston, which had a *patte
d'oie* to the south of the house radiating from a terraced bastion on which there
was a summer house (fig. 34).[55] At Carton House in Kildare, the straight, tree-
lined avenues were up to three-quarters of a mile in length, forming a great
patte d'oie that extended out from the court at the front of the house and into
the park and beyond. Railed gaps or *claire vue* in the stone wall around the
court enabled the vistas to be enjoyed from the house itself. *Patte d'oies* could
be linked by placing two or more around a circle to form elaborate star shapes,
as seen at Howth Castle, Gaulstown, Mount Merrion (see plate 3) and later
the Phoenix Park, where they performed their original function as hunting
rides. The matter is further muddled by the variety of sizes and formations
these features could take. There were two sorts of avenues and walks; those
with a primarily practical purpose such as a drive or approach to a house, a
walk to get from one point in the garden to another, and those with a more
predominantly visual and aesthetic purpose. The latter sort were useful for
framing views to and from the house or demesne, often terminated or
punctuated by buildings and monuments, and linking areas within the garden
either physically or visually. In addition to their decorative properties, avenues
created useful shelterbelts for the house and garden, with more tender plants
growing to the lee of thick rows of trees.

The avenue as an approach to a big house is probably the feature most
familiar today. From its humble beginnings as a track leading to a house, the
avenue became grander and more symbolic. It often stretched for over a mile,

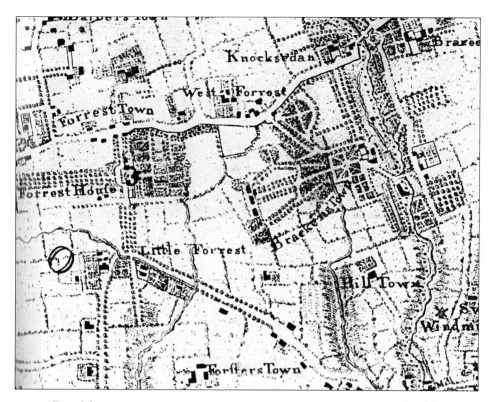

34 Detail from *Map of the county of Dublin* by John Rocque (1760) showing the *patte d'oie* to the south of Breckdenston House, radiating from a terraced bastion on which there was a summerhouse.

a topographical announcement of the visitor's arrival in the vicinity of the seat of a powerful family. The journey along the avenue gave the visitor or owner an opportunity to view the house ahead.

References to 'avenues' have been in existence since classical times – in Tudor England tree-lined drives were associated with ceremonial routes – and the earliest examples were the approaches to royal palaces.[56] John Evelyn is attributed with the first use of the word avenue as meaning a special tree-lined approach or walk.[57] Some very early avenues have survived in Ireland although, in most cases, the original trees have been replaced or absent altogether. Many of the old avenues were incorporated into modern road systems, such as Mount Merrion and Foster's Avenue in Dublin, and the avenue from Blessington village to the site of the old house. At Ballykilcavan, east of Stradbally, the 1700s layout and avenues were rearranged in the nineteenth century when a new road was built from Stradbally to Athy. A distant section

35 Stillorgan House from a drawing *c.*1830 reproduced in F.E. Ball's *History of the county of Dublin* (Dublin, 1902), p. 121.

of this road is now on axis with the front door of the late eighteenth-century house. The avenue at Lismore, described as 'ancient' in 1797, had 'tall dark trees [which] shed a gloom over the outer gate house'.[58] Today the avenue at Lismore remains rather gloomy and dark but none of the original trees survive.

The approach avenue did not always run along a direct axis to the house itself. For example, at Mount Ievers and Killruddery the approach avenues ran along the side of the house, meeting up with a grand avenue, which was created to frame the view of the house itself (plate 4). At the Turrets in Staplestown, Dineley's picture shows the main avenue on axis with a castle on a nearby hill. The house lies to one side of the axis fronted by a garden surrounded by trees, and a further avenue without trees runs down to the village.[59] At Blessington the avenue from the house ran on a direct axis with the village church, built shortly after the house was completed (see plate 8).

Of lesser importance in the hierarchy were the ancillary avenues, which often criss-crossed the demesne, and were simply approach roads to alternative points of access and egress. The visual importance of secondary avenues should not be underestimated; they marked out the landscape and asserted ownership, emphasizing their creators' power over their area of jurisdiction. Sometimes

36 Detail from *Map of the county of Dublin* by John Rocque (1760) showing the layout of the gardens at Howth.

avenues continued at the rear of the house, their purpose being to extend the axial symmetry of the approach avenue. This technique was used at Belan, Kildare, where 'the chief beauty is the bold avenue on both sides of the house, to the front between a noble walk of trees of decent width, and considerable height, so as scarce (take it all together) to be paralleled'.[60] John Rocque's map of Dublin shows Howth Castle having an avenue cut through thick woodland directly on axis with ancient ruins of Corr Castle (fig. 36).

As the seventeenth century progressed, avenues grew longer. At Burtonhall in Carlow, the avenue to the front of the house was described as 'very long and handsome' although, unsurprisingly, it had to be replanted 'several times and the trees do not thrive'.[61] The avenue on the first OS map from 1837 is indeed massive in scale and planted with a double row of trees. In 1748, Chetwood wrote that the avenue 'that leads to the beautiful house is at least an English mile long',[62] and in 1838, Fraser remarked that Burtonhall was still 'remarkable for the fine old straight avenue to the mansion'.[63] By 1996, when the area was re-surveyed, the house had been demolished and the trees were gone, but the avenue remains as a long straight road.

The external landscape became an extension of the house itself. Features were laid out to be viewed and enjoyed from the main salons, which were generally still on the upper floor of the house. At Dunmore a row of trees were planted in a direct line 'from the garden door' to the banks of the river Nore.[64] The planning of Dunmore was possibly influenced by the Ormond's temporary home in England, Moore Park, where the earl of Anglesey described a long walk extending from the dining room window leading out to 'a fair brick lodge' which gave a 'prospect of most of the park and country beyond'.[65] Sir William Temple had eulogized Moore Park when he 'knew about it thirty years ago', that is, in the 1650s, as being the 'perfectest figure of a garden' he ever saw 'either at home or abroad'.

Two characteristics of many avenues were the half-moon or turning circles to the front of the house and at junctions of avenues. These were to enable lumbering coaches to turn more easily, as coaches and carriages were not easily manoeuvrable. As with all practical interventions of the period, these were incorporated into the overall design and layout of the garden and made into a feature. Avenues terminating in a semicircle half-moon were equally popular in very grand houses and more humble country gentlemen's seats.[66] In Van der Hagen's painting of Carton House c.1738, a great half-moon is visible to the front of the house, edged with very wide grass lawns. A survey of the more modest house of Dr John Madden at Castle Waterhouse in Fermanagh from 1688 shows a long avenue to the front and rear of the house, with a turning circle off the avenue, and half-moon behind the gates to the front of the house.[67]

Other demesnes with prominent turning circles include Westown House and Luttrellstown in north west Dublin. At Ballynunnery in Carlow, Dineley sketched a half moon to the front of the house.[68] At the date of Dineley's visit, sometime in the late 1670s, the house was inhabited by Captain Edward Brabazon, later the 4th earl of Meath, who when living at Killruddery created an enormous turning circle at the front of the house. An example of a turning circle at the points where primary and secondary avenues meet can be seen in an image of the old Stradbally Hall in Laois.

Groves, wildernesses, angles and labyrinths

As with avenues, there is confusion over the nomenclature used to describe the different wooded features in the garden. Wooded areas were usually ranged at either side of the main vista. In Killruddery, the main vista ran along the axis of the twin fishponds, carrying on into a long avenue edged by two rows of lime trees. The terms 'grove', 'wilderness' and 'labyrinth' are often used interchangeably. A wilderness usually referred to an area of ornamental woodland, often a mix of natives and exotics, broadleaved and coniferous species. It could also refer to an area of woodland within the formal gardens, or a plantation of woodland for cropping within the larger area of the park. These features had two extremes. At one end of the spectrum they could be a loose, naturalistic grouping of trees; at the other end, they were composed of closely cropped evergreens forming narrow angular walks terminating in pieces of statuary or water features, the latter often reaching a complexity more akin to a maze or labyrinth. At a time when privacy was at a premium, these ordered areas of woodland and shrubs created a series of intimate spaces or cabinets, where men and women could walk alone and unseen. These green rooms often contained seating, statuary, ponds or fountains. The designer Stephen Switzer called wildernesses divided by walks, 'forest gardens'.[69]

A grove, in the context of a park or garden, was woodland with grass or gravel under the trees, whereas a wilderness was an area of woodland with an understory.[70] The wilderness at Killruddery fulfils this description, being a mix of broadleaved trees (hornbeam) and conifers with an understory level. Similarly, an area of naturalistic woodland with an understory survives in the Phoenix Park; devoid of any straight rides or walks, it was referred to as 'the wilderness'. Luttrellstown Park had two wildernesses, one west of the river Liffey and another south of the river. 'Grove' and 'wilderness' have been used interchangeably and hybrids existed. The Molesworths at Breckdenston had what Robert referred to as 'a thick grove' of trees in the north-east corner of the cherry orchard. In this case, he appears to have been referring to a group of trees with grass underneath, as he earlier referred to 'sodding the grove in the garden'.[71]

No matter how 'natural' or contrived the wilderness, regular maintenance was required. The wilderness at Dunmore had suffered throughout the exile of the Ormonds. In 1667 the duchess' servant, John Bryan, informed her that they were 'going about renewing what is decayed of the wilderness', adding that he proposed to supply the gardeners with trees from the Curragh for that purpose.[72] Groves, though undoubtedly decorative, were frequently composed of plantation timber trees, which were felled when mature and ready to be sold, and were replaced by saplings. At Castlemartyr, a former potato garden was given over to a plantation of 'a hundred of English elms'.[73] A description from 1754 of the groves to the south of the house at Castlemartyr says that they were composed of plantations of elm, chestnut and other 'foremost trees of a large growth'.[74]

James Boyle described the wilderness at Antrim Castle as extending over thirty-seven acres, and being 'a grove thickly wooded with very tall and tapering elms, interspersed with a few other trees and some shrubs, traversed by numerous perfectly straight alleys and walks, and these again intersected by several curiously contrived vistas cut through the planting and at the termination of two of them are handsome bases [vases] supported by pedestals'.[75] Cultivated groves could also be purely ornamental or composed of timber trees for harvesting. Groves of timber trees were often cut into 'decent and convenient walks and divisions'.[76]

Just as classical statuary and references in the garden displayed the owner's education and understanding of the classics, the presence of exotic species emanating from English colonies in the West Indies and the Americas, and through trade links with the Far East, was another indicator of the owner's access to the global fruits of colonial enterprise. Conifers gained popularity at the end of the seventeenth century as both plantation and ornamental trees. In purely economic terms, conifers with their faster growth provided quicker returns. Sir John Perceval of Burton in Cork raised several Scots pine from seed.[77] The Antrim Survey also mentions 'lofty scotch firs and shrubs' growing at Antrim Castle.[78] John Evelyn designed a 'grove' for his garden at Sayes Court, which in plan resembles what is known as 'the angles' at Killruddery, being a densely planted enclosed area of woodland intercut with geometric walks in the form of a union flag.[79] Another densely wooded park was that at

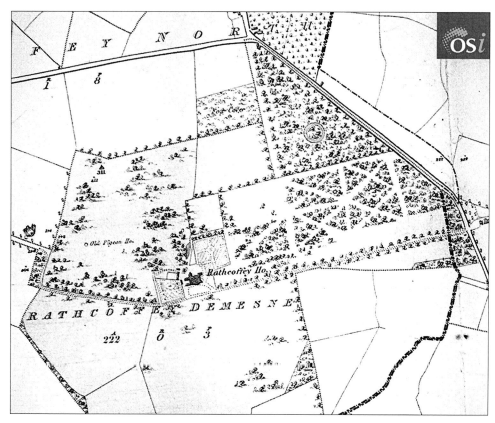

37 Elaborate woodlands with rides and walks at Rathcoffey, Co. Kildare
(courtesy of Ordnance Survey Ireland, permit ID 158).

Rathcoffey in Kildare, which had plantations cut into several rides radiating
from a central point (fig. 37). Evelyn filled his 'grove' with over 500 standard
trees of oak, ash, elm, service, beech and chestnut. However, he also planted an
understory of birch, hazel, 'thorn, wild fruits, greens, etc.'[80] At Killruddery
what survives of the angles today is composed of hedges of lime, hornbeam
and beech all within an enclosing hedge of yew. It appears that there was never
an understory planting as the walks are sharply clipped and formal, the
diagonal intersections interspersed with statuary. The 'angles' at Killruddery
have more in common with a labyrinth than a wilderness.

Labyrinths generally referred to mazes such as those at Castlemartyr and
Doneraile Court in Cork.[81] The latter was located at the site of the present
arboretum. George Rawdon created what was described as a labyrinth at
Moira, which had unfortunately been completely razed by the date of the first

OS. The garden was described by Charles Smith in 1754 as being 'adorned with a pretty labyrinth, ponds, canals and wood cut out in vistas, at the bottom of which is a decoy'.[82]

Spacing and layout of trees

There were exacting rules and regulations for the spacing and layout of tree planting. Detailed instructions as to how, where and at what distance to plant trees and shrubs for avenues and walks were prescribed by garden writers. In 1638, the French writer Jacques Boyceau's *Traité du jardinage* set out what he considered to be the proper dimensions for tree lined walks.[83] Both Evelyn and Moses Cook recommended that the width of the approach avenue should be proportionate to the length of the approach and to the width of the building to which it led. Cook suggested widths of 40, 50, and 60 feet for long avenues.[84] In a letter of instructions to his wife about the planting of the wilderness, Robert Molesworth insisted that 'the walks must be very narrow and close, yet the principal ones a little broader than the others'.[85] Molesworth came to regret this narrow specification. Just ten years after this letter was written, he complained that the gardener had allowed all the hedges 'both hornbeam and others to grow too broad; they are four, five, or six foot broad, whereas they should ever be suffered to be above two', thus spoiling the walks.[86] Excessively high hedges seem to have been popular. Loveday noted 'high hedges and long narrow walks' when visiting Antrim Castle in 1758;[87] the canal was edged with a lime hedge of eighteen feet.[88] At Breckdenston it was hoped to grow the hornbeam hedges in the gravel walk up to thirty feet or more, which required the gardener to climb upon long ladders in order to keep them trim.[89]

Moses Cooke's detailed directions on the spacing and placement of walks within the garden disclose the huge dimensions walks could take. The sizes advocated show the confusion that could arise over what constituted a walk and what constituted an avenue:

> Do not mask a fine front, nor veil a pleasant prospect (as too many do) by making the walks too narrow. If you make any walk that leads to any pleasant front of a house, or other object; if it be but half a mile long, let it be at least forty foot wide, but if longer, more, as 50 or 60 foot wide, or the breadth the length of our front; but if you be for walks of shade, then make three walks, the middle one 40, the two outside walks each 20 foot, or 50 and 25 the outside walks, or divide your front into two

parts, and let the middle be as broad as both the side-walks ... so will the trees range much the better, whether you set them square or triangular; the square to be the best, because then four trees in the four rows end all together, fit to end in either semicircle, segment of a circle, oval, triangle, or circle; for all walks of any length, especially in parks, should end in some one of these figures, or lead into some other walk; but where the doe fall into another walk, there should be a circle to receive them, or else they seem much defective.[90]

The spacing of the trees themselves depended on the root and canopy spread (which are generally broadly similar). Batty Langley suggested spacings of 30–35 and 40 feet for large or grand avenues and walks planted in elm, lime or beech. Cook, in describing walks outside the garden, suggested a spacing of 2 rods, or 33 feet.[91] Evelyn recommended a spacing of 18–20 feet for elm walks or avenues, and 10–30 feet for sweet chestnut avenues, although the spacing of 40–50 feet was given for walnut avenues 'to our country dwellings'.[92] Dézallier d'Argenville recommended a spacing of 12 feet for trees in walks and counter walks of elm, lime and chestnut, preferring it to the spacings of 9, 15 or 18 feet given by others. In the fourth edition of *Silva*, Evelyn noted that the trees in Spain were decayed because they had been planted too close to each other.[93] Switzer advised that the spacing should relate to the width of the avenue by a factor of two or three. For terrace walks he recommended walks 20 feet wide with trees 30 feet apart.[94]

Research done by Sarah Couch in Britain on surviving parkland and approach avenues shows a range of spacing, which falls between the limits prescribed by garden writers.[95] It is most unlikely that any of the lime present in avenues today are the original plants. However, elm, sycamore, yew and occasionally oak and sweet chestnut have survived in the landscape from the seventeenth century. The elm and ash avenue at Belan House, Kildare, was described in 1797 as being 'not strongly regular',[96] indicating that the avenue, which was planted *c*.1690, was poorly maintained as it is likely that the lack of regularity was due to age and decay. Palmerstown, Sir John Temple's house near Chapelizod, had a long avenue to the front of the house planted with ash and elm.[97]

Tree species used in the seventeenth-century demesne

Within the demesne, Ireland's native trees were supplemented by the addition of available foreign exotics.[98] Natives such as the wych elm, *Ulmus glabra*, were relegated to make way for more glamorous or stately trees. The 'wych elms' in the 'great avenue' at Breckdenston which led to Knocksedan were removed 'where they will not be taken so much notice of' and pollarded ('stubbed' or 'dehorned') to improve their ungainly structure and replaced with 'the best trees we have'.[99] Trees such as the common sycamore, *Acer platanus*, beech, *Fagus sylvatica*, lime, *Tilia*, and the horse chestnut, *Aesculus hippocastanum*, are all originally alien trees, which have adapted well to Ireland's climate and become naturalized. The horse chestnut, being the most recent, was a late sixteenth-century introduction.[100] Sycamore and beech were introduced in the sixteenth century as was the English elm.[101] Bishop King had both walnut and chestnut trees sent from Dublin to the palace in Derry.[102] There has been much debate over whether sweet chestnut, *Castanea sativa*, is native to England or Ireland, but writers such as Evelyn treated it as indigenous.[103] Most references to 'chestnut' refer to the sweet chestnut and not the horse chestnut. Another exotic tree from the temperate world was *Liriodenron tulipifera*, the tulip tree, emanating from English colonies in the West Indies and the Americas.

Young trees took time and care to establish and many were lost through planting in unsuitable soil conditions or through lack of sufficient irrigation. Letters between the countess of Orrery and her servant, William Cooper, disclose how several lime trees died after a particularly dry summer in 1669. Cooper thought that ash would be a more suitable replacement but was prevailed upon by the earl to secure more lime.[104] The letters between Robert and Lettice Molesworth contain frequent references to troublesome plantings at Breckdenston. In 1716, several of the elms in 'the great avenue towards Hatch Hall' died and had to be 'dug about and repaired with thriving trees'.[105] 'Fir' trees grown in another avenue were described as having been 'blasted brown', suggesting that they suffered from windburn.[106] 'Scotch fir' was proposed as a possible replacement, but rejected on the grounds that they were 'of the ugliest trees that is'. It also appears that several beech trees were lost in 1695. Lettice was directed by her husband to buy as many beech trees 'as will make good the avenue'.[107]

After a particularly hard winter in 1683, Lord Weymouth, who had planted 'about 10,000 trees', lost all his arbutus, which was native to Ireland. Sir Robert Southwell wrote to his friend Sir John Perceval back in Ireland requesting that he 'procure him some of them' to replace those lost. He had clearly researched the topic: 'his lordship says, and so does Mr Evelyn in his *Silva*, that they grow everywhere in Ireland'.[108] The 'most esteemed' of the 'dry' trees, according to Evelyn, were the 'oak, elm, beech, ash, chestnut, and wall-nut'.[109]

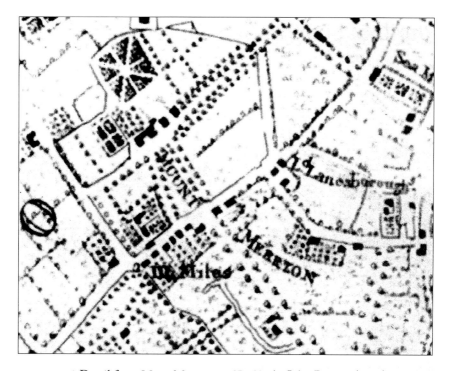

38 Detail from *Map of the county of Dublin* by John Rocque (1760)
showing Mount Merrion.

Lime and elm appear to have been the predominant species for use in
avenue planting although beech, chestnut and walnut did make appearances.
Beech was used in avenues at Doneraile, Breckdenston and Ardfert in Kerry.[110]
Avenues of both walnut and chestnut were seen at Ballybeggan in Kerry
(owned by the Hussey family), which according to Smith, survived well into
the eighteenth century.[111] Lime and elm were also planted in large quantities
at Burton in Cork.[112]

The great *patte d'oie* at Breckdenston was planted with six rows of elm. One
of the avenues at Mount Merrion, at the site of the present Foster's Avenue,
was composed of a double row of elm (fig. 38).[113] Elm was also used in the
avenue towards Mount Merrion at Stillorgan House[114] and at Ardfert.[115]
Avenues of elm were seen at Killruddery up until the 1850s but it is not
known where these were situated, though they probably lined the approach
avenue.[116] In his *Topographical dictionary* Lewis described the approach to
Castlemartyr from Middleton as being 'a magnificent avenue of lofty elms, one

mile in length, and terminating at the eastern gate of Lord Shannon's demesne'.[117] Elm was also used in municipal plantings, the Corporation of Dublin ordered both elms and sycamore for a proposed new park near Oxmantown Green in 1665 and in St Stephen's Green.

Along with elm, lime was popular for avenue planting because although it is naturally tall and fast growing, it lends itself to pruning and to training, and so was often close planted and pleached. Three species of lime were commonly available in the seventeenth century. *Tilia platyphyllos* is large leaved and red twigged, and is useful in parks because it is long-lived and tends not to sprout at its base. While Evelyn admired 'Dutch lime', which he observed on his visit to the Low Countries in 1641, he preferred to see native English small-leaved lime, *Tilia cordata*, the less vigorous and slower growing, being used in Britain. 'Dutch lime' referred to *Tilia x vulgaris*, a new hybrid between the two limes that was propagated in vast numbers in the Netherlands. This lime was easily propagated by layering whereas the native trees had to be gathered as seedlings from the hedgerows.[118] The Dutch lime was therefore widely used due to its availability from nurserymen. The great avenue at Killruddery consists of treble rows of lime, though it is unlikely that any of the original survive. It is possible that some of the avenue trees at Breckdenston were of Dutch lime as Molesworth instructed his wife to ensure that the trees in the avenue were 'cleansed from suckers'.[119] This contention is further supported by a letter dated 1695 in which Robert Molesworth referred to several Dutch elms being missing from a parcel he sent to his wife.[120] The popularity of elm and especially Dutch lime was probably enhanced by their apparent cheapness and easy availability. In 1669 Dublin Corporation noted that 'there is a great quantity of lime trees now within this city to be sold at reasonable rates'.[121] In December 1683, Sir John Perceval received a bill 'for 100 lime trees and 200 Dutch elm trees,[122] and in 1685 he received a parcel of '70 or 71' bare rooted elms from Bristol.[123] The minutes of the Royal Hospital in Kilmainham tell us that several hundred lime trees were planted about the grounds between 1690 and 1692.[124]

Hornbeam, *Carpinus betulus*, was used regularly for high walks and borders, as it was easy to maintain and dense, retaining some of its leaves throughout winter. At the Royal Hospital, the Committee recommended that elm and abeale should be planted for walks in the hospital grounds. The great avenue at Breckdenston was planted with what Molesworth referred to as 'spruce firs'.[125] These firs could have been either *Picea abies*, the common or Norway spruce,[126] or one of the new North American varieties, *Picea glauca* or *Picea mariana*, the black spruce, both introduced in 1700.[127] At Ballybegg spruce was used to edge a gravel walk where it was cut into pyramids, and the avenue was lined, unusually, with holly.[128]

Sir John Temple's gardens at Palmerstown had a fir avenue.[129] And Lixnaw in Kerry was described as having 'a noble avenue of lofty fir trees not ornamented or improved'.[130] Fir trees were sometimes planted as 'nursery trees' to provide shelter for the plants intended for the final avenue or walk. By planting this way the fast-growing conifers gave coverage and definition to the walk and protected the young trees from windburn; this practice was carried out at Castlemartyr where the gardener 'planted a great quantity of yew cuttings in rows between the fir'.[131] Worlidge stated that 'the fir-tree is rather for the woods than for the garden' by reason of its shape, which made it only suitable for planting in corners or at the termination of walks.[132] This description suggests that the 'fir' he referred to was *Abies alba*, the common silver fir. *Abies alba* is an unsatisfactory garden tree, it attracts aphids, is not frost hardy and looks shabby. Attempts were made to grow silver fir as a specimen tree in one of the parterres at Breckdenston for its 'beauty'; it failed to thrive though, and Molesworth directed its removal.[133]

What was referred to by Molesworth as 'Scotch fir', which he thought 'one of the ugliest trees that is', was probably *Pinus sylvestris* or Scot's pine.[134] It appears to have been the common term for Scot's pine until relatively recently. The Antrim Survey also mentions 'lofty scotch firs and shrubs' growing at Antrim Castle.[135] Sir John Perceval of Burton in Cork raised several Scots pine from seed.[136] The cedar of Lebanon, *Cedrus libani*, was introduced to England *c.*1659[137] and had certainly reached Irish gardens by the 1680s.[138]

Trees for the wilderness, when in the context of a 'forest garden', were ideally woodland trees that were shade tolerant and would suffer close spacing well. *Carpinus betulus*, the hornbeam, and *Sorbus* species and *Fraxinus excelsior*, ash, which were fast growing, were planted along with slower growing oak and elm. Understory plantings of yew, holly, briars and honeysuckles were added to create naturalistic woodland and to add variety and scent. Henry Boyle's gardener describes how he planted such a scheme at Castlemartyr:

> I have planted a great many yew and laurel on both sides in the walks for underwood and have left holes between the laurel and yew in order to plant holly in them ... [and] I have set a great quantity of filbert decorus and crabsticks with a good quantity of walnuts and chestnuts.[139]

Worlidge held that next to perennial greens, '*platanus*' was the best tree to adorn walks and groves. In this context, 'platanus' probably refers to *Platanus orientalis*, the oriental plane, a species in cultivation in England since the early sixteenth century, rather than the London plane, *Platanus x hispanica*. *Platanus hispanica* was first described in 1670 as growing in the Oxford Botanic Gardens. This was a hybrid between the American plane, possibly sent over by John Tradescant the younger, and the oriental plane.[140] In 1682, *platanus* was observed growing at Arthur Forbes' garden in Longford.[141] As the tree was described as the 'famous platanus' it probably was a specimen of the London plane.

The more formal elements of the garden – the walks, parterres and formal groves – were generally planted with evergreen trees and shrubs or beech (which keeps its form and some leaf cover in winter), although a chestnut walk was planted at Castlemartyr,[142] and Breckdenston had both fir and ash groves.[143] Evergreens with variegated leaves were highly regarded by some.[144] Evelyn asserted that of all the 'winter greens', cypress was the best, 'it being the most uniform, straightest, and most slender of any other, preserving its verdure throughout the year'.[145] Evelyn's reference fits the description of *Cupressus sempervirens*, the Italian cypress; this seems to be confirmed when he concedes that it was practically impossible to get the seeds to ripen in the English climate. However, he enjoined his readers to persevere with attempts to grow it from seed, hoping that it would eventually acclimatize itself to the colder conditions of England.[146] In the 1690s, Sir John Temple attempted to grow cypress but it did not survive the winter.[147] Italian cypress, *Cupressus sempervirens*, is a relatively hardy plant, and can cope with some frost, but will not survive very cold winters. Also the difficulties described in growing cypress may have been the result of a combination of cold and damp, fatal to the young plants. Evelyn displayed a stubborn streak, refusing to acknowledge that wet weather was the cause of the plant's failure, upbraiding Pliny's suggestion that cypress seeds 'prosper not, if on the same day they be sown, the rain falls on them: it is doubtless either a mistake, or some superstitious observation'.[148] Robert Molesworth tried to grow Italian cypress unsuccessfully in his garden in 1720s; again, this was probably due to the plant's failure to establish in the cold winds blowing in from the Atlantic. In 1750, Smith observed cypress trees at Mount Uniack in Cork, owned by Richard Uniack. It is most probable that this was raised in a greenhouse or cold frame and kept in pots to be wheeled out during the day until sufficiently hardened off to survive alone.[149]

The perfect alternative to cypress was yew, *Taxus baccata*. The Irish yew, in particular, could be clipped to give the same sense of vertical formality and intense dark green colour as the Italian cypress, while thriving in the Irish climate. In John Evelyn's plan for the duke of Norfolk's garden at Albury in

Surrey, he specified a series of unnamed tall pencil-like trees indicative of cypress. However visitors to the site found yew growing in its place.[150]

Yew was used extensively at Killruddery in the angles and wilderness where its red fruits give additional interest in autumn. Yew could also be shaped by topiary and used in mazes and parterres. At Antrim Castle, 'a yew tree 14 feet high in the form of an obelisk' was grown in the centre of a parterre.[151] In the gardens at Lismore, the remains of an early yew walk are propped up and wired into place, massively overgrown and shapeless – a pathetic travesty of the original planter's intentions. The Irish clergyman Rowland Davies, dean of Ross, was taught how to propagate yew by Evelyn himself on a visit to his garden at Sayes Court:

> I went with Dr Parr and Mr Higden to visit Mr Evelyn at Deptford; there saw his gardens and varieties of trees, with several rarities, and also drank some quince wine. He also assured me that the best time to remove any greens was in August or in the spring, and that yew grows as readily and easily from the slip as rosemary, being either twisted or bruised before it is set.[152]

Box, *Buxus sempervirens*, another plant traditionally associated with French and Italian gardens, fortunately thrived in the Irish climate. Box was most commonly used in parterres and as edging for walks. At Birr Castle, a thirty-five foot tall box hedge allée survives which is said to date from late seventeenth century (although this is debatable). Some massively distorted and overgrown box survives in the remains of a walled kitchen garden at the Bishop's Palace at Clonfert in Galway; these were once low box edgings to vegetable beds

In addition to yew and box, myrtle and bay were all excellent plants for use in walks and parterres as both are evergreen. *Myrtus communis*, the common myrtle, has aromatic leaves and deliciously scented white flowers in bloom from summer to autumn, followed by purplish black berries. The leaves of *Laurus nobilis*, or sweet bay, are used in cooking. Its dark glossy leaves are scented and it is an ideal plant for topiarizing. It too has the benefit of bearing scented yellow flowers in spring followed by black berries in autumn. The 'sylvan theatre' at Killruddery is surrounded by *Laurus nobilis*.[153]

When the early horticultural writers talk of 'laurel', they appear to be referring to *Prunus laurocerasus*, the cherry laurel, introduced to Britain in 1576, and *Prunus lusitanica*, the Portugal laurel, introduced in 1648. Worlidge also referred to 'Laurustinus', which is now identified as *Viburnum tinus*.[154] Evelyn went so far as to pronounce the 'laurel to be one of the most proper and ornamental trees for walks and avenues of any growing'.[155] The walks in Evelyn's grove were edged with laurel.[156] In January 1710, William King paid for '8 plants of laurel', which indicates that they were to be grown either as dot plants or in combination with other greens for hedging.[157] *Ilex aquifolium*, or common holly, was used as a hedging plant as well as for understory planting. Evelyn had holly hedges in his own garden at Sayes Court and holly hedges were observed by his son at John Temple's gardens in Palmerston.[158]

CHAPTER 7

Botanical developments and the physic garden

S EVENTEENTH-CENTURY IRISH LANDOWNERS sought to combine statuary, rare plants in their gardens reflecting the practice of the creation of *cabinets de curiosités* by royalty and nobility throughout Europe. With the penetration of the New World to the west, which began in earnest during the reign of James I, and the increase in travel and exploration eastwards, increasing numbers of non-native or exotic plants were introduced to Europe. The garden was a site where botanical and art collections could be organized and shown off.

Gardeners in Ireland were greedy for as many new species as possible. As well as being decorative additions to the garden, many of the new plants were, like earlier introductions such as the potato, useful food and cash crops. Plants were sent back and forth between English and Irish estates, and from abroad.[1] In a letter to Lord Conway dating from 1667, Rawdon referred to Conway's 'intended adventure to the Canaries'[2] from whence he may have sent plants home. Richard Bulkeley of Old Bawn in Co. Dublin visited the Oxford Physic Garden and took advice from its keeper, Jacob Bobart the younger.[3] His gardener, Harrison, had been 'bred up under Bobart' and Bulkeley expressed his hopes he would 'sub auspices of my Lord Capel[4] bring the more elegant cultivation of gardens and curious plants into fashion here'.[5] In 1694, Harrison was sent to England and it was hoped that he would bring back 'trees plants flowers, exotics' and other 'rarities'. The Molesworths also obtained plants from Lord Henry Capel, whose gardens at Kew Park in London were the core of what later became the Royal Botanical Gardens.[6] The mild climate of Cork allowed more exotic trees and plants to survive the Irish winters outdoors. At Castle Phillips in Ballymaloe, Charles Smith saw 'the *arbor vitae* of Gerrard, and several kinds of myrtle, which thrive here and flourish equal to those planted in a warmer and happier climate'; in addition to this he observed 'a bladder nut *nux versicaria*' at Aghada.[7] Smith was also fortunate enough to see some of the trees brought to Moira by the plant collector James Harlow,[8] such as the 'locust of Virginia', 'a tree 30 feet high, and of a body at least a foot and a half in diameter, bearing a pod larger than any pea, and full of honey'.[9] This probably refers to *Robinia pseudoacacia* which was introduced in the 1630s.

Sourcing and obtaining plant materials

The explosion of tree planting in large geometric layouts in the late seventeenth and early decades of the eighteenth century led to a huge demand for plant stock. By 1691 there were at least five commercial nurseries in London, including Brompton Park nursery in which George London and Henry Wise were partners.[10] In Ireland commercial nurseries were well established by the early-eighteenth century when Cork nurseryman Andrew Bridges provided plants for many of the estates around Munster including Lord Kenmare's Ross Castle in Kerry, Lismore in Waterford and Doneraile in Cork.[11] However, it was better economic practice for a landowner to raise trees in his own nursery as advised in the practical gardening manuals of the period. Where this was not possible or where a particular species was sought, the normal practice was to send to London or to exchange stock from other estates. The growth of the nursery trade indicates that many landowners did not raise sufficient stock for their own needs. Switzer directed what he considered essential for the establishment of a nursery:

> I suppose to find some thousands of oak, ash, beech, chestnut, hornbeam, scotch and silver firs, for walks, avenues and groves, raised from seed, ... I suppose to find some thousands of elms, limes, abeals, poplars, etc. raised from the layers.[12]

John Bryan wrote an account of his progress in planting oak and ash nurseries for the duchess of Ormond:

> I have advised with both gardeners at Dunmore and Adam Seix about planting the acorns and ashkeys. They are all of opinion that a large nursery be made, out of which the plants may be removed into any place or part that your Graces shall command it hereafter. And such a place for a nursery have I now ready, close and strong fenced. And for planting acorns and ashkeys by the pale sides in the park, where the deer can come at them, is thought to avail little. I have with both the gardeners viewed the grounds at Dunmore and (as we conceive) have pitched upon the most fit and convenient places for ornament and shelter, yet to be better satisfied I gave order to the new gardener, when Captain Martin comes to Dunmore to take his advice. Adam Seix is of

opinion that it will be to little purpose to plant acorns or ashkeys in Kilkenny meadows because of the cattle coming there, and where to get trees within less than 15 or 20 mile he knows not; besides that the season is so far spent.[13]

At Breckdenston, the Molesworths planted a nursery of oaks from acorns which appears to have thrived.[14] Molesworth prevailed upon his son John, then in Italy, to send him 'a small sack of acorns of the ilex, or evergreen kind, whereof there is a great wood near Pisa'.[15] Nick the gardener was also instructed to 'propagate as many Myrtles' as he could, and to 'dig, cleanse and increase all his nurseries' in preparation for Molesworth's 'great matters in view as to planting' for which he needed 'a fresh supply of all sort of trees especially elms and limes'.[16]

Whenever possible, seeds and whips were obtained from neighbouring counties and estates. In 1679 John Baxter informed the duchess of Ormond that 'yesterday the Lord Granard's servant came hither with seven score five trees of which care is taken according to your Grace's commands'[17] A letter of 1728 from Garret Fleming, a gardener to Henry Boyle at Castlemartyr, provided a good contemporary account of the purchase and of the planting of trees:

> Since your honour left home ... I got as many ash trees at Ballynacurron. And as many English elms as filled up the ground where the Dutch elms were in the walk, and have planted the Dutch elm inside the wall in the barren meadow. I have laid a great quantity of English and Dutch elms, and have set a great many English and Dutch cuttings of elm likewise a great quantity of French elm with some mulberry[18] cuttings. I got 4000 of English and Dutch elms from Mr Croker from the county of Limerick and have planted out by way of a nursery in Maurish Joyce's garden ... and I got from the same gentleman as many Dutch alder as filled up the ground next to Beecher's orchard where the ash did not thrive, and the high ground that is above that, I planted with Birch. The bowling green is planted with sycamore. I bought a thousand fir trees from Colonel Maynard and filled up the old nursery, and what remained I planted them in the garden above the nursery.[19]

Lord Conway purchased several plants from nurserymen in Dublin and had them transported by ship to Belfast.[20] It was advisable to seek out nurserymen

39 The remains of Finglaswood House taken from a 'Descriptive sketch of places visited', *JRSAI*, 27 (1897), p. 446.

on the recommendation of a trusted friend or colleague: Lord Massereene wrote the following in a letter to his cousin Sir Richard Newdigate:

> Upon the subject of roots and seeds to be begged out of your fine plantations, and same (if you please) to be bought also from any gardener yet I might trust; which enlargement you would excuse I hope as I would the freedom used on so innocent a design as that of partaking with you of such things as might reside in this climate.[21]

As well as importing from nurserymen on the Continent, gardeners also enlisted the aid of friends and relations in England. In the early 1680s Laurence Clayton, who owned an estate near Mallow, presented a relation in London with a list 'as long as a tailor's bill, which if you can procure among the virtuosi gardeners you will oblige me and the curious here'.[22] In particular, he requested evergreens, which could withstand exposure, including variegated forms of holly, *Phillyrea latifolia*, and privet. Also ordered were elm, lime, plane, Virginian acacia, cedar, lotus, olive and pomegranate. In an undated letter, probably from the early 1720s, William Boyle of Castlemartyr wrote: 'I have now made myself acquainted with some of the most noted nurserymen and gardeners, so that if you want anything that this country affords; command me and I will soon find out some ship bound to Cork'.[23]

Nicholas Plunkett, who at the time was residing at the court of the dowager Queen Mother in England, spent a lot of time sourcing plant materials for his friend Thomas Flower who had estates in Brecknock in Wales, Castle Durrow in Meath as well as at Finglaswood in Dublin (fig. 39).[24] In 1691, Plunkett updated Flower on his efforts:

> I have now, dear Thomas, performed my task with all the care, circumspection and valour that the King of France himself would have done it for you; I need not I suppose, give you any more than particulars of each parcel of tree nor what each parcel cost, but the fir trees came to much more than we thought at first; and thereupon my friend Mr Baddsley the gardener ... 7/6 for the fruit trees, for they reckon the 12 fir trees at 19/6 so as the trees came to £5 6s. 4d. and to make it even money I gave the gardener £5 8d. and for 2 mats 2s., and to a porter for carrying the to the inn 1/6 which in full you will find to be £5 15s.[25]

Plunkett also managed to ingratiate himself with one of dowager Queen Catherine's gardeners who was willing to supply him with plant materials:

> The only gardener here of my acquaintance is her Majesty's man at Somerset house; and he has the countenance and deportment of honesty, and promises to deal with me as reasonable and justly as any other, if this liken you? Pray dispatch your orders that your work may be despatched accordingly, set down the number the quantity.[26]

A further letter disclosed that he had obtained 12 fir trees which were to be sent 'for security in mats',[27] and an invoice of 1723 sent to William Flower includes delivery of 1,000 fir trees.[28]

Sometimes trees were stolen en route to Ireland; Molesworth wrote of a 'rogue Browne', who appears to have been a carrier, and was to be arrested 'for the knavish tricks he played us about our yew trees'.[29] Disloyal gardeners were also responsible for selling their master's stock to unscrupulous dealers. Theft by gardeners was so prevalent that in 1698 laws were enacted to punish the offenders.[30] The duchess of Ormond complained of a keeper at Carrick:

> [He] is not to be trusted, for a gentleman who is now here, told me that he offered him to sell him trees from thence and that he had sold unto diverse gentlemen in the county of Tipperary and Waterford; and so little he minds anything of the gardens but what does yield himself profit, as he lets all go to ruin, without taking any pains himself; and expects his wages and the profits of the place.[31]

Lord Massereene and Sir Richard Newdigate conducted a regular correspondence in which they discussed their shared interest in botany, dispensing and receiving advice on how best to grow trees. It is clear from the letters that both correspondents had nurseries of their own. They also sent seeds and stock to each other on a regular basis.

> My health is improved of late, and my greatest entertainment is planting, in which I saw you were curious and your nurseries fully stored; I therefore desire a paper of seeds of your greens of all your best and most curious kinds – at least of your pines, firs and other sorts of trees, with which you are well stock and so am I. But because your kinds are different from ours I beg some more variety from you, with your advice to sow and raise them and the best season. If any other trees or of your flowers or rarities can be spared and may be sent in seeds, I can hope safely get them planted here; which is a favourable climate. I want Spanish gessime [*Jasminum grandiflorum*]. But without pots know not how to convey it. If anything in root or seeds can be spared, that you think worth sending, my son will take care to transmit them and your directions therewith.[32]

The seeds were sent as requested; they proved to be a disappointment, and Massereene wrote 'none of the seeds you sent add to our plantation, because they do not come up'.[33] When Viscount Conway was in France on State business, he frequently sent plants back to Ireland; in 1669 he sent several unidentified trees from Bordeaux. Seeds were also sent home – one consignment of which Rawdon complained were 'very ordinary'. He was, however, confident that he would be able to get other seeds 'which were wanting' from Dublin, which indicates that seedsmen in the city were importing less 'ordinary' and more interesting plants from the Continent at this time.[34]

The Molesworth correspondence contains several references to seeds and stock, including bedding plants, being sent from abroad to the Swords estate.[35] There is one tantalizing reference to 'a great sale of trees of all sorts at Twittenham' by a gardener who is 'breaking up or dead lately'.[36] 'Twittenham' is a reference to Twickenham, which opens the intriguing possibility that some of the trees at Breckdenston may have originated in one of the great gardens in Richmond such as Twickenham Park. This piece of intelligence probably came via one of Molesworth's friends and fellow gardeners, possibly 'Secretary' Johnston who gardened at his home in Twickenham (later Orleans House), designed by John James (1672–1746) and famous for its gardens.[37]

Molesworth and his wife were both close friends of Johnston and clearly respected his gardening aesthetic, incorporating some of his designs in their own garden.[38] Alternatively, the information could have originated from the earl of Shaftesbury, also a close friend.

Richard Bulkeley sent his correspondent Lister whole catalogues of plants which he hoped he might procure for him.[39] By the 1660s seedsmen and nurserymen appear to have been well established in Dublin.[40] Archbishop King's accounts contain many references to payments for seeds for his garden,[41] and Robert Molesworth mentioned 'a salesman in Dublin where you may get more, [beech seed] and hornbeam seed too'.[42] It is unfortunate that details of the seedsmen have not survived. However, for exotics, one had to look further afield. The earl of Clarendon requested his friend Lord Willoughby, who was governor of Barbados at the time, to send him 'some seeds or nuts which may produce trees'.[43]

As well as exotics, the incomers took an interest in cultivating native Irish plants and sending them abroad. The Lane papers contain 'directions how to raise the cane apple by seeds otherwise called the Irish strawberry tree or arbutus'.[44] (An example of a very old *Arbutus unedo* can be seen at Killruddery.) Seeds of choice Irish plants were sent to England. Sir Thomas Southwell sent arbutus seeds to Coningsby at Hampton Court Park in Herefordshire.[45]

Edward Cooke, who took care of the duke of Ormond's business in England and at Moore Park, collected seeds from various estates he visited throughout the country. He wrote from Highnam in Gloucester in 1667, where he had been on 'partly business, partly visit and partly sports', that he had requested 'a sufficient quantity of acorns, beech masts, and walnuts; and if your grace can recollect anything else yet you have any inclination for'.[46] A few days later he informed Ormond that he had been in the Forest of Dean where he had collected further walnuts, acorns, and beech masts.[47] As well as seeds and young trees, cuttings were sent between English and Irish properties. Robert Southwell had several cuttings of fruit trees sent from his wife Elizabeth's family home, Surrenden in Kent, owned by her father Sir Edward Dering.[48]

An account of Castle Forbes in Co. Longford, written for the Dublin Philosophical Society in 1682, described how Arthur Forbes, Viscount Granard, had improved his estate and described some of the plants growing there:

> [He] hath by much industry managed the soil that it beareth all sorts
> of plants and flowers that are set or sowed there is now growing there
> in great order large groves of fir of all sorts with pine, juniper, cedar,

lime trees, beech, elm, oak, ash, aspen and the famous platanus[49] tree I suppose not growing anywhere besides in this kingdom, he hath built a fair and spacious house with lovely gardens of pleasure enclosed by high stone walls against which great plenty of fruit of all sorts grows, and in the said garden are all kind of flowers and flower trees that grow in this kingdom, as the lilacs, laburnum and many more, with phillyrea hedges, laurel etc., and the tuberose beareth here which is not to be raised but with the assistance of glasses.[50]

This entry is interesting as it is one of the first times the use of 'glasses' is mentioned (although here they were not necessary). In this case, glasses may refer to the glass bell jars or cloches used to protect tender plants as illustrated by van Hohberg in *Georgica curiosa* and Evelyn in *Elysium Britannicum*.[51]

The reference may also be to an early greenhouse. The seventeenth century saw the emergence of the first purpose-built greenhouses. In *Reflections upon ancient and modern learning*, William Wotton included a chapter entitled 'of ancient and modern agriculture and gardening' in which he wrote of the advantages the modern gardener had over the ancients, including the fact that 'there is far more variety in modern kitchen gardens, especially with their greenhouse culture'.[52] Conservatories, orangeries and hothouses were necessary to grow the influx of plants from East and West Indies, which were too tender to leave outdoors. It was further reported that there was a 'greenhouse' at 'Primate Boyle's old house' in Blessington, Co. Wicklow.[53] In his chapter on 'trees for ornament and shade', Worlidge suggested that imported plants should be taken indoors for winter, or that a 'repository' for tender plants be created, 'under the same construction as a pleasure house, called a green-house' because 'several winter greens are therein preserved'.[54] The term greenhouse presumably derives from the fact that it was somewhere sheltered to preserve tender 'winter greens' and need not necessarily correspond to what we understand of the term greenhouse today in that it was probably not constructed wholly of glass. Such houses were heated with stoves when tender plants were to be grown within them. The earliest greenhouses were developed by the Dutch at the university of Leiden's botanic garden. They were constructed of brick and wood with slate roofs and the south-facing wall was composed of large double casement windows. There they were heated with a wood or charcoal-burning stove,[55] with under floor heating using clay pipes and glass roofs being introduced in the late seventeenth century.[56] Chapter 15 of Evelyn's *Elysium Britannicum* was entitled 'orangeries, and conservatories of rare plants and fruits' and this included glasshouses.[57] In 1677, he described

40 Grafting trees from *A new orchard and garden* (1631) by William Lawson.

seeing a 'conservatory very long (some hundred feet) adorned with maps, as the other side is with the heads of Caesars all cut in alabaster' at Lord Arlington's garden at Euston Hall in Suffolk.[58] Worlidge suggested that 'repositories for tender plants', called 'green-house[s], as several winters green are therein preserved' be made at 'some remote angle' in the garden where they would have both 'air' and a view. These constructions, similar to 'pleasure houses' or 'banqueting-houses', should be 'glazed with the best and most transparent glass'.[59] Certainly there was a conservatory or glazed plant house, said to be the first such building in Ireland, at Moira by 1690[60] and, in September 1705, Brilliana Rawdon, daughter of George and sister of Arthur, wrote to Sir Hans Sloane relating that her sister had 'got a little green house this winter' having 'lost several plants last year which she raised of seed for want of it'.[61] The wide variety of tender fruits grown by the end of the century suggests that hothouses had become commonplace.[62]

Methods of propagation

Propagation of plants is used to multiply stock, either by seed or vegetatively, by cuttings of live plant material, or by grafting. Grafting, in most cases, involves one plant, such as quince, selected for its hardy and vigorous roots (the stock or rootstock), and another plant selected for its good stems, leaves, flowers or fruit (the scion) and joining the two together to create one stronger plant (fig. 40). Until the seventeenth century pears had been grown grafted onto pear stocks, crab apple stocks, and, occasionally, hawthorn stocks. Sir Thomas Hanmer and his friend, John Evelyn, were among the first in England to realize the value of grafting onto quince stock, which ensured that the trees remained small and sturdy, which is now the preferred method of propagation. The practice was already widespread in France and probably originated there. Fruit growers were occasionally frustrated in their endeavours by the difficulty and delays in transporting stock from abroad. In April 1683 Sir John Perceval wrote to Sir Robert Southwell that 'the westerly winds will make me lose the season for grafting a great many cuttings of fruit trees from Surrenden which are still detained in the river of Thames'.[63] Reliance was often placed on friends and acquaintances to ensure that stock reached them safely.[64] Plants were often damaged en route either through neglect or to the packet boats being held up in bad weather. On other occasions the stock arrived safely but the documentation accompanying them was damaged:

> The sciences have come safely and time enough but the labels being of paper, were rotted off, and we have had to guess at the various sorts, and I think have hit right of the golden pippins. I am afraid the greens must have been delayed at Chester.[65]

Obtaining and then maintaining healthy trees was fraught with difficulties. As with other garden plants, fruit plants and trees were imported from abroad or from other properties in England and Ireland. (Archbishop William King obtained some 'flower roots' from Chapelizod for his garden in Dublin, possibly from the Viceregal Lodge.)[66] Entire trees were purchased as well as scions for grafting.[67] One of the many duties of the literate gardener was to locate fruit requested by his master or mistress.[68] Nicholas Plunkett gave Thomas Flower's gardener 5s. for 'his pains in going choosing and bringing' fruit trees for planting in his garden at Finglas. Plunkett himself bought several fruit trees in London for Flower in 1691.[69]

William Temple instructed the gardener that he should 'take the greatest care and pains in preserving your trees from the worst disease, to which those of the best fruits are subject in the best soil, and upon the best walls'.[70] Despite the best efforts of gardeners to protect and nourish their precious plants, fruit trees often succumbed to the rigours of climate and disease. Temple described how his fruit developed a 'soot or smuttiness upon their leaves', which indicates one of the fungal diseases still called 'sooty mould' today. He went on to say that he knew of some collections of orange trees 'quite destroyed by it' and, demonstrating his scientific curiosity, observed, accurately, that the vector for this disease was a scale insect, 'a small insect of a dark-brown colour, figured like a shield'.[71] Several trees at Portmore and Lisburn Castle perished in the Spring of 1667.[72] In March 1691, Edmond Doyne, Thomas Flower's gardener at Finglas, wrote that many of the trees, both wall and orchard, had been infected by 'a great blast' but was relieved to report that 'the apricots were all spared'.[73] His relief was short-lived as by July, they too 'were all blasted and are turned very small and hard'.[74] Mrs F. Keightley, a kinswoman of Lettice Molesworth, who lived at Killester, received some rather suspect advice from a Frenchwoman called Madame Bourchier on protecting her pear trees. Madame Bourchier suggested mulching the roots of pears with 'the rags of all sorts, silk, linen and woollen'.[75] This would, apparently, encourage trees that had been barren to bear fruit. Some landowners began to experiment with different varieties to assess their hardiness; Rawdon noted that 'sweetings' apples failed to produce more fruit than the more reliable 'red strakes'; Francis, the gardener at Portmore, requested that red strake scions be sent which he could then graft onto the almost 1000 stocks he had, stating that this was 'the surest, easiest and cheapest way'.[76]

The ever-cheerful Richard Bulkeley saw the infestation of his fruit trees by pests as an opportunity to make scientific observations:

> I have been but since this day two years (at which time my father died), owner of this habitation so that I cannot pretend to so great a stock of experiments as longer time perhaps affordable to others, but coming over so late in spring I had the opportunity of having the experiment fully before my eyes. The observation is, that among 4,300 and odd young grafts of apples – which I have now in ten days' time taken up and planted again (of which above two thirds were the small golden pippin, and about 400 red shoakes) – I find the number of red shoakes that have been wounded, whether you'll call it stung, or bored ... to exceed (two for two) the number of golden pippins that have been so dealt with by the insect as aforesaid. So much as the matter of the fact, and the circumstances of their former place differed not, for they were grafted promiscuously. I imagine yet from hence may be concluded something in favour of the declining red shoake (although I declare I will never be its champion against the golden pippin). I have tried this two summers last past to accelerate or [a]meliorate the fruit of my walnut trees by inoculating (for that sort of hollow tree will not graft),

the notwithstanding it I have each season budded at least 500 young trees of about seven or eight years old. Yet I could never get one to hit. Pray sir give me your thoughts at your leisure, whether in those hollow trees the motion of the sap and the position of the vessels be the same as in the other trees yet are not so. I shall continue to renew to you my complaint of my quince trees, which notwithstanding that they are yearly full of blossoms and yet by my diligent observation I have not found the worm of the blatta[77] viola to be near so numerous upon them as upon my apricot trees (which yet are very often full of fruit) yet upon 300 bearing trees we have not had thirty quinces these five years ... Yet I am fallen out with the species, and am resolved to graft them all with pears, unless you can inform me of some further experiment to make.[78]

Again, in June of that year he wrote:

My late coming has given me occasion to make an observation in natural history. I have been very curious among my trees, and must acknowledge the moths eggs laid on the leaves to be one cause of want of fruit, but not at all the greatest: for the last year in my apricot trees were extremely full of fruit the leaves were as full of caterpillars and the cherry trees had much fewer of both. This year I have been much more curious in observing, and in which I have of cherries a hundred for one I had the last year and of apricots not one for a hundred. I do find notwithstanding yet the moths did fancy to lay much more this year on the cherry trees than the apricots, so that they are but one and not the greatest case of bareness but I have suffered a much greater loss, there has not been a week since spring, in which a whole arm of a cherry tree, (which blossoms with leaves, or with green fruit) has not been struck dead.[79]

To try and prevent the spread of pests and diseases, orchards were carefully managed and trees were spaced meticulously to avoid transmission of rust, canker and other diseases. Markham suggested that trees in the orchard garden should be set at 'thirty yards asunder'.[80] At Portmore the trees in the tunny orchard were set thirty-two feet apart, almost a third less than the distance recommended by Lawson.[81] The fear of disease also provided a reason for planting trees throughout the pleasure garden, rather than confining them to just one spot. Temple prescribed cutting out all diseased wood, pruning the trees tightly and washing the trunks and branches in order to remove all insects. 'Without these cares and diligences, you had better root up any trees that are infected, renew all the mould in our borders or boxes, and plant new sound trees, rather than suffer the disappointments and vexation of your old ones'.[82] Pride was taken in keeping orchards and gardens in good repair.[83] Grass was mown regularly to keep a neat and tidy appearance and to decrease chances of destructive fungi and vectors breeding. Lettice Molesworth regretted the fact that she had to mow her new orchard, cutting down the cowslips in the process.[84] A most interesting entry in a letter from Richard Bulkeley to Lister[85] refers to an attempt to inoculate fruit trees against disease; whether this was successful or not is not known, but it shows how advanced scientific thinking was in matters botanical. (In 1707 Robert Molesworth also wrote of attempts to inoculate fruit against disease.)[86]

Even if they were absentees, many landowners liked to be kept informed of developments in the fruit garden. Garret Roche sent regular bulletins to the 1st earl of Burlington about the fruit trees growing at Lismore,[87] while George Rawdon's letters to Lord Conway are filled with accounts of the progress of the orchards.[88] While abroad (possibly hiding from his many creditors), Lucius O'Brien of Corofin House in Co. Clare asked his wife, Catherine, to ensure that their fruit trees were being tended to in the appropriate manner:

> Pray order the ground to be well stirred about all the trees, great and small, in the orchard, and if any of the wall trees in the pleasure garden have fallen, let the best of the same kind that are to be had in the county be got to supply their places.[89]

As there was a French colony at Corofin, it is possible that Lucius O'Brien may have used or sought advice from some of these Huguenot refugees for his garden work.[90]

The most interesting plant collection in Ireland at this time was that of George Rawdon's son and heir, Arthur, at Moira. Arthur Rawdon was a close friend of Hans Sloane, to whom he wrote when on a plant-collecting mission to Jamaica in 1688:

> I have heard yet in Jamaica on the tops of the mountains 'tis usual to have frost, I desire to be resolved where tis so or no, and must beg the favour of you by the first ship comes to Dublin if you would send me some seeds, direct them to Mr Robert King at his house in Skinner Row in Dublin, and if you can by any convenience procure seeds out of New England, New York, etc. They will I believe agree much better

with our climate than those of Jamaica, and I am informed they have several sorts of cedars pines etc.[91]

On his return to England in 1689, Sloane brought with him a large collection of specimens and some seeds Many seeds and cuttings were conveyed to Rawdon at Moira.[92] At this time it appears that Rawdon was already experimenting with propagation, and was sending seeds out of Ireland for Sloane to try out at Chelsea:

> I received yours, and some days ago gave a packet of seeds to be sent or carried you by Mr Dunbar in which are at least forty several seeds, and if you please to sow the dust as well as the larger seeds, there will certainly rise a great many of them, and if you please to bestow large watering, I believe it will be so much the better, for that in the countries where they grow, a fortnight's rain together, so that the whole face of the earth is covered (and consequently the seeds) with water, never misses to bring a plentiful spring. When you are settled anywhere about gardening you shall not want all the seeds I can scrape together for you.[93]

The success of Sloane's voyage and the excitement generated by the new specimens appears to have been the impetus for Rawdon planning his own expedition to the West Indies. Sometime in 1689 Rawdon commissioned James Harlow, a plant collector, to go to the West Indies to gather specimens to bring back to Moira. James Harlow arrived in Carrickfergus in April 1692 with his cargo of plants. Rawdon was delighted and immediately wrote to tell Sloane:

> James is safely landed here, he tells me he sent over a great parcel of seeds which I suppose Mr Sherrard writes to you this post about it, and the disposing of some of them.[94]

At this time, the botanist and associate of Sloane, William Sherrard,[95] was resident at Moira. Sherrard briefed Sloane on the condition and contents of the cargo:

> James Harlow is at last returned; he came last week to Carrickfergus, with twenty cases of shrubs and trees, each containing about fifty, well-conditioned, and considering the advantage of the season they come at,

1 Detail from the overmantel painting at Howth Castle showing a garden building at the centre of the walled garden. Straw bee skeps can also be seen in the garden to the left of the building (courtesy of Mr and Mrs Julian Gaisford St Lawrence).

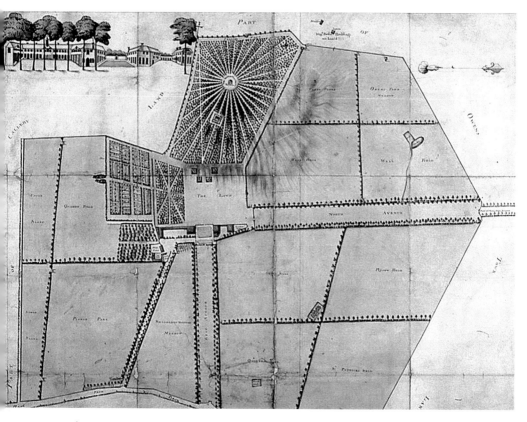

3 Avenues and groves at Mount Merrion, Co. Dublin (courtesy of the National Archives of Ireland). The shell house can be seen in the centre of the woodland, which was known as the 'cartwheel' due to the number of rides radiating from its centre.

2 (*facing page*) Johann van der Hagen, view of Carton House (*c.*1738) (courtesy of Christies), showing the great *Patte d'oie*. The mount can be seen in the foreground. To the front of the house is a large turning circle, and to the rear are a series of formal parterres and gardens laid out on a geometric grid.

4 Killruddery Hunt and the gardens at Killruddery in the background (courtesy of the earl of Meath).

5 Stradbally Hall (private collection).

6 Mount Ievers as seen in a painting at Mount Ievers House (courtesey of Norman Ievers).

7 Old Bawn moat as seen in the Lordship of Tallaght, by Robert Newcomen (c.1654) in the maps of the estates of the archbishops of Dublin (courtesy of the Representative Church Body Library).

8 Blessington House (courtesy of the British Library). Note the avenue running on an axis with the church.

A North Prospect of *BLESSINGTOWN*, A Seat, belonging to the R.t Hon.ble

he Earl of BLESSINGTOWN, Visc.t Mountjoy, Baron of Ramelton and Baronet t

9 The now-overgrown remains of
the great pond at Breckdenston
looking eastwards.

I hope they will continue so ... He has brought little else, not above six shells and but one new, to the little knowledge I have of them. His dried plants are pretty well preserved, and he has missed few trees or shrubs in the Island: his collection of ferns very large, but as for herbaceous things and grasses very few. Seeds he has not above a hundred (of which I will send next week for London) having sent his whole collection last fleet, which we have not yet heard of, and must desire the favour of you to enquire after.[96]

Sherrard promised to give Sloane cuttings from Harlow's herbarium collection. It is also notable just how many plants, including ferns, survived the arduous trip, almost 150 years prior to the introduction of the Wardian case in 1829.[97] In his catalogue of Jamaican plants, Sloane acknowledged the co-operation of Rawdon and Sherrard. Specimens were also sent to Jacob Bobart at the Oxford Physic Garden.[98] On Sherrard's recommendation Rawdon engaged a gardener from London called Thomas Harrison.[99] It would be interesting to know whether Richard Bulkeley's gardener at Old Bawn, a Mr Harrison, 'bred up under Bobart', was Thomas Harrison. Curiously, the gardener at the Royal Hospital in 1694 was also called Thomas Harrison; it is possible that Harrison worked at all three places consecutively.[100]

After the death of Arthur Rawdon in 1695 the collection diminished despite the best efforts of his son Sir John and sister, Brilliana. Anxious about the survival of his father's work John wrote to Hans Sloane:

[A]s for the plants you take notice of, I find that, whether the climate is not so proper, as allowing them (after a great deal of trouble) only to live, without any degree of flourishing or perfection, or by the carelessness of servants, and death of Mr Harlow, not long since, whom my father employed into Jamaica. I find that most of those foreign southern plants are dwindled to nothing. I am sorry I can't give you a better account of them, but of the books I can, all which I have together in good order, I believe my occasions will carry me into England next summer when I shall pay my respects to you in person, but in the mean time I should be very much.[101]

Despite the tragic loss of the collection at Moira, Arthur Rawdon's legacy survived through the many plants propagated from the original collection that found their way into botanic gardens across Europe and the British Isles.

CHAPTER 8

Use and control of water in the seventeenth-century garden

THE NEED FOR THE LANDSCAPE TO BE productive, as well as decorative, offers an explanation and rationale for the creation of water features. The necessity of water in the garden was emphasized in London and Wise's *Complete gardener*: 'rainwater, or rivers, or a canal, or pond well stored with pipes, to distribute water into several parts of a garden, are the soul of vegetation'.[1] Stephen Switzer asserted that water was 'indeed the life and spirit of all country-seats without which they are dull and flat'.[2]

The importance of water as an ornamental feature is indicated by the prominent positioning of many ponds, canals and fountains in the overall design of gardens between 1660 and 1720. Long, straight canals were aligned on axis with other features in the garden and round or '*rond*' ponds were placed in focal points and in the middle of the meeting points of walks. In many gardens, a canal or pond is the primary feature around which all other interventions are staged. The twin canals at Killruddery (fig. 41) and Thomascourt in Tipperary and the large elliptical canal at Westown House all date from the seventeenth century. Wherever the terrain permitted it, canals were seen on the central axis of the geometric garden with groves, walks and wildernesses radiating off the long flat sheet of water that dominated the landscape.[3]

The canal at Santry Park was aligned on the south-west axis of the house. (In the late eighteenth century the park at Santry was re-made in the English landscape style.) Decorative waterworks were often fashioned from existing features – rivers and streams could be dammed or redirected;[4] the eighteenth-century writer Charles Smith described how at Doneraile in Cork, water from the river Awbeg was 'retained in a fine basin for supplying the cascades'.[5]

Simple, plain fishponds were developed and worked into great decorative ponds. The necessity for good drainage to facilitate 'improvements' often dictated the extent and number of waterworks in a garden. Robert Molesworth, the owner of Breckdenston in Co. Meath, made several great hydraulic interventions, and reflected that nothing could be 'so beneficial to our trees and garden stuff as large and effectual draining everywhere'.[6]

41 The twin canals at Killruddery; the vista terminates in a long tree-lined avenue running south to the Wicklow mountains.

Fishponds

The fishpond was the most basic water feature, common to all demesnes, no matter how modest. The simplest fishpond was merely a dam, with a bypass to divert flood-waters around the pond.[7] More elaborate ponds had rows of compartments for various species or fish at different developmental stages. Some of these ponds had leats[8] for controlling the water independently in the different compartments of the ponds.[9] That the highly decorative canals and ponds of the classical seventeenth-century garden were designed as ornamental interventions on the landscape cannot be doubted but they invariably retained their underlying original purpose of providing fish for the table, and frequently water features evolved from fishponds that pre-date the period under examination.[10]

The ready availability of freshwater fish was seen, like the provision of venison, as a status symbol, and was commented upon by observers.[11] In a letter to his father, John Evelyn's son John wrote that Sir John Temple's[12] garden had 'many terraces one above another on the side of a hill ... the Liffey and green meadows below it with canals and fish ponds'.[13] When the duke of Berwick visited the earl of Longford in 1690, Longford, wanting to impress his elevated guest, ordered his staff that Berwick 'must be furnished with the best ale and fish; if there be any fish left in the fish ponds'.[14] Angling became a popular sport among the upper classes; in the dedication to his book *The compleat angler*,

Izaak Walton (1593–1683) noted that 'there be now many men of great wisdom, learning, and experience, which love and practice this art'.[15] Popular fish for the table were carp, roach, bream and tench. Some of these were better suited to breeding in ponds than others, either because they grew larger in confinement, or because they were more valuable and needed protecting. For instance, Walton related how he heard of a gentleman who had 'sixty or more large carps put into several ponds near to a house, where by reason of the stakes in the ponds, and the owner's constant being near to them, it was impossible they should be stole away from him'.[16] At Francis Aungier's house in Longford in the 1680s there were 'most pleasant fishponds and canals in which are tench in great plenty, and carp with store of trout roach etc.'[17] According to Charles Smith, Curroaghmore House in Co. Waterford, built in 1700, had 'the advantage of water on three sides, laid out in large elegant canals and basins, well stored with carp tench and perch'.[18] Robert and Lettice Molesworth stocked their ponds at Breckdenston with tench and carp in the summer of 1704.[19] Gentlewomen kept 'receipt books' detailing recipes for the best way to cook these delicacies.[20] At Birr Castle, one can read Dorothy Parsons's 'Booke of Choyce Receipts', dated 1666, which includes instructions on how to stew and dress carps and 'collar ells' (probably collected in the dammed river at Birr).

Most treatises on husbandry published up to 1760 dealt with fishponds at some length.[21] In most instances, these works deal with the construction and management of the large breeding ponds, known in the medieval period as *vivaria*. Works on fishponds advised on where they ought to be sited. John Norden suggested using an overgrown sedgey area of a field, which was of little value as pasture or arable, 'for it is a desert bottom … yielding now little or no benefit … it could with some cost to be bestowed here [make] a fishpond … it would make at the least two or three, one below the other'.[22] Gervase Markham also suggested using 'land "marshy" boggy, a land full of springs unfit for grazing and other profit', for the reason that 'spring water give clear water, marshy areas are good for fish, and boggy land prevents stealing'.[23] Early OS maps confirm that fishponds were frequently placed in odd, out of the way sites. John Taverner wrote of the benefits of converting poor land into fishponds:

> I do not think that ground would yield unto the owner any other way so much benefit, as to be converted into such ponds with heads as is aforementioned. If only fish were spent upon the days by law ordained for that purpose in this realm, the whole thing if it were observed, no doubt would turn this realm into incredible benefit, many and sundry ways. But now those that should spend such fish, will rather bestow their money in rabbits, capons, or such like.[24]

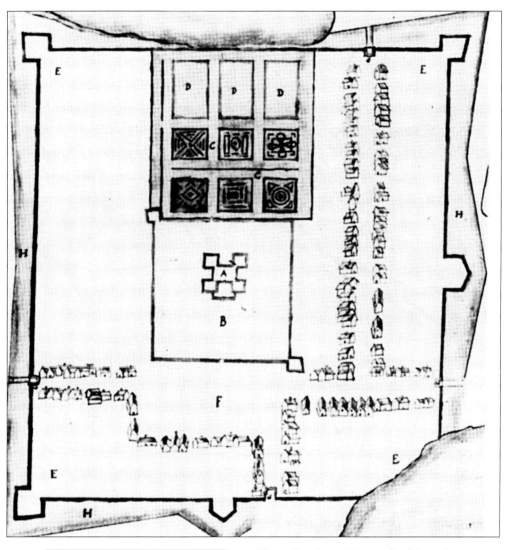

KEY:
A the Kinges castell
B the bawne being built all of stone
C the garden
D the fishponds
E the towne
F the market place
G the gates
H the diche
I the loughes

42 Plan of projected layout for Monaghan town and castle (courtesy of the Trustees of Trinity College Dublin, TCD MS 1209/32B), showing elaborate parterres and knots. Note how the three fishponds are incorporated into the overall layout of the garden.

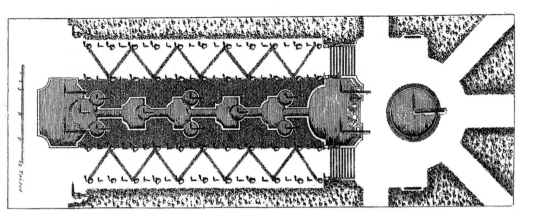

43 Designs for cascades taken from Dézallier d'Argenville, *The theory and practice of gardening* (1712), p. 218.

Most demesnes contained several ponds which made for the most efficient method of farming fish:

> So in our large and ample fields, it is as convenient for us to have ponds with many partitions, that the fish young in years and weak in strength may be separated from the bigger and stronger ... To this end and purpose, threefold ponds are sufficient enough.[25]

Taverner stressed the necessity for building two or more ponds; 'the greatness [of the ponds] may be according to the patens of the place ... and to the cost he meaneth to bestow'.[26] One reason for having at least two fishponds was that ponds were alternately allowed to drain. This was to allow grass to grow or sods to be placed in the bottom of the pond as it was 'a great advantage in the feeding of the fish'.[27] Draining the pond also provided an opportunity for repairs to be made and excess pondweed removed, thus ensuring good water quality was maintained. The sludge found at the bottom could be used as a fertilizer for arable crops grown on the pond bed while dry. Worlidge noted that 'there is likewise very great fertility in the residence of all channels, ponds, pools, lakes, and ditches, where any store of waters do repose themselves, but especially where any store of rain-water hath a long time settled'.

A map of the 'King's Castell' in Monaghan, dated sometime early in the seventeenth century, illustrates well how working fishponds were incorporated into the overall layout of the garden with an undoubted decorative aesthetic underlying their placement (fig. 42).[28] The plan depicts a walled garden lying behind the castle. The garden was Tudor in appearance, being small in scale with each element laid out geometrically. There are six parterres in two rows of three. Each parterre, presumably of herbs and vegetables, is laid out in knots, each one a different and elaborate design. Behind each pair of parterres are rectangular 'fishponds'. The entire scheme was clearly thoughtfully laid out to please the eyes of those viewing it from the house.[29]

The fishpond in the pleasure garden acted as a store from which the fish were easily caught, ready for the table. Roger North wrote the following about ornamental ponds:

> [they] maintain fish for the daily use of your house and friends, whereby you may with little trouble, and at any time, take out all, or any fish they contain; therefore it is good to place them in some enclosed grounds, near the chief mansion-house. Some recess in a garden is very proper, because the fish are fenced from robbers, and your journey to them is short and easy, and your eye will be often upon them, which will conduce to their being well kept, and they will be an ornament to the walks.[30]

North would have approved of Edward Stratford's garden at Belan in Co. Kildare.[31] Writing in 1709 it was described as:

> a very handsome improved garden of greens, grass and gravel very pleasantly situated by the banks of a small river which is very prettily cut into canals and fishponds and well sheltered by well grown trees.[32]

Fishponds were also placed in kitchen gardens and orchards which were designed for ornamental as well as practical value.[33] In 1665, Sir George Rawdon, who managed the estate of Portmore, Co. Antrim, for his brother-in-law, Viscount Conway, wrote:

> I have taken the advice of William Hoole, John Totnall, and Francis all together at the Tunny Park, and we have laid out the orchard plot. It will doubtless be excellent mould for fruit trees, and we think it would afford a place for a fish pond, and the soil be very agreeable for carps.[34]

Keeping fish for consumption in ponds close to the house continued well into the eighteenth century. In 1732 Loveday observed that the seventeenth-century ponds at Belan were still 'well stocked with fish'.[35] On the first OS a truly enormous fish pond is visible south-east of the house; similarly, there was a massive canal at Dangan Castle in Co. Meath, home of the Wellesley family.

As late as 1750, Charles Smith noted that Mount North, near Mallow, had 'a noble canal well stocked with fish' to the front of his house.[36] The inventory of Orrery's household goods at Castlemartyr, dating from 1677, includes a curious reference to a 'fishpond room'.[37] This was possibly a pavilion or banqueting house, where the owner could entertain guests. The angler could engage in his sport in comfort and shelter from the house, and nets and equipment could be stored in it. Such houses appear to have been common since the middle of the seventeenth century. A picture of Stradbally Hall dating from the early part of the eighteenth century depicts what may have been such a house. This two-story building, now in ruins, was positioned on the edge of one of the canals created by diverting the Stradbally river. The second story took the form of a pavilion, with open sides to allow for the taking of air, but roofed to protect from rain. It may have been close enough to the water to allow anglers to fish from it without getting wet. Numerous examples of these pavilions exist in England; for example 'fishing lodges' appear at Abbot's Hall and Somerleyton in Suffolk[38] and at Snitterton Hall in Derbyshire.[39]

As the seventeenth century progressed the fishpond evolved from its humble beginnings. Waterworks grew in scale, size and complexity. The simple rectangular fishpond was stretched into long, elegant canals or transformed into circular basins. Another popular configuration for waterworks was the 'ace of clubs' shape seen in early estate maps of Killruddery,[40] and also at Rathcoffey in Kildare (though somewhat diminished in shape by the time the first Ordnance Survey was made). The ace of clubs was a long canal with one end terminating in a round basin. This shape can also be seen in gardens in England – Clarendon Park in Surrey, Wrest Park in Bedfordshire[41] and Westbury-on-Severn in Gloucestershire.

By the end of the seventeenth century, Ireland had waterworks as fantastically elaborate and impressive as those at Rathbeale House in Co. Dublin and Stradbally Hall in Laois (see plate 5).[42] Even allowing for an exaggerated perspective being taken by the artist, the early eighteenth-century painting of Stradbally contains many topographical features and local landmarks that have been accurately represented. This adds veracity to the painting, which is supported by the archaeological evidence and by Lewis's 1837 description of the demesne as being 'highly embellished'.[43] The remains of buildings such as the waterside lodge, watermill and millpond (fig. 45) are

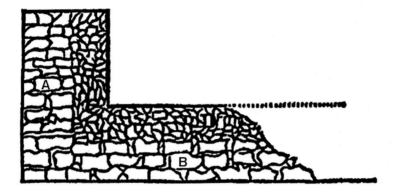

44 'Begin with raising and backing up against the ground, cut perpendicularly the wall of masonry, *A* of a foot thickness, which must go to the bottom and should be built with shards and rubble-stones laid in a mortar of lime and sand. This wall being made al round you begin the filling of the bottom, *B* a foot thick, and work it with the same materials and mortar, as the wall *A*. You then back up, against this wall the solid work or lining of ciment, nine inches thick.' Basin of cement, taken from Dézallier d'Argenville, *The theory and practice of gardening* (1712), p. 209.

45 The remains of the canals at Stradbally.

46 Mount Ievers by Thomas Dineley from Shirley and Graves (eds), 'Dineley's journal', *JKSIAS*, 6:1 (1867), p. 75.

47 Mount Ievers.

all consistent with the painting. The painting shows a network of canals and lakes with miniature ships and fishing boats sailing on the water. The positioning of the water at the front of the house is rather like a moat, access to the courtyards and house being via a bridge. This layout is also seen at the eighteenth-century Mount Ievers in Clare, and in Dineley's drawing of the

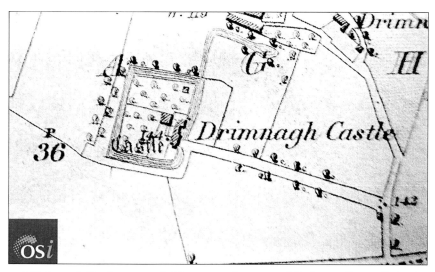

48 Drimnagh Castle surrounded by a moat (courtesy of Ordnance Survey Ireland, permit ID 158).

original Mount Ievers house with a bridge, perhaps a drawbridge, over a moat.[44] In fact, many of the landscape features identified by Dineley can be seen in a later eighteenth-century overmantel picture of the new house (figs. 46 & 47).

The scene at Stradbally would delight Roger North who, in 1713, argued for a return of moats for fish-keeping and as an 'ornament and delight to a seat beyond imagination', saying:

> The view of it [the moat] is a delicacy the greatest epicures in gardening court, and we hear of it by the name of canal. Then the moving upon it in boats … after a romantic way; and thus circling a house, taking the variety of walks and gardens here and there … are pleasures not given to be understood by any, but statesmen laid aside for their honesty, who by experience are taught the variety of greatness.[45]

From this, it can be seen that moats were not always created for defensive purposes, but as useful repositories for fish and to provide a source of delight to the inhabitants of the house, the sparkling reflections from the water lighting up the rooms overlooking it. Moats were seen around several houses in Ireland including Old Bawn in Dublin (see plate 7). The moat at Drimnagh Castle in Dublin survives intact to this day and is still stocked with fish (fig. 48). Another common feature was a canal with a large circular basin in

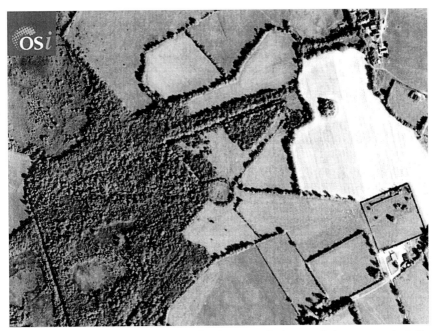

49 The remains of the great canal at Gaulstown with the wooded mount to the left
of the photograph and the huge circular basin in the central foreground.

the middle, the remains of which can be seen at Gaulstown in Westmeath
(fig. 49).

Methods for controlling hydraulic circulation

Methods of hydraulic management that had been developed for mining,
transportation, urban development and agricultural improvement were all
modified for use in gardens, and while they were aesthetic enhancements, they
retained their underlying practical and economic purposes. Technology,
developed to create sea walls and flood barriers, was used in demesnes and
gardens. The benefits of such works could be manifold. Floods at high tide
frequently submerged the earl of Inchiquin's land at Rostellan in Cork. The
inundation of salt water would have rendered the soil useless and infertile and
created an unpleasant stench. The earl built a sea wall 'at great expense in
keeping out the tide from overflowing', which had the additional benefit of
being 'of advantage to the harbour of Cork for small vessels'.[46]

Apart from their use for holding fish, ponds and basins were used for
drainage and irrigation purposes. Water was necessary for the usual domestic

50 The now-overgrown remains of the great pond at Breckdenston looking eastwards.

purposes, and by the early eighteenth century, piped domestic water was *de rigueur* for great houses. If water could be pumped to the house, why not use it in the garden using the same technology? Waterlogged land was useless for cultivation of crops or keeping of livestock. Good drainage schemes could make such unviable land profitable. At Lismore Park in Waterford, the earl of Burlington had 'trenches and watercourses in the park to drain the lowlands and make it more useful for the deer'.[47] At Breckdenston, water was used to irrigate the gardens and the 'great pond' was for the storage of 'waste water' (fig. 50). During periods of excessive rain, the pond would overflow and the water 'conveyed in cascades down the hill again to the ponds'.[48] The runoff from the orchard, kitchen gardens, parterre and woodlands drained into the canal and from thence via the cascades into the river Ward. It was not unusual to exploit excess water from canals. The energy created by a cascade could be harnessed to power a mill. Almost forty years earlier, John Evelyn described a canal at Viscount Hereford's estate which was 'full of carps' with a 'cascade at the end of the canal', which was used to turn 'a corn-mill which finds the family, and raises with water for the fountains and office'.[49]

The mere proximity to springs and rivers could not guarantee a constant regular supply of water. Apart from the dangers posed by flooding, summer droughts could prove fatal to crops and garden plants. Robert Molesworth made his intentions for the waterworks at Breckdenston clear when he wrote:

> I warrant you we shall have water enough and enough again before I have done at Breckdenston. I shall not depend altogether on the river water though I am sorry to hear it is so dry already.[50]

The extent and sophistication of water features depended on the availability of water – the more water available, the more elaborate the waterworks. At Breckdenston, for example, Molesworth was able to plan and carry out extensive hydraulic interventions because, in his words, there was 'no seat in Ireland to all parts of which water may be with more ease and plenty be brought'.[51] As the Ward river ran through the estate, water was available to be harnessed and channelled around the various features in his gardens. By 1720, a 'reservoir or large basin in the 16 acres' was built at Breckdenston that was capable of supplying 'constant running water even during the height of a dry summer';[52] oddly there is no sign of this basin in Arthur Neville's survey of 1775.[53]

Where water was scarce, it could be conveyed to the garden from springs via a series of pipes. Worlidge recommended asking a local 'rustic' to direct you to the nearest spring, suggesting that when it was not possible to have a stream or rivulet 'glide' through a garden that water could be raised by a machine at some distance or by 'an aqueduct conveyed through it'. This, he argued, often proved more convenient than having a natural stream, as an artificial current was not 'subject to those extravagances, that the natural usually are by over-flowing' after rainy conditions. Water brought by such means could be conducted around the garden and directed into canals.[54] Where the spring was on the same level as the garden Switzer recommended that the water was best conveyed along a rough stone or brick drain for cheapness, but when it was necessary to carry water over undulating country, lead or wooden pipes were to be preferred. Switzer also recommended that a reservoir should be built to collect a store of water that could then be conveyed to the garden by pipes when there was no water close to the house to make ponds. If the reservoir was intended to serve ornamental fountains, then it should be situated high enough to build up a sufficient head of pressure.[55]

At Rathcline in Co. Longford, laid out in the mid-1660s, an extra trench with sluices was added to the great canal that ran along the length of the castle in order to supply water for a fishpond. The canal itself was supplied with water from Lough Ree.[56] Whereas at Breckdenston, 'the great large pond by the river' was filled with water brought via an aqueduct or, in Molesworth's own words, 'brought in a narrow channel from the tuckmill race quite thro' the grove on the hillside and conveyed over the river by a trough as soon as ever the banks are finished'.[57]

Where a spring was located below garden level, it was necessary to erect a cistern filled by 'a machine moved by men, horse, or wind'.[58] Carrying water uphill presented problems and overly optimistic plans often had to be modified. Pococke described how Lord Shannon's[59] work at Castlemartyr had been frustrated by gravity:

> [The] gardens are laid out in lawn gravel walk, parterre and canal in the middle, which by flood gates might be carried near a mile to the south west to this lake, and would join a rivulet which was worked into a kind of canal by the late lord, but they found that the lake was much lower than the ground about his lordships house.[60]

Molesworth built a cistern to supply water to his gardens, which proved more successful.[61] The cistern was filled with water pumped uphill by a watermill and gravity was used to send it back down to the gardens.[62] Worlidge suggested that cisterns be made of lead and concealed in a 'lodge or grot'.[63] Molesworth's cistern, designed 'to hold fifty or sixty ton', was 'set a top of a water house', located at the 'west end of the long walk in the middle of the garden, near the bowling green wall', at the 'beginning of the terrace walk'. The housing for the cistern was to be disguised as 'a handsome open summerhouse upon pillars under it facing the sea and Swords steeple'. It was to be 'about 24 foot high' with 'pipes of alder tree' sourced 'easily out of the county of Wicklow pretty cheap' to connect it to the tuck mill which presumably pumped the water up out of the valley to the pond high above. The alder was expected to last 'as long as leaden pipes'.[64]

In a 1660 diary entry, Pepys recorded that he had been '[t]o walk in St James's Park, where we observed the several engines at work to draw up water, with which sight I was very much pleased'.[65] Water engines had clearly been in use since the early part of the seventeenth century, and Switzer refers to a water engine at London Bridge (fig. 51):

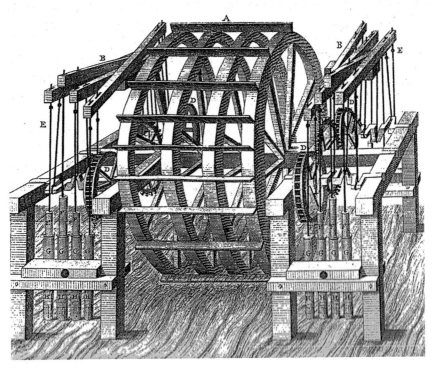

51 A perspective of the London Bridge water engine from Stephen Switzer's
Introduction to a general system of hydrostaticks.

which for curiousness and contrivance, the length of time it has went;
without any other than very necessary repairs, and the great quantity of
water it throws up towards the supply of that great metropolis, may very
well be parallel ... to that great engine of Marley itself and which ...
being as I am told the work of one Mr Sorocold, a very good engineer,
in the reign of King Charles I.[66]

The leading expert in the creation of water engines was Sir Samuel Morland,
who created a water engine at Windsor Castle for the King. This engine
brought water from Blackmore Park near Winkfield to the top floors of
Windsor Castle. Morland showed John Evelyn a 'pump he had created, that
serves water to his garden'.[67]

   Various methods could be used to raise water. The duke of Ormond had a
horse-powered water engine to supply Kilkenny Castle with water, described
by Dineley in 1680 as a 'curious artifice'.[68] As work progressed on the Castle

and gardens a more capacious engine was needed. In 1681, the 2nd duke of Ormond sought Morland's advice about sending 'a man' over to build a water engine at Kilkenny. At this time, Morland was at Windsor, 'about the King's water engine', and unable, or possibly, unwilling, to help. The earl of Longford commented that 'Sir Samuel keeps the business of waterworks a great mystery and has performed great wonders for the King at Windsor, having brought the water from the river on which his engine is placed to the top of the castle with great facility'.[69] Less elaborate water engines were used to power fountains and small water features. Plot discusses a water engine designed by John Wilkins, warden of Wadham College, Oxford, 'whereby but a few gallons of water forced through a narrow fissure, he could raise a mist in his garden, wherein a person placed at a due distance between the sun and the mist, might see an exquisite rainbow in all its proper colours'. He then relates how this device was 'based on the writings of Descartes', which rather neatly illustrates how technological progress was expressed in garden works.[70]

The capacity of the tuckmill and cistern at Breckdenston must have proved insufficient for Molesworth's increasingly elaborate plans, as in 1717 he decided to build a version of a water engine that he described, rather grandly, as being 'somewhat bigger than that at Chelsea'.[71] At Breckdenston the water engine was to be used to draw up water from the river Ward to solve water shortages. His long-suffering gardener, Nick, was sent to see the engine house at Chelsea and Molesworth hoped, rather uncharitably, that he was 'not such a blockhead but he can give some light into that matter'.

The water engines were housed, like Molesworth's cistern, in buildings to hide and protect the mechanism, which were themselves turned into ornamental features. The Kilkenny water house was particularly elaborate. Dineley observed the 'delightful waterhouse' sited next to the bowling green:

> [It] hath a pleasant summer banqueting room, floored and lined with white and black marble, which abounds here, with a pointed sky roof with angels; in this is seen a fountain of black marble in the shape of a large cup with a jet d'eau or throw of water arising mounts into the hollow of a ducal crown which but hangs over it, and descends again at several dropping places around.[72]

Molesworth's design for the house to contain the Breckdenston water engine was less elaborate. It was said to exceed the Chelsea water house dimensions 'not above 13 or 15 foot square'. Being 'very secure, both roof and walls', he thought that it 'would last for ages and prevent that attempts of the most

52 A water jet in the circular pond at Killruddery. The pond is on an axis with twin canals to the north and an avenue into the countryside beyond to the south.

malicious'. It had 'two strong doors' and 'narrow loopholes' for windows to prevent any creature from 'creeping under the wheel or coming in any way'. This was not 'too large, nor too little to turn in and repair the work upon occasion', with 'about two foot and a half space to go round it'.[73] Molesworth had 'no stone proper' for covering the house, instead using stones 'like great slates laid upon a kind of vault or arch'.[74] O'Kane identifies two small riverside buildings shown on the maps as being the tuckmill and water engine.[75]

Fountains and cascades

Fountains and water jets were added to ponds in Ireland after the Restoration (fig. 52).[76] Fountains and cascades, in addition to being highly decorative, also served to oxygenate water, keeping it from becoming stagnant and therefore benefiting the fish. Francis Bacon, in his essay on gardens, asserted that pools of stagnating water should not be tolerated: 'water should be in the form of

53 Some designs for fountains
by John Worlidge from
Systema horticulturae.

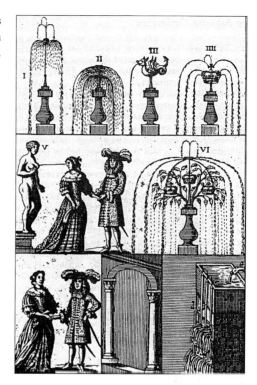

lively fountains and sparkling bathing pools'.[77] The king and members of the aristocracy were clearly keen to banish all traces of the plain puritan style publicly espoused during the interregnum. Statuary and fountains abounded in the latter part of the seventeenth century.

William Temple, who lived for a time at Staplestown in Carlow, advised that the 'dryness' of a garden should be relieved by fountains.[78] Temple's brother John, who had an extensive estate at Palmerstown near Dublin, clearly took this advice to heart; as John Evelyn's son noted, his gardens had many 'canals and fishponds'.[79] Worlidge's *Systema horticulturae* included an entire chapter on water features, grottos and fountains. He suggested several forms that the fountain itself could take; these included some popular motifs such as dragons, crowns and the royal oak:

> into some the water is cast by pipes from the sides out of the mouths of several figures representing animals or out of the pipes or ewers of stone standing on the brim of the fountain, or the water is cast from some figure or statue erected in the middle of the fountain or from pipes standing upright in the midst of it.[80]

54 The duke of Ormond's fountain at Kilkenny Castle by Thomas Dineley, taken from Evelyn Philip Shirley and James Graves (eds), 'Dineley's journal', *JKSIAS*, 4:1 (1862), p. 106.

More tediously, Worlidge displayed a then commonplace taste for rather crude practical jokes, suggesting one build '[a] statue of a woman that, at the turning of a private cock, shall cast water out of her nipples into the spectator's face' (fig. 53).[81] Strolling through a late seventeenth-century garden, such as Wilton House in Wiltshire, could prove something of a trial. Worlidge suggests another hilarious trap for the unsuspecting visitor by means of a 'secret pipe' hidden underground, 'the ends not appearing above it, that when any ladies unawares or casually walk or stand over them, by the turning of a stop cock you may force the water upright under their coats to their sudden surprise'.[82] The natural philosopher and member of the Royal Society, Dr Robert Plot, mentioned waterworks designed to 'sportively wet any persons within it'.[83] Worlidge also described how one could arrange waterworks in such a way as to create 'music' with them, claiming rather fancifully that they could emulate the sound of nightingales.[84] Another popular feature, as described by Plot, was 'a ball tossed by a column of water, and artificial flowers [which] descend at pleasure'.[85]

In 1664 a fountain was planned for the courtyard of Kilkenny Castle. The duke's son, the earl of Ossory, wrote that the 'French gardener is very laborious and hath undertaken within ten weeks to make a fountain in the centre of the court yard where the allées meet at Kilkenny which shall perpetually rise twenty-four foot high'.[86] It is not known who this gardener was, or whether he was resident in Ireland or brought over specially to work on the duke's garden. The fountain, which was of black marble and spouted high jets of water was illustrated by Thomas Dineley (fig. 54), who observed a similar one in the courtyard of Powis Castle in Wales. Manuscript evidence discloses that the duke had commissioned a new Triton fountain designed by Willem de Keyser, a well-known Dutch sculptor.[87] The fountain was clearly expensive and a highly impressive piece of work; in a letter dating from December 1681, the earl of Longford referred to 'Mr du Keizar's work about the fountain', which he reckoned would 'exceed all works of that kind in this kingdom'.[88] The Triton fountain was probably the one identified as remaining in the basin at the castle in the 1860s. Longford hoped that the duke would not 'put up the Triton fountain yet as there are a variety of pipes for waterworks to be fitted to the same socket which is to be fastened to Triton's shell which issues out of its mouth'.[89] This indicates that the fountain referred to by William Robinson a year later was the de Keyser fountain:

> I was then at Kilkenny setting things in order there, the fountain is set half up and the rest will be up in a month at furthest. The brass works which your lordship sent over I believe will not be useful there, the reason thereof is, if the fountain being at least twenty two feet high above the garden it will be difficult to get to the top thereof on all occasions to shift the several sorts of spout, nor will it be safe to raise ladder against it, lest the work be injurious. Nevertheless if her grace please to have any figures made about the basin below they may be useful there.[90]

Construction of water features

As water features were often used to control land drainage and irrigation, it was essential that they were sited and constructed competently. In areas with a high water table, flooding had to be avoided; similarly, in dry soils, what water there was had to be contained and directed as and when necessary. Wooden sluice gates were used to control water levels in the ponds and canals. North insisted that an experienced carpenter should be used to construct sluice gates, and the surviving manuscript evidence suggests that carpenters were employed for this purpose on Irish estates.[91] Oak, 'all of one piece', was recommended as the best wood to use for making sluices. The sluice vent was protected by 'large perforated boxes so that the fish cannot escape' when the sluices were opened. North noted that 'some do not bother with sluices but cut out the bank when they wish to drain the pond'. He argued that this was a bad policy because such cuts were difficult to secure afterwards as 'you shall scarce ram it up so well again, but it will perpetually leak about the place where the fissure was'.[92]

Water was channelled to ponds and basins via pipes. As lead pipes were comparatively rare and expensive, and iron pipes were not popular in England before the eighteenth century, wooden pipes were most commonly recommended.[93] Oak, alder and elm were traditionally used for pipes as they tend not to rot in water. Alder from the Wingfield estate at Powerscourt in Wicklow was used to make the pipes for the great pond at Breckdenston.[94] Clay pipes were used in areas where that material was readily available. Lord Shannon recommended a 'good potter' he knew who 'serves all Cork and the county about it' who had made pipes for him 'as also flower pots for the garden'.[95] The 'fountain in the middle of the parterre' at Breckdenston was supplied 'by carrying on the large pipe to the basin' as this 'would have made the water spout in the middle carry up the water as far as the spout of the cistern in the water house within less than a foot and with a large strong stream'.[96] Because of the complexity of hydraulic systems and the limitations of technology, fountains were only operational at selected times, usually to impress guests when walking in the garden. The jet was turned on and off by means of a valve when necessary.

Overflow pipes or gutters were created to take off surplus water in times of heavy rain. North refers to these as 'grates'. For larger ponds, he suggests that one should be placed at each end of the dam bank. If they were made of wood, he suggested that they should have diagonal bars, 'like window-bars so that rubbish does not block them so easily', and the water is able to flow out 'freer'.[97] The importance of maintaining static water levels is well illustrated in a letter from Robert Molesworth to his wife, Lettice, in 1712. Heavy rains had caused an increase in the speed and depth of the river Ward which had a catastrophic effect on the water features at Breckdenston:

> I am sorry for the floods carrying off your cascade and damaging the banks because a good deal of our fish especially those in the basin must be carried off. I thought I had given passage enough for the water by the channels on both sides but I really see the banks about the cascade and basin must be raised higher above the new pond and the walks to it.[98]

Molesworth asked Lettice to ensure that the workmen 'put stops across the water in the course which runs round the pond' which would prevent it from becoming 'very shallow and dry in some places in summer time'.[99] This course was a channel that kept the level of the water in the pond constant, and thus provided a controlled environment for cultivating fish, filling the pond when necessary and preventing the fish from being flushed out of the pond in times of flood. The channel could be filled when necessary by drawing up the sluice gates and allowing excess water to flow into a rill surrounding the pond, preserving the level of the water within the pond itself, ensuring that 'we may not be surprised by the floods at any time'.[100] When, however, the canal at Breckdenston was 'brimful' and in 'fear of overflowing', water was released from 'a gap or trench cut in the end next the house to carry the surplus water down the hill towards the sweep of the cascade'. This trench was eventually fashioned into another cascade falling 'down the hill to the low cascade', which in turn fell into 'the octagon basin', the remains of which still exist today.[101] Robert Plot observed a similar device to that at the pond in Breckdenston at the series of ponds at Cornbury, owned by the earl of Clarendon:

> [It had] a side ditch cut along by them, and sluices out of each, may be any of them emptied, without letting the water into, or giving the least disturbance to any of the rest; which being a convenience that I never met with before, and perhaps unknown to many, I thought good to mention.[102]

The canal at Breckdenston could also be drained by means of a pipe in order to give it a thorough cleaning or to repair leakages. Basins containing fountains required rather more complicated pipe work, for reasons summed up by Worlidge:

> There must also be waste pipes or cavities to convey the water from such fountain, which must be so made that at your pleasure you may drain your fountain and cleanse it and must be of a capacity to carry off all the water as it comes, lest it annoy your garden, for the greater quantity of water you have the more pleasant it will appear.[103]

The size of water features depended on a number of factors: the taste of the owner, the purpose of the pond, the topography and availability of water. According to Dézallier d'Argenville, 'the larger the better' was the rule with basins, probably for ornamental value.[104] This rule was applied by rich landowners such as Robert Molesworth who, in 1720, was advised by a consultant, Mr Costelloe, that two or three smaller basins might be more efficient than one large one. Molesworth was dismayed by the suggestion and stressed his determination to make the reservoir as large as possible and 'one of the finest things about Breckdenston'.[105] As this was a reservoir to provide water for irrigation, Molesworth probably felt that less water was likely to be lost from evaporation if the pond was as large as practicable. On a practical level, North suggested that the best size for holding ponds was 'two rods wide [c.10m] and three rods long [c.15m]'.[106] This presumably was the best size for the convenience of gathering fish quickly and efficiently, rather than breeding efficacy. Landing fish was made easier according to North 'by cutting the sides down somewhat sloping, and carrying the bottom in a perpetual decline from end to end, so as you have a convenient mouth ... for taking out your nets when you draw for fish'.[107]

The depth of ponds varied depending on their use. Switzer believed that five or six feet (c.2m) was the 'greatest depth necessary for any pond' for keeping fish. He also indicated that these were best suited to gardens on clay soil rather than gravel.[108] The canal at Breckdenston was to be 'four foot depth in the shallowest part',[109] whereas the large basin, constructed around 1720 to serve as a reservoir, was 'five or six foot deep, shelving from the sides towards the depth in the middle'.[110] Taverner suggested that ponds be no more than six feet (c.2m) deep 'to the end that one of them may be dry one year and the other the next year'[111] and Markham suggested a depth of six to eight feet (c.2 to 2.7m).[112] Dézallier d'Argenville recommended a depth 'ordinarily from 15–18 inches, or two feet (c.60cm) at most' for small basins. This was considered 'sufficient to protect [the] bottom from frosts'. For large basins, canals and ponds in which fish were to be kept, he recommended a depth of four to five feet (c.1.2–1.5m).[113] This runs counter to Dézallier d'Argenville's suggested vertical, rather than sloping, side walls for clay lined ponds, which would indicate, along with the fact that there was another large basin at Breckdenston, that fish were not to be kept in the reservoir. Today, purpose-built fishponds seldom exceed a depth of six feet, as greater depths do not allow sunlight to penetrate to the pond bed. Shallow waters provide more plant life and consequently richer feeding for the fish.

Such exact sizes were rarely incorporated into gardens, but used rather as a guide. The size of pond was generally dictated by the topographical character of the ground and altered to suit the overall design of the garden. As design considerations became more prominent (and transport of fish to markets improved), the strict needs of fishery management may have become less important. Sometimes, the scale of waterworks and fishponds became overwrought. The works in progress at Gaulstown in Co. Westmeath were described in 1709:

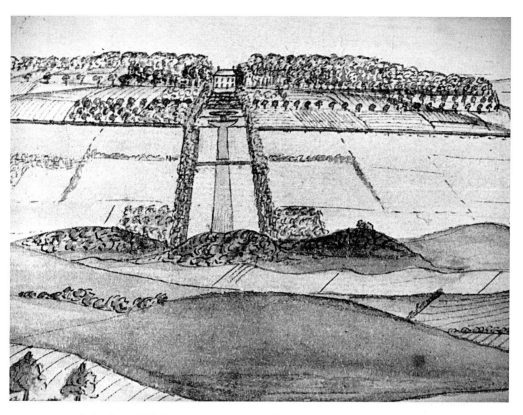

55 Pakenham Hall by Edward Pakenham (Tullynally Castle, Co. Westmeath),
showing the series of canals and basins.

A canal already almost finished; 'tis the most noble canal by far I ever
saw and cousin Dopping[114] assured us as fine as he had seen in
England. It has three noble large basins one at each end and one in the
middle. 'Tis twenty one yards broad, and 1000 long. [There is] a terrace
walk on each side planted with lime trees in the furthest basin from the
house stands an island [and] a pretty summer house which very
agreeably determines your view.[115]

While conceding that Gaulstown was 'a most noble improvement', he felt
'however this canal I think is longer than it needs be'.[116] The remains of the
great canal can still be seen (although the water is no longer present) and it is
huge in scale (see fig. 32). The terrace walk can still, with some difficulty, be
promenaded and is interspersed with small lime trees that may be descendants
of the original trees. Gaulstown was immortalized by both Jonathan Swift and,

later, Dr Delany, who each stayed there on a number of occasions – Swift in *The country life, part of a summer spent at Gaulstown-House* and Delany in *On Gaulstown House*.[117]

The description and outline of the canal at Gaulstown was similar to the remains of what appears to have been a canal at Eyrecourt Castle, although the Eyrecourt canal was considerably shorter (at less than 200 metres) and did not have basins terminating each end. There is no proof that this canal was seventeenth or early eighteenth century in origin; the house and gardens were laid out in the 1670s[118] and Loveday described great 'improvements' there in the 1730s.[119] The remains of the canal are consistent with other works carried out at the time and it is reasonable to suppose that the canal dates from this time.

At Antrim Castle, laid out in the 1660s by Sir John Skeffington, the canal is 660 feet long and 30 feet wide. The larger of the two circular ponds is 175 feet in diameter.[120] At Killruddery, the canals are a more modest 550 feet long. Pakenham Hall (fig. 55) had an enormous circular basin which was described by George Pakenham in 1736:

> 300 feet wide; from this is a cascade falling into another basin at the head of a canal, 150 feet wide and 1,200 feet long, on each side is a large grass walk planted with trees. From this canal there runs in a direct line another near a mile in length, equal in breadth to the first, and terminates in a large basin at the foot of three or four beautiful hills.[121]

It has been argued that the large size of many of the later geometrical ponds reduced their usefulness as holding ponds for fish and that therefore it can be deduced that they were designed primarily to be ornamental.[122] This argument is not really convincing as natural ponds and rivers vary in size and scale. Larger ponds may have made fishing less predictable, but the evidence is that the massive fishponds found on the early Ordnance Survey maps held fish and were used to provide fish for the table.[123] The theory is further undermined by the many paintings, depicting fishing taking place from the banks or from boats on large sheets of ornamental water, which certainly continued well into the eighteenth century.[124]

The ponds and canals of the post-Restoration garden were laid out in a rigid geometric fashion. Where possible, long ponds or canals were sited on an axis from the house towards a feature beyond the confines of the pleasure gardens. If the topography did not allow for this, canals were built in the most practical spot. If the technology was available, canals could even, as at

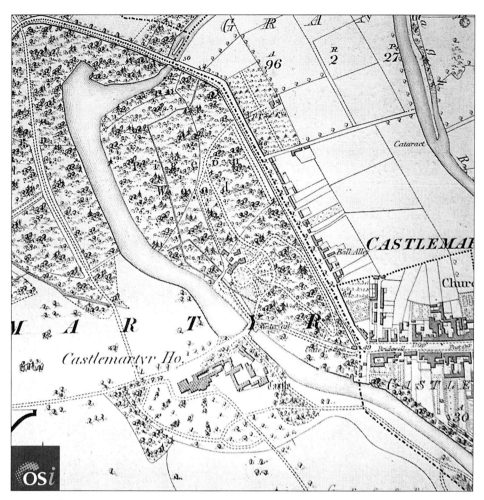

56 Castlemartyr, where the canals were 'made picturesque' (courtesy of Ordnance Survey Ireland, permit ID 158).

Breckdenston, be sited on top of a hill.[125] The long, narrow shape of the canal coupled with the position of an eye catcher was a visual trick, drawing the eye beyond the garden walls into the countryside beyond, giving an elongated impression of scale. The eye catcher could be a feature of natural beauty, a piece of statuary or a pond or an old ruin. The enormous canal built by the Molesworths at Breckdenston in 1719 was centred on axis with the round tower at Swords. At Killruddery, the central feature is the 'long ponds', two parallel canals 550 feet long extending from the rear of the house. These ponds on axis with a lime avenue, which continued out of the formal garden, into the deer park beyond towards the Sugar Loaf Mountain. The double canals are an unusual feature but were not unique in Ireland; twin canals are also indicated on the first OS map of Thomastown in Tipperary.

The 'large beautiful canal' opposite the house at Castlemartyr in Cork was said to form 'a vista to that side of the county, through a venerable grove of lofty trees'.[126] In the mid-eighteenth century the classical geometric garden of Castlemartyr was 'made picturesque' and included an artificial river created by Henry Boyle (fig. 56).[127] The remains of this canal are possibly a straight section of the existing river that is now serpentine and informal. At Castle Ward in Co. Down, the view over the single long canal is terminated by the ruins of a fifteenth-century tower. Another feature seen in canals at Gaulstown and Rathcline was an artificial island called a 'redoubt',[128] which provided a safe haven for wildfowl. Sometimes a small building or 'duck house' was included, as at Castle Durrow.[129]

Smaller, decorative basins and fountains were usually positioned within parterres close to the house where they could be viewed from the main salons – although Dézallier d'Argenville cautioned that fountains should be kept away from the house as 'in the summer, there rises off the water vapours so corrupt as may communicate a malignity to the air we breathe, which is very injurious to health'.[130] Ponds for holding fish were often to be found in kitchen gardens where they were easily accessible to the house.[131]

Even where water was freely available, the creation of elaborate waterworks was costly and labour intensive. In 1682, Nicholas Plunkett, who appears to have been acting as agent for his good friend Thomas Flower at Castle Durrow, suggested that 'some little addition … I fancy might be added to your water in bringing it a little further', but recognizing the costs involved felt that 'without commission I must not be free of another man's purse'.[132] As water had often to be carried long distances, over difficult and unsuitable terrain, it was occasionally necessary to employ people with some expertise in mechanics and engineering; for example, Thomastown had 'two large pieces of water' which were 'supplied from a distance of several miles'.[133] Loveday also commented that the water at Thomastown had been 'brought with no small charge from a great distance'.[134] Apart from the labour needed to dig out the ponds and dispose of the spoil, it was necessary to employ specialist tradesmen such as plumbers and carpenters to execute the designs envisaged by the landowner. The cost of personnel combined with the monies outlaid on materials such as pipes, spigots, and specially commissioned statuary could be

57 The site of the great canal on the high ground at Breckdenston.

excessive. Molesworth initially estimated that the construction of the great canal at Breckdenston 'with the fine water summerhouse and leaden large cisterns upon it, and the five or six basins in the gardens and wilderness with pipes etc. could not stand in £500 sterling' (fig. 57).[135]

Where money and influence allowed, the best architects and experts in hydraulics were employed to design water features. William Kenn,[136] who was engaged by Sir John Perceval to build the house at Burton in Co. Cork, was responsible for designing the waterworks necessary to create the ornamental ponds in the gardens.[137] Other less wealthy landowners would combine their own expertise and knowledge gleaned from books available on the subject, with that of local tradesmen. Contemporary gardening literature gives us a useful guide as to how water features were used and constructed. It is known that Robert Molesworth supplied his wife Lettice with a book for help during the canal's design and construction.[138] The title and author of the book is unclear: it may have been Dézallier d'Argenville, Worlidge, Switzer or London and Wise's abridged translation of de la Quintinye's *The complete gardener* (London, 1704) – all of which gave detailed instructions for the creation of waterworks.

The difficulties faced in the construction and execution of water features is well illustrated in a sympathetic letter from William Boyle to his cousin Henry Boyle at Castlemartyr.[139] The letter also describes how important the writer felt it was to personally supervise workmen and to be sure that all interventions were carried out in the correct manner:

> I sincerely retract from what I said in relation to your trees and fishponds 'tis certain your works will not add on nor the designs be so well executed, if you have not a watchful eye, nay two. Therefore once you have so great an undertaking in hand, I think you absolutely in the right not to absent yourself from the workmen. I have experienced what it is to leave one's affairs to other people, having paid for what they ordered, and been forced to the expense of demolishing what they had done to make all new again. This has happened to me within these two months and in the compass of three acres; how might you suffer in 250 [acres]. I wish you success in what you are about and may you long enjoy the pleasure of those innocent country amusements.[140]

The best workmen were not always those from abroad. In his *Sketches*, George Holmes observed that Castlelyons in Cork, owned by Lord Barrymore, had 'a large canal' filled by 'a very curious aqueduct which conveys water from the river, contrived by a common miller, at a trifling expense, after the exertions of a celebrated artist from England had failed in bringing the water by another course'.[141] George Rawdon referred to employing a local plumber for work at Portmore.[142] Mr Stewart, a 'gardener', was engaged in 1714 to go to Breckdenston and take 'instruments with him' so he could 'come to town full of knowledge and good demonstrations and to be able to finish such a plan of that work' as to enable his wife Lettice to oversee the works in his absence. Stewart had already created 'a most noble canal of 300 or 400 yards long' for another client.[143] Lettice assured Molesworth that 'there are many outstanding workmen in this country to be had, so that you need not be at the expense of bringing anyone out from England for it'.[144] Work on fountains was more complicated and required tradesmen with more specialized skills. Molesworth used an English plumber called Bell as he claimed that there was 'nobody in Ireland' for work on the construction of the parterre fountain.[145]

Molesworth requested that before any work was carried out on the canal at Breckdenston, the ground be 'entirely laid out and contrived and levelled before they break ground', and 'some computation made' of all the earth that had to be moved and 'how to dispose of it'.[146] Despite this, the construction of the canal was delayed by the workmen's inability to ensure a consistent level for the entire length of the canal. Five years after the excavations commenced, work on the canal began again. The unfortunate gardener Nick was held to be at fault as he had 'not carried the bottom of his canal upon the true level nor deep enough', and by 'sodding' the banks, which Molesworth alleged had caused him to understand that the 'water would rise at the house end upon level with the uppermost sod'.[147] The canal was finally completed in 1722 when it was described as being 'top full' and 'the engine and pipes and cistern and sluices' 'all in good order'.[148] The banks of the great pond at Breckdenston were to be 'raised not cut'.[149] This method was also used at Gaulstown and at Eyrecourt Castle in Galway, where the remains of the raised banks are still visible.

Planting around water features

The orthographic composition of the seventeenth-century garden was reinforced by intensive, regimented soft landscaping. Avenues of trees, bosquets, 'wildernesses' and groves cut with vistas added interest and depth to the gardens. Water features were placed strategically among the planted elements of the garden, frequently in breaks in ornamental woodlands called *cabinets*, as advocated by writers such as Dézallier d'Argenville.[150] The visitor was frequently lead by a series of walks and enticing views through the soft landscaping to come upon a water feature almost by surprise. Versailles is the archetypical example of this sort of plan, the tapis vert created by Le Nôtre, being studded with basins, fountains and sculptures. Robert Molesworth wrote to his wife in 1709 with instructions for planting and laying out a wilderness with the specific injunction that she was to 'remember to leave ronds or ovals in the middle of each for a basin and also near the corners for some small ones. The walks must be very narrow and close, yet the principal ones a little broader than the others'.[151] At Gaulstown, a large pond was sited at the centre of the wooded area or wilderness with allées radiating outwards from it. The fishponds at Thomastown in Tipperary were placed one above the other on a hill terminating the vista at the end of a long avenue, planted with treble rows of trees.[152] This is not clearly illustrated on the first Ordnance Survey map, as the avenue no longer appears but its remains can be discerned on axis with a thick row of trees between two long canals.

Taller trees or hedges often bordered water features, adding a strong vertical element to the design. These were more than just stylistic gestures. As well as being attractive and adding structure, they acted as windbreaks and

gave shelter to the pond, screening it from noise that might disturb the fish
and lessening the action of sun and wind, which caused evaporation from
ponds. Molesworth's gardener, Costelloe, suggested that willows or 'sallies' be
planted about the basins to protect them from exposure. Molesworth
disagreed, insisting that such planting would 'spoil the beauty' of his new
basin.[153] It was important not to plant trees too close to the banks of static
water features, as this could cause deterioration in water quality by casting
excessive shade. Deciduous trees were potentially problematic in waterside
plantings as their leaf litter could cause stagnation. Despite this, deciduous
trees were frequently planted adjacent to water features, but at a sufficient
distance to avoid creating trouble. The great canal at Breckdenston was
planted in a traditional fashion with a double row of elms on either side. It was
described as being 'thirty yards broad' and flanked on each side by primary and
secondary walks, 'a lower and a higher', only the higher walk 'to be planted
with trees' while the lower walk was 'twenty or thirty foot broad at least to
prevent the trees (when grown) from casting their shadows too near the
water'.[154] The canal at Antrim Castle was described as having 'a splendid lime
hedge 18 feet high' extending along each of its sides.[155]

A letter from Molesworth describing his plans for planting around the
ponds and basins illustrates that the gradual loosening up in style, which began
around the 1720s, had not yet been adopted at Breckdenston. The layout of
the garden remained formal, with many of the geometric elements of the
earlier century in place

> the great round one in the sixteen acres shall be ... free from all
> encumbrances because from the rising bank about it will be the longest
> prospect of the sea from any place about Breckdenston and a great
> circular or oval basin is a most beautiful thing. The elms about it shall
> be planted thirty or forty foot asunder, in double rows, by which means
> all the fine prospect will appear under their branches, and between the
> intervals of trees, till they grow exceedingly old.[156]

This letter suggests that the lower branches of the trees would be pruned to
create a series of standards allowing views to be seen underneath their
canopies.

In the first half of the eighteenth century, fishponds and waterworks
became increasingly more elaborate as gardens of great estates became
monuments to displaying the wealth of the new merchant classes. The
utilitarian role of waterworks declined as the century progressed, with grand

decorative schemes becoming the driving force for the creation of water features. This period saw the development of the purely ornamental water garden. Charles Smith's description of the gardens at Doneraile in Cork shows how far the waterworks of the Restoration era had evolved by the mid-eighteenth century:

> [Doneraile is] situated on a rising ground of south end of the town facing the river Awbeg, which is formed into a fine cascade with reservoirs. In the front court on a pedestal stands the statue of a gladiator, with other lesser figures ... the gardens [are] well laid out, and of a very considerable extent; in them is a wilderness and labyrinth, and towards the foot of the gardens is a canal of 370 yards long and 140 broad, well stocked with fish; the water is constantly supplied by a large well, that casts up a part of the river Awbeg into a reservoir which is conveyed underground into the canal, and returns back over a cascade.[157]

To the north of the house was 'a most delightful spot, called the water garden, with cascades, [and] jets d'eau', while the ponds in the water garden were 'adorned with fountains, statues, and other decorations'.[158] Doneraile's elaborate water garden typified those being constructed in late seventeenth- and early eighteenth-century Ireland, and demonstrates their complexity and decorative value to the demesne as a whole.

CHAPTER 9

Field sports and hunting

I need not tell you whether summer or winter here, but here is plenty of corn, great store of conies, and very good fowling.[1]

Deer parks

THE SEVENTEENTH-CENTURY UNDERSTANDING of a 'park' was of land specifically for the preservation of game (although, as we shall see, other domestic animals and agricultural activities also took place within parklands). A park was defined by the lawyer Joseph Chitty as 'an enclosed chase, extending only over a man's own ground'. The most important feature of the park was that it was enclosed 'by pales, wall or hedges', and must contain 'best [beasts] of the park, bucks and does'.[2] Occasionally, the creation of new deer parks necessitated the removal of tenants. When Lord Conway's park was being enclosed at Portmore, George Rawdon wrote to him on how the plans were progressing:

> I cannot yet come to reasonable arrangement with some of the tenants who hold part of the land which is to be enclosed. This should not, however, hinder going on with the pale, and I hope that next year they [the deer] will be made to understand themselves better. I saw ten brace of deer and antler [stags] in two herds and believe most of them came in at the leaps and the keeper will I think prove good and serviceable.[3]

Deer are extremely strong and agile so the pale had to be sturdy and secure. The pale was the most expensive element of the park's construction. It took various forms; the park could be enclosed with ditches, palisade fences or walls of 'lime and stone'. The usual method of enclosure was a large bank three or four metres high topped by a strong wooden fence. At Killruddery, Edward Brabazon had a 'treble ditch' made outside the walls of the pleasure gardens and planted quicks, which refer to hawthorn or other thorny hedgerow plants, in order to contain the deer.[4] A ditch inside the bank stopped them from trying to escape by jumping; this ensured that they did not stray into the pleasure gardens and cause damage.[5] The earl of Antrim's deer park was enclosed by man-made and natural methods:

> The south enclosed with a wall of lime and stone to the west with natural rocks (only a door to enter) and so the northwest except five or six perches with post and rail and all the rest with the sea.[6]

Evidence for the proposition that the Restoration sparked an interest in the development of parks in Ireland can be found in the many manuscript references to new or improved parks created in the years following 1660. James Ross of Portavoe in Co. Down was lauded for establishing, 'since his Majesty's happy Restoration', a 'great house and large office houses all of stone brick, and lime slated gardens walled in', designed with 'convenient places for a deer park, a warren and other chases'.[7] The St Legers at Doneraile established what was described as a 'fine ... park' in the time before the 1680s.[8] The duke of Ormond had deer parks at all of his estates, including his English seat, Moore Park, where in 1663 the earl of Anglesey found it 'to be still the same sweet and pleasant seat I knew it before, and had a taste of the goodness of your Grace's venison'.[9]

The status conferred on the owners of great deer parks is evidenced by the awestruck description by William Chetwood of Thomastown, the estate of George Mathew, half-brother of the duke of Ormond:

> I cannot find words to describe this place. What think you of walls nine foot high, composed of lime and stone, that girdles in above two thousand acres, and Irish acres, that make almost a fourth part more than our stinted measure; these walls, with innumerable lofty gates, that would not disgrace the portal of a fine house. Within these secure enclosures you see the deer trotting after one another.[10]

Parks were for recreational hunting and other field sports. Within the great parks domestic and feral game were encouraged to breed and managed sustainably. The park at Howth Castle (see plate 1) had 'great store of conies, and very good fowling',[11] while that at Portmore in Down had 'strong covey of partridge'.[12]

In 1758, perhaps expressing the taste for open parkland that had become the fashion, Pococke described Lord Shannon's park at Castlemartyr as being 'finely wooded' with 'beautiful ridings in it, and it commands a charming, though, I think, too distant a view of the lake'.[13] These, though at first glance apparently 'natural', wood and pasture lands were very carefully planned and stocked. Books and treatises such as Moses Cook's *Manner of raising, ordering and improving forrest-trees* (1676) were consulted as to the best trees to be planted, and others detailed how the land was to be ploughed and levelled.[14]

Deer parks, which were common throughout the late Middle Ages, had declined until the Restoration period when they were re-popularized by Charles II. Some of the great medieval parks survived, such as the earl of Thomond's park at Bunratty, but extensive poaching in both English and Irish parks throughout the Commonwealth era meant that they had to be restocked with deer. Sir John Davies, writing in the early seventeenth century, recorded that such was the decline in deer parks that Dunmore was the only park in Ireland stocked with deer.[15] Davies had clearly not made a complete tour of Ormond's estates as the then dilapidated house at Carrick had an excellent park 'fully stocked with fine large fat deer' during the early part of the century.[16] Certainly by the late seventeenth century, well stocked deer parks were commonplace on Irish demesnes. Sir George Rawdon informed Lord Conway that 'red deer come into the Tunny Park. There are nine of them now in all, and many brave old bucks'.[17] Two of the grandest and most famous palaces and gardens in Europe started life as small hunting lodges in areas rich in wildlife; Versailles in France and Het Loo in Holland, built for William III and Mary II. Charles II, like his grandfather James I, was a very keen huntsman – deer stag and otter being his preferred quarry. Where the monarch led, his subjects followed. Despite never visiting Ireland during his lifetime, the King kept buckhounds on Crown estates in Ireland – for example, the Phoenix Park. The Treasury accounts for Ireland for the year 1662–3 disclose that Sir William St Rauy, master of the Royal buckhounds, was paid £1 20s. and Mr William Peter, master of the 'bows and string hounds', was paid £61 13s. 4d.[18]

Medieval deer parks tended to be composed of dense natural woodlands; their seventeenth-century counterparts were designed to make the chase easier and to encourage breeding. The preferred layout was a park with clumps of trees and woodland and these woods were sometimes cut through with geometric avenues or rides and interspersed with open pasture for grazing.[19] As the craze for geometric precision reached its height, forest chases were expressed by the creation of formal wildernesses that were carefully planted and cut through with long allées, in geometrical symmetry. These were intended to emulate rides through hunting forests. The enclosure and careful management of large areas of parkland outside the curtilage of the main house and gardens and the transformation of game reserves and habitats into ornamental features were not merely expressions of wealth and sophistication, but also a means of gaining rational order and control of the otherwise wild countryside.

Ireland, constitutionally a kingdom, was subject to the common law prerogatives of the Crown. As the fountain of privilege, the King was the possessor of various powers, one of which was the right to confer lucrative game franchises on his subjects.[20] The law catered for many different types of game franchises depending on both the nature of the game and the means of pursuit. Game franchises included forests, parks, chases, and warrens.[21] Franchises could be vested in natural persons or bodies politic, such as corporations; for instance, at the north-east side of Limerick was a great salmon weir belonging to the Corporation.[22] Patents for game and fishing were valuable and often the subject of disputes. In 1677, the earl of Burlington's agent wrote asking him to direct his attention to securing the patents for fishing at Lismore, where a successful fishery was established.[23]

It is important at this point to note the nomenclature of the period. The word 'forest' did not necessarily refer to a piece of woodland; in fact it need not contain any woodland at all. A forest was described as 'a certain territory or circuit of woody grounds and pastures, known in its bounds and privileges, for the peaceable being and abiding of wild princely delight, replenished with beasts of venery and chase, and great coverts of vert, for succour of said beasts, for preservation whereof, there are particulars, laws, privileges, and offices, belonging thereunto'.[24] A chase was defined as 'an unenclosed place',[25] similar to a right of way or other easement which often lay across another person's land. Chases came into existence when landowners sold land but reserved the right to the chase for themselves. For example, by a lease of 1665 the earl of Arran assigned land in Galway to another, while reserving his right to 'hunt, hawk etc.'[26] The owner of the chase had the right to hunt game as opposed to the owner of the land itself. What was called a free chase was a right to hunt and kill game over a certain district. The value of chases and game reserves can be seen by their exclusion from several leases. Land would be assigned to lessees with hunting rights reserved to the lessor.[27] Conversely, a landowner in need of money could lease a chase for a considerable sum. Chases were valuable commodities. The existence of game and sporting facilities increased the value of land.[28] Granting visitors the use of game reserves showed hospitality.[29] In 1670 the Ormonds loaned their house at Carrick to a Ralfe Freeman and his wife while they were waiting to have their estate 'freed'; the duchess ordered that they were to be given the house 'with liberty to make use in his absence of the pigeon house warren and gardens also'.[30]

Apart from poachers and wild animals, the parks were subject to trespass by unauthorized hunts. The earl of Burlington wrote regularly to his agents to try to curb this liberty. The chief culprit appears to have been his cousin, Lord Shannon,[31] whom he heard had hunted for a whole season at Lismore without his permission.[32] He was particularly annoyed as he said that he would never refuse a day or two's hunting to a 'gentleman of the country or neighbourhood'. The earl was also fair handed, disapproving of any favouritism on the part of his agent. 'I don't allow my agents to oblige some more than others out of partiality' in relation to the use of the park.[33] In England where sworn enemies would display their contempt by hunting openly in each other's parks, the crime of 'park-breaking' was regarded as the supreme affront.[34] To ensure that there were ample stocks of game, stringent laws were passed to prevent unauthorized hunting. The acts targeted poachers and the smaller landowner, who may have attempted to 'rise above himself' by aping the upper classes and thus diminishing stocks. The Game Preservation Act of 1698 was passed by the Irish parliament to preserve game and fish which were 'very much destroyed by many idle persons, who afterwards betake themselves to robberies, burglaries, or other like offences'.[35]

Parks created in the Restoration period were often established at some distance from the house or even outside the demesne (but within the estate). The density of tree planting was greatly reduced and wide areas of pasture became more prominent. The more open nature of the park, with its associated ornamental rides and vistas, allowed the owners and guests to enjoy extensive prospects and thus to appreciate its full size. The overall 'natural' or wild irregularity of the park provided pleasing contrast to the strict geometric order seen in the gardens about the house. This was especially relevant in England where there was a more marked contrast between the park and the rest of the countryside which had been far more extensively enclosed and tamed than in Ireland, Scotland or Wales.[36]

Deer were hunted with deerhounds followed by men on horseback with crossbows. Venison was highly prized meat, eaten at celebrations and grand entertainments.[37] Deer were bartered in return for favours granted or presented as gifts. For instance, in return for his 'wisdom and kindness to me' the earl of Thomond ordered that his cousin, Sir Donat O'Brien, and his 'friend Macnemara of Crattallagh' be presented with a buck each.[38] Ambrose Upton writing to Sir Donat O'Brien enclosed a warrant to the keeper of Deer Island to deliver 'a fat buck' to Sir Donat for Lord Thomond's twenty-first birthday.[39] In 1690, the 1st earl of Burlington, on hearing that the duke of Wurttemberg intended to take his winter quarters in Youghal, asked his agents

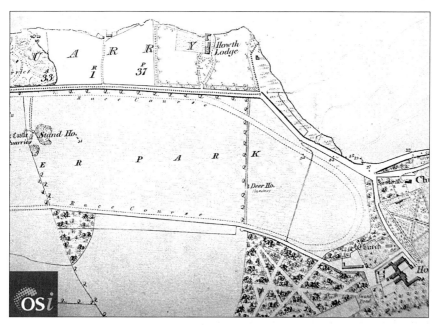

58 A deer house and horse course at Howth (courtesy of Ordnance Survey Ireland, permit ID 158).

to ensure that he be given 'the best accommodation in my house for lodging as the poor plundered place can afford, and that he may be frequently supplied from my parks at Lismore with does and salmon'.[40]

The deer that were hunted within the parks were not there due to mere luck. A variety of species were stocked and a lot of judicious trading and cadging of deer took place among friends, family and neighbours.[41] When Ormond bought Moore Park in Hertfordshire, one of the first things he attended to was the stocking of the deer park. Some of the stock came as a gift from the King himself.[42] Ormond's servant James Buck wrote that 'I did, in several letters, humbly desire your grace to direct two or three lines to me, for the King's Sergeant Trumpet, for the delivery of those deer and ducks His Majesty promised out of St James's Park'.[43]

The deer, unlike their wild cousins found in the Scottish highlands, were regarded as domestic animals, and treated as such. They were provided with warm quarters to shelter[44] in and were sometimes fed hay or bread to supplement their diet during winter.[45] The papers of the Lane family of Lanesborough include undated early seventeenth-century accounts that note the costs of providing 'bread for the dear' [sic], which indicates that they were treated much like cattle or other domestic beasts.[46]

Notwithstanding their idyllic pastoral appearance, parks were highly contrived landscapes, which were well planned and expensive to maintain. They were not quiet sylvan oases where nature was left undisturbed; on the contrary, they were places bustling with activity, people, animals and their associated buildings. Accounts in manuscripts of the time make constant references to expenses outlaid on keeping parks in repair.[47] Trees had to be guarded to stop the deer from damaging them, while trees grown to provide faggots or small 'boote' were either pollarded or coppiced and fenced off. Meadows were fertilized and mowed for hay.[48] The parks were prevented from becoming waterlogged by extensive drainage schemes. All this maintenance demanded a resident staff and most parks had a hunting lodge, which was a small house in which people often dined and stayed overnight. The lodges at Burlington's estates in Cork and Waterford were well maintained and expensively glazed.[49]

The park was managed by a keeper, whose duties are delineated in an interesting manuscript dating from the sixteenth century in Trinity College Dublin:

> The keepers of my lord's parks not to keep any more cattle than they are allowed, and to have special care of the coppices and that no cattle roam into them of kind so ever. That they create no houses for continuance without my lord's special warrant, and that they have good care to feed their deer, with the hay provided for them, not giving it to other cattle and to look that their pales and fences being well made be well looked into.[50]

The position of park keeper was one of trust and responsibility, and as such well remunerated. In 1687, James Edmonds, the keeper of Lord Burlington's park, was paid £15 a year, a quite substantial sum, especially when the other perks that came with the job such as a lodge to live in and access to game are taken into consideration.[51] Managing the deer population was one of the main duties of the keeper, with friends and neighbours helping each other to restock their parks. With breeding plans and imported stock in place, Captain Henry Boyle wrote to the dowager countess of Orrery that he expected Charleville Park to be fully stocked with deer in three years' time, 'there already a good quantity there'.[52] By 1683, the countess of Donegall had 'a very fine park well stored with venison'.[53] Ormond, who appears to have had the most lavish lifestyle at the time, was always generous with his deer; he ordered his keeper at Carrick to provide John St Leger with 'six brace of deer and one brace of sows of the season'.[54] The importance placed on the maintenance of deer parks can be gauged by the amount of interest taken in them by their owners. Busy men of state were kept closely informed about the condition of their parks and their stock. Instructions were sent from London or further abroad as to what work was to be undertaken and how the parks were to be managed.[55] Sir George Rawdon kept Lord Conway informed about the park at Portmore Castle, which was well stocked with game for hunting. For instance, in 1665 he wrote that 'the deer in both parks are in great case and the lean white buck we had from Antrim is exceedingly mended since we had him'.[56] Breeding and training of hounds was another of the gamekeeper's duties.[57] It was important that only trained hounds were allowed into the deer parks as wild dogs and domestic pets could cause havoc.[58] In the seventeenth century, wolves and eagles were still common in Ireland so in addition to contending with human poachers, gamekeepers had to deal with a variety of wild beasts that stalked the parks by night.[59] Wolves were so prevalent that during the Commonwealth it was felt necessary for parliament to pass an act prohibiting the export of 'wolf dogs' from Ireland as it was noted that 'wolves do much increase and destroy many cattle'[60] and, in 1686, a wolf was killed at Burton.[61] In addition to wolves, one of the Dublin Philosophical Society's correspondents, Roderick O'Flaherty, observed an eagle in Connaught that killed deer 'by grappling [them] with his claw and forcing him ... headlong into precipices'.[62]

Falconry

The park was also a site for falconry, an ancient practice, which involves the taking of wild quarry, such as rabbit and game fowl, by means of trained birds of prey. The most popular hawks used were the peregrine falcon, the hobby, the merlin, the goshawk and the sparrow-hawk.[63] Hawking was said to be the duke of Ormond's favourite sport, and he had a particular fondness for hunting at his ancestral home, Kilkenny Castle: 'I am gotten hither', he wrote in August 1667, 'and am yet in the happiest calm you can imagine. Fine weather, great store of partridge, a cast of merlins, and no business, and this may hold for a week'.[64]

During his second term as lord lieutenant, when he was particularly bogged down with work, Ormond liked to escape from the city to enjoy country pursuits such as racing at the Curragh.[65] In 1668, he wrote that he was 'taking the opportunity of the king's going to Newmarket' by spending time with his friends 'to divert myself with country sports and have not my papers by me'.[66] The Curragh in Kildare was said to be ideal for 'hawking or hunting or racing, for in the clearer and finer air the falcon goes to a higher pitch or mint'.[67] Prey was plentiful in the countryside, but near congested cities it was more difficult to find. In the 1630s, the earl of Strafford found partridge so scarce about Dublin that he had to take to hawking blackbirds.[68] In November 1662 a proclamation ordered that for the preservation of game for the benefit of the lord lieutenant (Ormond) and officers of state, all persons were forbidden 'to take any pheasants, grouse, hares, or any prohibited game whatever by hawks, nets, guns, setting dogs, greyhounds or any other engine whatsoever'.[69] When in Derry, Bishop King made occasional payments to a falconer George Delap, for various work, possibly for the purposes of pest control.[70]

A statute was passed as early as 1480 to prevent the exportation of hawks from Ireland. It noted that 'hawks of diverse nature as goshawks, tiercels, and of other names were of great plenty within the land of Ireland' but that unscrupulous merchants were selling them out of the country, thus depriving the Irish population from purchasing hawks for themselves. The Act imposed fines for the sale of hawks abroad of 13s. 4d. for a goshawk, 6s. 8d. for a tiercel and 10s. for a falcon.[71] The value of hawks can be measured by the frequency that they appeared as consideration in leases and conveyances. For instance, a lease for forty messuages[72] and two windmills in Co. Monaghan was granted in return for a sparrow hawk.[73]

Good hawks were much prized and were often subject to theft.[74] In a letter of 1677, the earl of Barrymore wrote to Daniel O'Donovan at Ardagh thanking him for a hawk and asking 'if you could get me a rock merlin you would do me a great favour'. O'Donovan received further letters from Lord Orrery and Lionel Beecher referring to further gifts of hawks.[75] During his tenure as bishop of Derry, William King sent hawks to Dublin.[76] The use of hawks for hunting declined with the availability of firearms, but continued to be used for racing.[77] Documentary sources reveal that although the popularity of falconry began to decline in the mid-seventeenth century in England, it remained very popular among the aristocracy, and especially so in Ireland.[78]

Hunting with horses and hounds

Fox hunting with hounds had been formally established by the latter half of the seventeenth century, and parks, with their ground cover, proved ideal hunting areas and contained many foxes. Ross in Bantry was described as being 'good for hunting and hawking, there being good riding and plenty of game especially hare, pheasant, grouse and partridge' and 'too many foxes'.[79]

Then, as now, the animals were hunted with dogs.[80] Fox hunting was not merely good sport, it was necessary to control these effective predators and protect livestock. The earl of Burlington paid a 'fox ketcher' for killing 18 foxes in his park in 1683.[81] Hunters were brought to and from England so their owners could take part in field sports when free from business at Court.[82] Some estates had their own 'horse courses' for exercising bloodstock within the parks. For example, in 1709, it was reported that 'the countess of Donegall hath a very fine park well stored with venison and in it a horse course of 2 miles'.[83] A course can also be seen in the first Ordnance Survey map of Howth Castle.

Good horses were often hard to come by in England, so Ormond's servant Edward Cooke vowed that he would 'rally together both skill and diligence to provide your grace with a supply of that so material want of horseflesh'.[84] The duke also bred bloodstock himself, importing 'barbs and Arabs' (although it was reported that he was not very successful).[85] Ormond kept a pack of hunting dogs at the Phoenix Park[86] and at Kilkenny which were alleged to have been so well trained that they were said to always turn homewards on the sound of the castle dinner bell.[87] Cooke established a further kennel for Ormond's beagles' use when at Moore Park.[88] The 1st earl of Burlington had his hounds sent over from England to Lismore.[89] Good hunting dogs were at a premium and often presented as gifts. Lord Ossory received a lurcher and greyhound from his father.[90] In 1683, Adam Loftus (later Lord Lisburn) wrote from Rathfarnham Castle to Thomas Coningsby at Hampton Court Park in Herefordshire asking him to buy him a setter dog.[91] Hare coursing was another sport carried out within the walls of the park. When Sir Ralph Freeman was resident at Carrick, he was allowed to 'take a hare or two' for himself.[92]

Warrens

Another feature of the park and demesne landscape, which has all but disappeared today, was the rabbit warren. As late as the mid-nineteenth century, the German writer Kohl noted that all the Irish estates had rabbit warrens.[93] The wild rabbit, or coney as it was commonly called, is not native to Ireland and is thought to have been introduced by the Normans in the twelfth century for their meat and fur. As rabbits were valuable and useful, they were desirable commodities to keep on demesne lands.[94] In law, a warren was described as 'a place privileged for the keeping of bests and fowls of warren'.[95] Warrens were artificially constructed enclosures containing groups of undulating artificial mounds, or 'pillows', established on suitable land to appeal

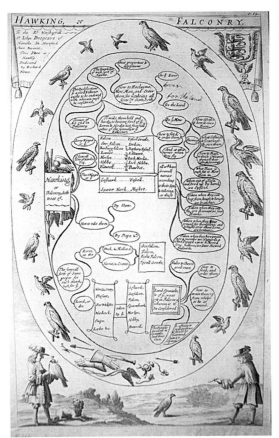

59 Hawks and hawking, a plate from Richard Blome's *The gentleman's recreation* (London, 1686).

to rabbits and wild birds (figs. 59 & 60). Warrens were established on many estates, often created artificially in order to encourage breeding. For example, Lord Conway's servant John Oliver suggested making 'two or three burrows' in the park at Portmore, close to the lough, as it was 'a good place for rabbits by the lough side'.[96]

Breeding was promoted by the laying down of pipes to encourage the rabbits to burrow and establish colonies. The warren could take a more naturalistic form, where the rabbits were confined by a large bank and ditch topped with furze and regularly patrolled.[97] An example of this type of warren can be seen in the first OS map of Bessborough.

Alternatively, warrens were created in a more formal and decorative style in an enclosure whose walls retained a bank in which the burrows were set. The wall was made of brick or stone and contained small arched entrances to the burrows. John Worlidge explained the workings of warrens in *Systema agriculturae* as follows:

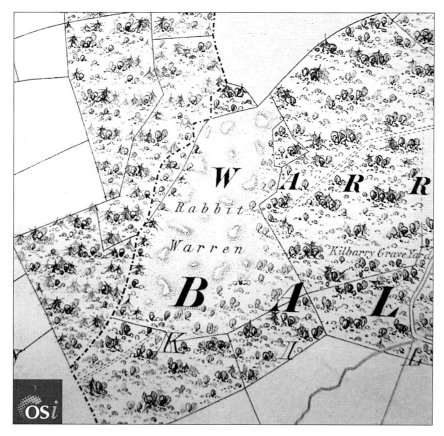

60 A warren at Warrenscourt (courtesy of Ordnance Survey Ireland, permit ID 158).

Besides the wild, which are very profitable in warrens, tame conies may be kept to a very great advantage, either in hutches or in pits, which is much to be preferred. These pits are sunk about six or seven foot deep, in a good light mould; or in chalk or sand they delight most. These are to be made round or square, and walled with stone or brick, to preserve the earth from foundering, in leaving places on the sides for the conies to draw and make their stops or buries. At the one end or side, make a hollow place for the buck to rest in, chaining him to a small stump, that he may have liberty to go to the rack to fees, and then to his den to rest. On the other side or end, let the places be left for the does to make their stops in. About the middle of the pit may you place the rack to feed them in; the buck on the one side, and the does on the other. In a pit of about ten foot square may be kept two or three does, (besides the buck) which will bring each of them about fifty or more young ones in a year, sometimes seventy or eighty. When they are about a month old, you may take them out of the pit, and either spend them, or feed them in another pit or place made for that purpose. If you have much garden-ground, and a good soil free from water, clay or stone for them to breed in, they will thrive exceedingly, and doubly repay your care and trouble.[98]

There were probably several warrens on Burlington's lands as accounts relating to the estates in Cork and Waterford make several recurring references to the maintenance of the warrens.[99] The warren at Lismore was on the site that now lies behind the cathedral.[100]

The keeper of the warren was called a warrener. His duties were described in a sixteenth-century manuscript as follows:

The warrener to look well to my lords warrens, to keep no ferrets, to maintain his nets and traps in good repair, and to set them in good sense to overlook his grounds. Not to suffer his game to increase or run further than to those rounds allotted for conies, and to deliver his conies to the clerk by tally or bill indented.[101]

The warrener lived in a warrener's lodge where skinning, butchering and salting would take place. Occasionally, trespassers proved too much for the warrener to manage alone and outside help had to be called in. At Lismore, a night watchman was paid to watch the warren by Garrett Roche.[102] In the 1680s, the warrener at Lismore, a John Liddle, was paid a salary £4 a year.[103]

As with other game reserves, great care was taken to maintain the warrens, by fencing them in (or even establishing them on offshore islands). Rabbit warrens were cultivated, usually on dry soil such as heathland, although one was planned for the water's edge at Portmore.[104] Building raised mounds ensured drainage. Magilligan in Co. Londonderry was noted for its rabbits:

In it there is one of the best warrens in Ireland, for from Solomon's porch to the Rowfat is ten miles in length and reasonable well stocked so that you will buy here a couple of conies for 2d. ... (but without skins) ... in which warren are abundance of juniper shrubs.[105]

The duke of Ormond developed a warren at Kilkenny in the 1660s, but it was not a success (perhaps the soil was unsuitable) and plans were made to build a new one at a more suitable site.[106]

Warrens sometimes became the casualty of campaigns to level and plough the parks, as flat terrain was considered more suitable for deer parks; making the sport less arduous for the huntsman. In 1673, the warren in the deer park at Lismore was levelled and ploughed to make 'the ground even'.[107] Twenty-five years later, the earl wrote to Congreve again regarding levelling the park, which also illustrates the gentile nature of hunting:

> I have read our proposal about the park, and to the best of my under-standing in those matters it seem a reasonable one. What I would have, is to have the grass made as good as possible can be for the deer, and to have the ground laid as smooth as you can, for the conveniency of hunting.[108]

The park had many other economic functions: it was a useful place in which to site plantations of timber trees and other wood. The timber was managed with some areas being coppiced. This meant that areas within the park would sometimes be further divided by banks and ditches so that certain sections were closed off from the deer as and when new shoots were developing from coppiced stools.[109] Often the park provided grazing for cattle, although this was strictly controlled in order to protect timber and meadows.[110] The fishponds in the parks tended, on the whole, to be larger and less regular in design than those found closer to the house.[111] Parks such as that at Dunmore also included pheasantries and paddocks for horses.[112] Ormond's younger son Ossory collected live pheasants from Arklow with which to stock his father's parks.[113]

Duck decoys

The introduction of decoys to ensnare wildfowl was one of the most interesting contributions of the Dutch to seventeenth-century Ireland.[114] In addition to farms, fisheries and deer parks, a useful source of food and financial income was the creation of, what was then a relatively new innovation, the duck decoy. Wild ducks were a much-prized delicacy. At a time when religious observation was taken very seriously, wild duck was very important as an alternative to meat as it was not classified as meat so could be eaten with impunity during lent and fast days.[115] Prior to the introduction of decoys, the main method of catching wildfowl commercially was 'ducking'. Ducking involved hunting the birds in natural wetland during the summer months when mature fowl were rendered more-or-less flightless because they were moulting. There were, however, many disadvantages to ducking. It required a lot of manpower and, more importantly, it caused extensive disturbance of the birds and could not be repeated in same area for a long time. It was very destructive of stock, killing many immature birds. It is unclear whether ducking was ever even carried out in Ireland.[116] Firearms were rare, expensive and cumbersome. Shooting ducks with hand-held 'fowling pieces' was practised primarily for sport, but was inefficient for commercial purposes. Firearms became more widely available during the English Civil War of the 1640s, but continued to be rare and expensive to use.

The most refined and simple way to catch ducks in quantities was by using duck decoys. Decoys to entice wildfowl originated in the Netherlands; in fact the word decoy comes from the Dutch words *eende* and *kooi*,[117] which translated means duck and cage,[118] and in turn, the word 'decoy' is an abbreviation of 'duck-coy'. Hundreds of decoys were constructed in the Netherlands during and after the sixteenth century.[119]

When on a tour of the Netherlands in 1641, John Evelyn observed 'decoys where they catch innumerable quantities of fowl'.[120] Decoys had already begun to appear in England early in the seventeenth century.[121] Sir William Brereton (1604–61), the early seventeenth-century traveller, noted many 'coys' both in Holland and England.[122] Brereton was said to have built one of the first decoys in Britain at Dodleston, south west of Chester.[123] Shortly after his Restoration, Charles II set about the creation of a decoy in St James's Park. John Evelyn wrote, on 9 March 1665:

> I went to St James's Park: the park was at this time stored with infinite flocks of several sorts of ordinary, and extraordinary wildfowl, breeding about the decoy, which for being near so great a city, and among such a concourse of soldier[s], guards and people, is very diverting … the withy pots[124] or nests for the wildfowl to lay in, a little above the surface of the water, [were] very pretty. [125]

On 29 March 1665 he noted that 'His Majesty is now finishing the Decoy in the Park'.[126] The St James's decoy was said to have been designed by Sydrach Hilcus, a Dutchman.[127] The decoyman was called Storey, and he gave his name to Storey's Gate in the Park.

John Ray wrote in 1678 of decoys being a 'new artifice' lately introduced by the Dutch and, in addition to describing the workings of a decoy, he also alluded to the great number of fowl caught in a decoy in the winter. This was the great beauty of the new decoys – they did not depend on catching fowl during the moulting season when they were vulnerable, they could be caught at any time of year.

At the same time as decoys were being introduced to England they began to appear on Irish estates. As early as 1635, Brereton wrote a description of a 'coy' in Wexford.[128] At the time of the completion of the St James's Park decoy, several decoys were already well established on estates in Ireland and many more were in the process of construction or under contemplation. In 1664 the duke of Ormond's younger son, Richard Butler, the 1st earl of Arran, was building a decoy at Sherwood Park in Co. Carlow.[129] Arran's uncle, George Mathew, also had a decoy on his estate at Thomastown in Tipperary.[130] Thomas Dineley wrote of 'a great decoy for ducks belonging to James Fitzgerald of the Middle Temple' in Parteene in Limerick in 1681.[131] The Killruddery decoy was built in 1682 and Doneraile, in Cork, seat of the St Leger family, had a decoy 'to the east of the house'.[132] Rathbeale also had a decoy prior to 1699.[133]

Those who could afford to do so, hired Dutch men to supervise the building of their decoys.[134] The Dutch were experts in water management. Martin Jansen van Heyninge (known locally and referred to hereafter as Martin Johnson), a Dutchman, created the decoy at Portmore, Lord Conway's estate on the eastern shores of Lough Neagh in Co. Antrim. Johnson worked for other landowners in Ulster, giving advice to Lord Massereene on the creation and maintenance of his decoy at Antrim Castle.[135] Rawdon himself had a decoy at his own estate in Moira, Co. Down,[136] which was most likely constructed according to Johnson's prescription. Johnson and Rawdon appear to have worked together on the design of the decoy at Portmore. The Dutchman oversaw the technical side of the construction, while Rawdon was responsible for the design and layout. In May 1665 he wrote:

> I received this report from Mr Mildemay yesterday from which your lordship may see what is doing at the decoy. He is skilful and I write to him to advise with Johnson about it. I have had an exact plot drawn of Sir Edward Rodney's decoy in Somersetshire. It is one of the best in England.[137]

The best and most complete early account of how decoys were constructed dates from 1752 and describes one seen in Lincolnshire:

> What are called decoys are generally confined to the fenny counties. Decoys are large ponds, dug in the fens, with four or five creeks, running from them to a great length, and each growing gradually narrower till it comes to a point. The banks are well planted with

willows, sallows, osiers, and like of underwood … boughs are so artfully managed, that a large net is spread near the tops of the trees, among the branches, and fastened to hoops which reach from side to side. This is so high and wide, the room is so much below, and the water so open, that the fowls do not observe the net above them.[138]

Decoys were ideally established in quiet places. Willughby wrote in 1678 that 'a place is to be chosen for the purpose remote from common high-ways and all noise of people'.[139] The decoy at Doneraile, constructed by Arthur St Leger, 2nd Viscount Doneraile (1694–1733/4), was situated in 'a dense thicket in the park', as was the Thomastown decoy.[140]

In April 1665, Conway, Rawdon and Martin Johnson, the decoyman, were deciding where their decoy should be situated. The first site fixed on was close to an old church, but the Irish custom of loud 'keening' at funerals ruled it out as being too noisy:

> I have seen the ground by the old church. The place would be good, but the Irish do come there to bury their dead bodies and do make such a noise that they will spoil the duckcoye. Therefore, I have found out another place in my lord's park between the little lock and the great lock and the park house, upon the meadow that lies near the lock. I find it a better place, as it is more in the air than the place by the church, and for flying to the great lock. It is calm before the north wind and north west. It is sweet to roost in and it is better pleasure for his lordship to have it in the park; but it will be a little more cost to stock the wood. We have the advantage of not having to plant wood, which is a great advantage for the coy. I like the country so well as any country I have seen, so I do not doubt but with the help of God I shall catch fowl enough.[141]

The decoy, completed in October of that year, was constructed at another site within the park between two lakes. Rawdon wrote about how the plans were progressing:

> I spent Monday last with Martin Johnson [the Dutch fowler] and had with me John Totnam (sic.) and also Travers the gardener and Mr Mildmay, who pretend some skill in a decoy. We viewed the little lough both by water and land and at last agreed in deciding that the best and most private place for it was between the Tunny mouth and your

meadow in the park. On that side, the fowl do most haunt, being sheltered from the north wind; and Johnson approves it as the best he has seen in any country. He saw the other possible spots, the other side of the old church and the great lough side, but for these and other reasons he thought within the park the fittest and most private, and that our lordship would take more pleasure of it there than of another place out of your hands ... Your lordship has not computed the charge in your letter. It will be £300, and some think it will be more. I should be glad to hear if our lordship approves of this expense. Meantime we shall be getting tools and providing workmen and shall cut the wood in that place, which must however, be cleared. He speaks of three or four acres for a pond, and his pipes that must be digged, and the earth taken away to raise banks and walks about it, and the lough being yet high it cannot be wrought or begun till about a fortnight or three weeks hence, that the lough fall.[142]

The decoy pond at Portmore, at four acres, was a particularly large one. Payne-Gallwey suggested that decoys should be between one and three acres. The work was expensive and required a lot of manpower as is well illustrated by the following letter from one of the project's overseers:

Sir, as for the coy, I hope it will go on apace. We have sat the pond to dig by the great lake. We have divided it into four quarters and have four men at every quarter, which will be a great cause to make it go on apace if the water be not very wet. It will be expensive for I think the digging of the pond will cost about £140. We are to give them thirteen shillings for a square perch and there will be 160 perch to be digged three foot deep besides the skoupes and the pipes; and Mr Johnson intends to make a moat about the pond twelve foot broad and to cast it all one way, which will be great charges. We have ten men casting up a large highway from the dry ground down to the decoy, which is set out sixteen foot broad and the tranches, both sides are seven foot broad and four foot deep.[143]

The moat mentioned would have kept the nesting ducks safe from foxes, similar devices were made for protecting rabbit warrens.

Ponds usually had a depth of two or three feet with sloping banks surrounded by trees and shrubs. The banks around the main decoy pool were generally steep in order to discourage birds from resting on them. A more suitable resting place was usually provided near the entrance to the pipes beneath the nets. Planting around the decoys and ponds was as natural as possible, generally composed of alder, osiers and other willow species.[144]

In areas not blessed by nature with suitable lakes and ponds, considerable skill was exercised in creating artificial ponds and managing the hydraulics. It was important to keep the pond from drying out. Viscount Molesworth expressed his concern about the decoy at Breckdenston: 'I hope James Hand takes care to keep all his string of high ponds and decoy ponds as brimful as possible'.[145] Breckdenston's decoy was said to be 'very convenient' – whether because it was close to the house, or because it made the catching of wildfowl easier, is difficult to gauge as there is no sign of a decoy either on the ground or on the maps available.[146]

The complications involved in ensuring water supply can be seen in this account by Rawdon, who was anxious to ensure that works on Lord Massereene's land which would affect the water table would not cause the decoy pond to dry out:

> He and I have made a plot of the whole work and I fear it will come to more [than £300]. I was so ignorant I thought such a work might have been made by cutting pipes out of the lough itself; but he will not understand any other way but by making a pond and by cutting the pipes out of it. I hope he understands his trade fully and that your lordship hath received good testimony of it. This place is over against the priest's house, close by the little loughside, and if the great lough, and so consequently the little one, should fall three or four foot by any good project either of Lord Massereene's or any other, which I do not hope to fall out, this pond would be supplied with water from the river, which can easily be turned into it by the new ditch made through the wood. Unless, however, the lake falls, there is no fear but that this pond will be troublesome. He thinks they may be kept out by a close pale without the walks. If this can be done this summer (which I question) it will drain some of the money which your lordship makes account of.[147]

And again a week later:

> My last letters were about the decoy; and I spent Wednesday with William Hoole and John Totnall devising the best way to carry it out, and think now that it will not cost so much as the first estimate of £300. We think to bring in the river by the new trench and so to avoid the

61 Decoyman putting ducks into a net, from Ralph Payne-Gallwey's
The Fowler in Ireland (London, 1882), p. 94.

expense of making the pond and pipes about two feet deep, but to raise
the banks and let in water in summer from the river by turning some
part of it at the head of the meadow into the pond.[148]

Radiating from the pond were 'decoy pipes'. There could be one or as many as
eight such pipes (fig. 62).[149] Killruddery decoy appears to have only one pipe,
while Doneraile's had four. These consisted of curved, tapering ditches with a
wide mouth, narrowing to a width of only about two feet at the end. Over the
ditches were arched wooden hoops, which gradually became lower as the ditch
narrowed; the hoops were covered in nets or a lattice weave of willow. The
pipes were well disguised by trees and shrubs. Alongside the decoy pipes, were
screens made or reed or willow hurdles. The screens were to enable the
decoyman and his dog to hide out of sight.

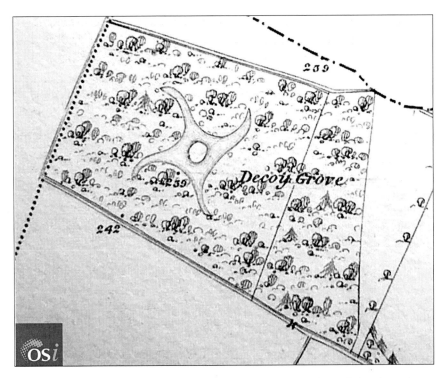

62 A four-pipe decoy at Kilbrew in Meath, built for the Barnwell family in the
seventeenth century (courtesy of Ordnance Survey Ireland, permit ID 158).

The decoyman also had a hut situated somewhere behind the screens in
which to keep his nets and other equipment. Writing in 1886, Payne-Gallwey
recorded seeing the remains of the decoyman's hut at Doneraile, together with
the channels cut for flooding the pool from the river Awbeg that flowed beside
it.[150] When Edward Brabazon was creating the garden at Killruddery, his
father, the 3rd earl of Meath, was informed of the progress of the decoy and
construction of the screens by his agent Oliver Cheney:

> The decoy will be the finest in the kingdom or I believe in the three
> kingdoms. The pond is already made and the reed wall is making, round
> about which he will build a wall at so great a distance that the fowl shall
> not be frighted thereat.[151]

The wildfowl were enticed up the decoy pipes by throwing food from behind
the screens up along the pipes, or by sending the decoy dog called a 'piper'

(from the Dutch *pijper*) up the pipe to be followed by the ducks. The ideal decoyman's dog was said to be one 'as similar in appearance to a little fox, red in colour with a bushy tail with a frolicsome and affectionate disposition and obedient'.[152]

The Dutch developed their own breed of dog for working the decoys, the *kooikerhondje*. It is not known whether any of these were imported into Ireland.[153] At Portmore Joseph Stroude wrote that he would assist Mr Johnson 'with two or three small dogs' for training as decoy dogs.[154] When the ducks reached the end of the decoy pipe, which by this point was cramped and narrow, the only way of escape was to go forward through a small hole and into the hands of the waiting decoyman and his basket.

Decoys took at least a year to establish. Johnson was perhaps overly optimistic about the decoy at Portmore. He hoped that it would be providing ducks before the decoy was even finished.[155] This was not to be as Rawdon wrote in disappointment to Lord Conway that only 'one unfortunate duck was sent me three days since as the first fruits of the decoy. It is near completed and likely to do well, but much cannot be expected this year'.[156]

Allurement was achieved by the simple means of making the decoy an attractive place for wildfowl to settle and colonize. This was done by first establishing a colony of tame decoy ducks. These tame ducks were to entice other wildfowl into the decoy.

In 1699, Lettice Molesworth informed her husband that 'wild ducks and teal are on the decoy' and that despite a scarcity of water, the decoy 'occasions is to be furnished with several sorts of fowl ... I saw, I believe, thirty or forty snipes, abundance of plover and herons and I don't know what besides'.[157] Lord Massereene of Antrim Castle supplied the Portmore decoy with twelve decoy ducks in return for advice from Johnson on how to improve his own decoy.[158] Johnson suggested that Lord Conway's decoy needed 200 decoy ducks.[159] Lord Massereene's ducks proved to be both fecund and attractive to wildfowl as by September 1665 the target had been achieved.[160]

The decoy ducks were kept in the decoy and trained to come in for food whenever they heard 'a low whistle from the decoy man'.[161] In Ireland in the late seventeenth century, hemp seed was a popular choice of duck food, although expensive.[162] Sir George Rawdon wrote to Lord Conway asking 'as to hemp seed, be pleased that Garrett bring as much as he can get. It will be good for sowing as well as for the decoy, and is much dearer here than at Chester'.[163] With over 200 tame ducks to feed, the decoy was proving expensive to run. Rawdon suggested that crops of suitable seeds should be sown on the estate to keep costs down, asking Conway:

Pray direct Garrett to buy two or three barrels of buckwheat at Chester. Some call it French wheat. It is almost as good for feeding decoy ducks as hemp seed, and far cheaper. We could sow some of it in March if we had it.[164]

The decoy, like any other element of the demesne landscape, was expected to pay for its own upkeep. As more varieties of food became available, transport methods improved and tastes changed, decoys fell out of fashion in the nineteenth century as they became economically unfeasible. By 1721, the decoy at Breckdenston was proving to be economically unsustainable:

I wish that [the] decoy could be set or ordered so that at least it should maintain itself in repairs and the man's wages that looks after it. If it will not do this, it were better to abandon it, though I am loath to lose my so many years' trouble, expense and delight … Try what good way you can contrive to put it in that it may not be too heavy a burden upon our hands. Now it [the decoy] takes away almost all the rent of James Hand's farm, the very best we have in those parts.[165]

By 1886, when Payne-Gallwey published his treatise on decoys, only a handful of functioning decoys remained in Ireland. Many decoys were lost along with the razing of the great seventeenth-century deer parks to make way for the more 'naturalistic' eighteenth-century landscape parks. For instance, Thomastown had most of its formal layout turned into parkland in the late eighteenth century. Dunmore's decoy was allowed to become overgrown. Eyrecourt decoy existed and was in use until about 1860.[166] Other decoys such as Clonfert, Ballinakill and Beaulieu had also fallen from use by the mid-nineteenth century. The decoy at Killruddery is no longer visible, many others are overgrown and the decoy pipes clogged up. Perhaps the most poignant loss is the decoy at the Portmore estate in Co. Antrim, which was so minutely documented by Sir George Rawdon in his letters to Lord Conway. Not a trace of the works carried out by Martin Johnson remains.

Epilogue

A THEME UNDERLYING THIS BOOK is that improving Irish landowners of the late seventeenth and early eighteenth centuries were guided by the principle of *utile et dulci*, integrating the pragmatic into their design. Their landscape interventions were guided by three main concerns: first, to make the Irish landscapes more 'English like', and to follow the same Continental styles that were *à la mode* in England; second, to manage their demesnes in such a

63 Russborough House, detail from *Map of the county of Dublin* by John Rocque (1760).

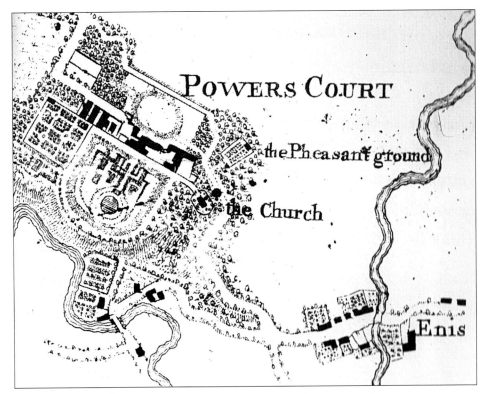

64 Powerscourt House, detail from *Map of the county of Dublin* by John Rocque (1760).

way as to make their fruit growing endeavours, timber plantations and parklands economically profitable and sustainable as well as aesthetically pleasing; and third, to create idealized landscapes for retreat and leisure pursuits away from the business of government.

The geometric landscape adopted in seventeenth-century Ireland did not simply cease to be in 1740. As discussed in chapter 2, the early landscape gardens as promoted by Addison and Pope, and espoused by Jonathan Swift and Mrs Delany, were stiff and formal affairs, some of which lasted into the early nineteenth century. The addition of the occasional serpentine path was the first step in a long progression culminating in Capability Brown's English landscape parks in the latter part of the eighteenth century. By the mid-eighteenth century, the demesne landscape had begun the process of dramatic alteration; however, geometry was never completely abandoned and many great gardens such as Stowe, Chatsworth and Blenheim Palace retained elements of formality and symmetry within or on the edges of their great parks. In Ireland, Mount Ievers, built in the 1730s, was designed with a huge formal garden to the rear of the house, and Palladian houses such as Russborough and Powerscourt had formal gardens in addition to large parklands (figs. 63 & 64).

Very little of the landscapes described in this book remain today. Many of the great geometric wooded gardens of the late seventeenth and early eighteenth centuries were incorporated in the latter half of the eighteenth century into new supposedly 'naturalistic', but no less contrived, landscape parks, which consisted of large areas of green, undulating ground as opposed to densely planted flat landscapes.[1] However, earlier features still remain. The many ponds and canals at Stradbally were dug out into one great lake and Thomastown and Castlemartyr had most of their formal layout turned into parkland in the late eighteenth century. Many estates, such as Gaulstown, were broken up and redistributed, fracturing and disengaging the constituents of their planned landscapes. Dunmore Park, like Gaulstown and Garryhunden, simply fell into ruin. At Ormond's house at Garryhunden, Co. Carlow, a report for the Dublin Philosophical Society in the 1680s described 'a very pretty new improved garden of grass, greens, gravel, etc.' with 'a large basin and fountain in the middle of the garden and a noble canal at the end of it'.[2] By the 1740s Garryhunden lay neglected and derelict. 'However, though in ruins', wrote William Chetwood, 'this still keeps an appearance of its ancient magnificence, particularly in a noble park, a fine wilderness of lofty fir trees, and vast canals, malls, and fishponds. The whole seated in a country which is a perfect garden, and full of fine plantations'.[3] In 1838, d'Alton wrote of how the Archbishop's Palace at Tallaght had been improved, noting with approval that although 'its ancient yews, cypresses, laurels and above all some magnificent walnut trees' remained, 'the former stiff plan of those pleasure grounds is pleasingly metamorphosed, with all the taste of modern improvement'.[4] George Bennet, visiting the late seventeenth-century Palace Anne in Cork in 1864, noted that 'the fish-ponds have run dry, the parterres have become obliterated, and the gardens entirely possessed by weeds'.[5]

The ghosts of the old landscapes are hinted at in names of places today: Pigeonpark, Warrenstown, Warren Point, Coney Island, Deer Park, among others. The importance of warrens to demesne life declined after the mid-eighteenth century though many coastal warrens survived into the nineteenth century.[6] As farming methods progressed and food became more plentiful, rabbit warrens became impractical and an unnecessary expense.

In a moving postscript to an article recollecting her visits to Belan as a child, an anonymous source wrote of its destruction in the late nineteenth century; her description is characteristic of the fate of most of the gardens discussed above:

> Beautiful Belan lies in ruins; the wind blowing where it listeth, sighs over the desolate grounds and gardens, once so beautiful. A herd lives in the yard, sole occupant of this once lovely demesne.[7]

Abbreviations

Add. MS	Additional manuscripts
AH	*Analecta Hibernica*
ANH	*Archives of Natural History*
BHJ	*Bandon Historical Journal*
BL	British Library
BNHPSP	*Belfast Natural History and Philosophical Society Proceedings*
Bodl.	Bodleian Library, Oxford
CARD	John T. Gilbert (ed.), *Calendar of ancient records of Dublin*, vol. 4 (Dublin, 1894)
Council Book of Cork	Richard Caulfield (ed.), *The council book of the Corporation of the city of Cork: form 1609 to 1643, and from 1690 to 1800* (1876)
Council Book of Kinsale	Richard Caulfield (ed.), *Council book of the Corporation of Kinsale* (1879)
Council Book of Youghal	Richard Caulfield (ed.), *Council book of the Corporation of Youghal* (1878)
CPRI	*Calendar of patent and close rolls of chancery in Ireland for the reigns of Henry VII to Elizabeth I, and Charles I*, ed. James Morrin (Dublin, 1861–3)
CSPD	*Calendar of state papers relating to English affairs, Domestic*, ed. R. Lemon & M.A.E. Green, 12 vols (London, 1856–72)
CSPI	*Calendar of state papers relating to Ireland*, ed. H.C. Hamilton, E.G. Atkinson & R.P. Mahaffy, 24 vols (London, 1860–1912)
Dézallier d'Argenville, *Theory and practice of gardening*	Antoine Joseph Dézallier d'Argenville, *The theory and practice of gardening*, translated by John James (London, 1728)
'Dineley's journal'	Evelyn Philip Shirley & James Graves (eds), 'The journal of Thomas Dineley', *JKSIAS*, 1:1 (1856), pp 143–6, 170–88; 2:1 (1858), pp 22–32, 55–6; 4:1 (1862), pp 38–52, 103–9; 4:2 (1863), pp 320–38; 5:1 (1864), pp 40–8; 5:2 (1865), pp 268–90; 5:3 (1866), pp 425–46; 6:1 (1867), pp 73–91, 176–204
DNB	*Dictionary of national biography*
Garden History	*Journal of the Garden History Society*
Glynns	*Journal of the Glens of Antrim Historical Society*
HMC	Historical Manuscripts Commission

IESH	*Irish Economic and Social History*
IHS	*Irish Historical Studies*
IMC	Irish Manuscripts Commission
JCHAS	*Journal of the Cork Historical and Archaeological Society*
JCKAS	*Journal of the Carlow and Kildare Archaeological Society*
JIGS	*Irish Architectural & Decorative Studies, the Journal of the Irish Georgian Society*
JKSIAS	*Journal of the Kilkenny and South-east of Ireland Archaeological Society*
JRSAI	*Journal of the Royal Society of Antiquaries of Ireland*
Moorea	*Moorea: Journal of the Irish Garden Plant Society*
NAI	National Archives of Ireland
NLI	National Library of Ireland
OED	*Oxford English dictionary, 2nd ed.*
OKR	*Old Kilkenny Review*
OS	Ordnance Survey
PRIA	*Proceedings of the Royal Irish Academy*
PRO Kew	Public Records Office, Kew
PROI	Public Records Office of Ireland
PRONI	Public Records Office of Northern Ireland
QBIGS	*Quarterly Bulletin of the Irish Georgian Society*
RSLC	*Record Society of Lancashire and Cheshire*
SIH	*Sussex Industrial History*
TCD	Trinity College Dublin Manuscripts Library
TNNNS	*Transactions of the Norfolk and Norwich Naturalists Society*
TRIA	*Transactions of the Royal Irish Academy*
UAHS	*Ulster Architectural Heritage Society*
UJA	*Ulster Journal of Archaeology*

Notes

1   T.C. Barnard, 'Gardening, diet and "improvement" in later seventeenth-century Ireland', *Garden History*, 10:1 (1990), pp 71–85.

CHAPTER 1
The political, intellectual and economic background to landed estates

1   The barony of Onealland in Portadown described by William Brooke for the Dublin Philosophical Society in the 1680s, TCD, Dub. Phil. Soc. 883/1 (I.1.2) fo. 223. One of the earl of Orrery's avowed missions was the 'planting of a wild and dangerous country with industrious and faithful English'.
2   *CSPI, Sept. 1669–Dec. 1670*, p. viii.
3   8 Sept. 1685, duke of Newcastle to earl of Clarendon, in S.W. Singer (ed.), *Correspondence of Henry Hyde, earl of Clarendon* (London, 1828), p. 157.
4   James Butler, 12th earl and 1st duke of Ormond (1610–88), was appointed lord lieutenant of Ireland on three occasions. Ormond was commander of Royalist forces during the Confederate War in 1641 and went into exile following defeat in the battle of Rathmines in 1649. During his exile he became one of the chief confidants of Charles II. On his appointment as lord lieutenant in Jan. 1664 he became the first Irish chief governor in over a century. S.J. Connolly (ed.), *Oxford companion to Irish history* (Oxford, 2002), p. 418.
5   By order of parliament 1653 Dunmore was set apart from the Ormond estates for the use of the duchess and her children. See T.J. Clohosey, 'Dunmore House', *OKR*, 4 (1951), pp 44–58, p. 44.
6   On 27 February 1661/2, it was ordered that Lords Massereene and Kingston, Sir George Lane and Sir Audley Mervin, who had 'been entrusted with and diligently prosecuted the Settlement of Ireland' each be granted 'a convenient dwelling fortified house such as each shall choose of in Dublin'. *CSPI, 1660–2*, p. 234.
7   To give but a few instances of the web of intermarriages between Irish, Anglo-Norman and Cromwellians, the Anglo-Norman Sir Adam Loftus was married to the English earl of Cork's daughter Dorothy, who when she was widowed married the Catholic Anglo-Norman Colonel Talbot. The English George Lane married Dorcas Brabazon, the daughter of the 3rd earl of Meath, in 1664. The daughter of Sir Walter Coppinger, a rich Roman Catholic from Cork, married a Cromwellian man. The Irish aristocrat Morrough O'Brien married Elizabeth St Leger, daughter of the president of Munster, Sir William St Leger. The Irish 2nd earl of Inchiquin was married to Margaret Boyle, another daughter of the earl of Cork. See Jane Ohlmeyer, *Making Ireland English* (New Haven, CT, 2012), p. 420.
8   Jane Austen, *Persuasion*. See also A.P.W. Malcomson, *The pursuit of the heiress: aristocratic marriage in Ireland, 1750–1820* (Belfast, 2006).
9   The Dillon papers contain a lease by William Talbot of Carton dated 27 July 1617; Edward MacLysaght (ed.), 'Report on the Dillon papers', *AH*, 20 (1958), p. 36. William FitzGerald writing about Carton's history in 1903 stated that William Talbot, grandfather of Richard Talbot, duke of Tyrconnell, built Carton sometime after 1623, and that the house formed 'the nucleus of the present mansion'. Walter FitzGerald, 'Carton', *JCKAS*, 1 (1903), pp 2–34.

10   Sir William Dongan, later earl of Limerick, came from an old Catholic family, and was the eldest of three sons of Sir John Dongan of Castletown. His mother was a sister of Richard Talbot, who became earl of Tyrconnell and later lieutenant governor of Ireland. He was attainted of high treason in 1687; the attainted land was described as 446 acres in Castletown and 224 acres in Kildrought. TCD, MS 1460. Dongan's younger brother and successor, Colonel Thomas Dungan, became governor of New York.

11   Arthur Capel, earl of Essex (1631–83), appointed lord lieutenant in 1672. He committed suicide in 1683 after being imprisoned in the Tower of London.

12   22 July 1673, PRO, SP/63/334, fo. 38.

13   Sir William Petty (1623–87). Petty was a true polymath; a scientist, philosopher and inventor and member of the Dublin Philosophical Society. He first came to Ireland during the Commonwealth where he carried out the 'Down Survey' – the first thorough mapping of the country.

14   William Petty, *Political anatomy of Ireland* (London, 1691), p. 89.

15   As a measure of this success he stated that 'the poorest now in Ireland ride on horse-back, when heretofore, the best ran on foot like animals'. C.H. Hull (ed.), *The economic writings of Sir William Petty* (Cambridge, 1899), p. 203.

16   Keith Thomas, *Man and the natural world* (Oxford, 1983), p. 42.

17   Ibid., p. 228.

18   TCD, Dub. Phil. Soc. MS 883/1 (I.1.2), fo. 298.

19   Bodl. Carte MS 229, fo. 70 'The improvement of Ireland' c.1690. The author of the pamphlet is unknown, but thought to be Nicholas Plunkett, the younger son of the 2nd earl of Fingall. Patrick Kelly, 'The improvement of Ireland', *AH*, 35 (1992), pp 45–84, p. 46.

20   Burton House was destroyed by fire and plundered in 1690. 'In 1690, when the owner of Charleville was a child and absent, the duke of Berwick, having dined in the house, ordered it to be fired and stood by to see it consumed'. Richard Bagwell, *Ireland under the Stuarts*, vol. 3 (London, 1963), pp 310–11.

21   25 Oct. 1690, 'The house at Lismore being most destroyed and possessed by the soldiers'. NLI, Lismore MS 13226 (1).

22   Nicholas Plunkett to Captain Thomas Flower, undated, 1691. 'My two eldest sons are in rebellion and that I put my youngest son into King James's army that being sent with others into England he from there escaped into France and I followed him hither'. His son later returned 'home into Ireland and was killed under the walls of Derry', NLI, Flower MS 11,472 (2).

23   Throughout the reign of Charles II, there remained an undercurrent of Catholic agitation. Chancellor Maurice Eustace wrote to Secretary Nichols that 'seditions, treasonable or Roman Catholic tracts' and 'books of controversy and libels' were being illegally imported into Ireland from France, 18 Sept. 1661, *CSPI, 1660–2*, p. 425.

24   John H. Kennedy, *Thomas Dongan, governor of New York (1682–1688)* (Washington, DC, 1930), p. 102. For example, Hillsborough (1662), Baltinglass (1675), Portarlington (1679), Longford (1680) and Blessington (1681): *Appendix to the report of the commissioners appointed to inquire into municipal corporations in Ireland* (HC 1835: 25).

25   For example, Charleville, Kenmare and Eyrecourt. Other plantation towns were resettled and redesigned such as Phillipstown (now Daingean) and Bandon.

26   Sir Laurence Parsons sought to fill Parsonstown (Birr) with English: 'If there be any persons about you that wants farms and can bring stock with them I can supply them with land in Ireland on easy terms ... I have also a want of good tradesmen in the town of Birr, pray tell our neighbours and if any come over let them be such as are able for our kingdom is over

stock with beggars', undated, post 1660, Birr Castle, Rosse MS163. Roger Boyle, the 1st earl of Orrery, brought over forty Dutch families to Limerick in 1661, 'It did my heart good' he wrote to Secretary Nichols 7 Sept. 1661, 'to see them so busy in their manufactures and plantations', *CSPI, 1660–2*, p. 415. See also Thomas Gimlette, 'The settlement in Waterford, the French settlers in Ireland', *UJA*, 4:4 (1856), pp 198–221, 201; Charles Nicholas de la Cherois Purdon, 'The French settlers in Ireland, no. 1: the Huguenot colony at Lisburn, county of Antrim', *UJA*, 1 (1853), p. 209.

27 Robert Molesworth to Lettice Molesworth, 16 July 1712, NLI, P3753. Abeles or abeals refer to the white poplar, *Populus alba*.

28 Roger Boyle was very sectarian in his views: he changed the name of the original village on which Charleville was built from Rathgogan and stated that 'I admit neither presbyter, papist, independent, nor, as our proclamation says, any other sort of fanatic to plant there, but all good Protestants'. See Smith, *Cork*, vol. 1, p. 303.

29 A member of the Dublin Philosophical Society at Trinity College and brother of Arthur Dobbs of Castle Dobbs in Antrim.

30 Sir George Rawdon (1604–84); Rawdon was the 1st baronet of Moira in Co. Down.

31 Jimmy Irvine (ed.), 'Richard Dobbs, notes for his description of Co. Antrim written in 1683', *Glynns*, 7 (1979), pp 35–49.

32 Pole Cosby (1703–66), owner of Stradbally Hall in Laois. The father to whom he refers to is Dudley Cosby.

33 Pole Cosby, 'Autobiography of Pole Cosby, of Stradbally, Queen's County, 1703–1737 (?)', *JCKAS*, 5 (1906–8), pp 79–99.

34 Earl of Burlington to William Congreve, 1698, NLI, Lismore MS 13,226 (2).

35 Several references to such ships appear in the *Council Book of Kinsale, 1652–1800*, pp 40, 57, 63, 72.

36 In 1662, the duke of Ormond brought before the Irish parliament 'An act for encouraging Protestant strangers and others to inhabit Ireland'.

37 Sir Richard Bulkeley (17 Aug. 1660–7 Apr. 1710), 2nd baronet of Old Bawn.

CHAPTER 2
The changing appearance of the Irish landscape in the seventeenth century

1 'Soon as the English had subdued the martial spirit of the Irish, and obtained for themselves the peaceable enjoyment of the lands which they had won with their reeking swords, they introduced the formal style of gardening, which then, and for some years before, prevailed in England', Joseph Cooper Walker, 'Essay on the rise and progress of gardening in Ireland', *TRIA*, 4 (1790), pp 3–19, 10.

2 'Lord Sunderland's seat at Althorp [since burned and well rebuilt]; tis placed in a pretty open bottom, very finely watered and flanked with stately woods and groves in a park with a canal, yet the water is not running, which is a defect. It was moated round after the old manner, but is now dry and turf'd with a sweet carpet: above all are admirable and magnificent the several ample gardens furnished with the choicest fruit in England, and exquisitely kept. Great plenty of oranges, and other curiosities. The park full of fowl ...' 14 July 1675, E.S. de Beer (ed.), *John Evelyn's diary*, vol. 3 (Oxford, 2000), p. 207.

3 1 Oct. 1661, Guy de la Bédoyère (ed.), *Diary of John Evelyn* (Suffolk, 1995), p. 123.

4 '[N]ow planted with sweet rows of lime-trees, and the canal for water now near perfected, also the hare park. In the garden is a rich and noble fountain, of sirens and statues etc. cast

in copper by Fanelli, but no plenty of water. The cradle walk of hornbeam in the garden, is for the perplexed twining of the trees, very observable etc. Another Parterre there is which they call Paradise in which a pretty banqueting house, west over a cave or cellar; all these gardens might be exceedingly improved, as being too narrow for such a Palace', 9 June 1662, de la Bédoyère (ed.), *Diary of John Evelyn*, p. 129.

5 '[W]ent to dine at my Lord Arlington's, who had newly built a house of great cost (his Architect Mr. Pratt) I believe little less than 20,000 pounds, seated in a park, with a sweet prospect and stately avenue, water still defective'. 21 July 1670, de la Bédoyère (ed.), *Diary of John Evelyn*, p. 176.

6 Sir William Temple (25 Apr. 1628–27 Jan. 1699), son of Sir John Temple of Dublin, was a diplomat and politician. He lived for a time at Staplestown in Carlow.

7 Temple, *Upon the gardens of Epicurus*, p. 20.

8 Chandra Mukerji, *Territorial ambitions and the gardens of Versailles* (Cambridge, 1997), p. 2.

9 Nigel Everett, *The Tory view of landscape* (New Haven, CT, 1994), p. 7.

10 For a discussion of Robert Molesworth and Whiggism in gardening see Finola O'Kane, *Landscape design in eighteenth-century Ireland* (Cork, 2004), pp 30–1, 34–5, 37, 42–3.

11 O'Kane believes that Breckdenston expressed the force of the Irish Whig ideal. See O'Kane, *Landscape design in eighteenth-century Ireland*, p. 2.

12 For a discussion see David Hayton, *Ruling Ireland, 1685–1742* (Woodbridge, Suffolk, 2004), pp 35–7.

13 Ibid.

14 Hayton, *Ruling Ireland*, p. 37.

15 *The Spectator*, 28 June 1712.

16 O'Kane, *Landscape design in eighteenth-century Ireland*, p. 37.

17 John Turpin, 'Continental influence in eighteenth-century Ireland', *Irish Arts Review*, 4 (1987), pp 50–7, 54.

18 The eighteenth-century Dromoland House was demolished in the 1830s to make way for the present castellated mansion.

19 See, for example, Batty Langley, *New principles of gardening* (London, 1728). Langley discussed the 'niggard breadth' of walks in early gardens, but goes on to describe how to design similar, broader walks, pp 4, 197.

20 Augusta Hall, *The autobiography and correspondence of Mary Granville, Mrs Delany*, vol. 1 (London, 1862), p. 315.

21 Walker, 'The rise and progress of gardening in Ireland', p. 18.

22 Brewer, *The beauties of Ireland*, vol. 1, pp 219–20. In 1760, Delany expressed her alarm at the destruction and obliteration of the formal gardens at Longleat by Capability Brown.

23 David Leatherbarrow, 'Character, geometry and perspective: the 3rd earl of Shaftesbury's principles of garden design', *Garden History*, 4:4 (1984), pp 332–58.

24 Campbell (1676–1729) was an architect who is credited with introducing classicism to Britain and Ireland. He produced the first of three volumes of *Vitruvius Britannicus* in 1715 in order to market his architectural services. He expressed contempt for the baroque and promoted the classical ideals of Roman architect Vitruvius and the sixteenth-century Italian renaissance architect Andrea Palladio. Richard Boyle, 3rd earl of Burlington, hired Campbell to remodel Burlington House in Chiswick in 1717.

25 Carole Fry, 'Spanning the political divide: neo-Palladianism and the early eighteenth-century landscape', *Garden History*, 31:2 (2003), p. 181.

26 A certificate dated 25 Feb. 1661 by Captain John Purdon testifies to the loyalty of Thomas FitzGerald of Glin who never fought in the wars but 'being an unwealdy man'; i.e., fat, he

lived quietly on his own estate 'without intermeddling with the affairs of those times', *CSPI, 1660–2*, p. 275.

27   See chapters 4 and 8 below.

28   A Persian waterwheel was mentioned by John Worlidge in 'the explanation of the frontispiece' in *Systema agriculturae* in 1668: 'In yonder vale hard by the river stands a water-engine, which the wind commands to fertilize the meads, on the other side a Persian wheel is placed both large and wide to the same intent'.

29   Young, *A tour in Ireland*, p. 65. Molesworth commented that '[t]he Persians are and always were the best contrivers and drawers of aqueducts underground by reason of the dryness of their country', R. Molesworth to John Molesworth, 27 Feb. 1722, NLI, P3753.

30   Jacques Boyceau, *Traité du jardinage selon les raisons de la nature et de l'art* (Paris, 1631), chapters 14 and 15, pp 82–3, discussed in Vanessa Bezemer Sellers, *Courtly gardens in Holland, 1600–1650* (Amsterdam, 2001), p. 45.

31   E. Charles Nelson, 'Sir Arthur Rawdon (1662–1695) of Moira: his life and letters, family and friends, and his Jamaican plants' *BNHPSP*, 10:2 (1981), pp 30–52.

32   Rawdon to Sloane, 4 May 1692, BL, Sloane MS 4036, fo. 121.

33   Sir Hans Sloane (1660–1711). Sloane was born in Killyleagh, Co. Down. He was a physician, botanist and collector of antiquities. He founded the Chelsea Physic Garden in 1673. In 1687 Sloane embarked on a hugely successful expedition to the West Indies to collect plants, retuning in 1689. The trip is chronicled in *Voyage to Jamaica* (London, 1707).

34   Nelson, 'Sir Arthur Rawdon', p. 41.

35   A member of the Dublin Philosophical Society described the houses of gentlemen in Co. Wexford as being 'fortified with castles of quadrangle form, some sixty feet high within walls five feet thick' and we are told that 'not many of these were ruinous', TCD, Dub. Phil. Soc. MS 883/1 (I.1.2), fo. 52. The development of Scottish gardens was somewhat similar to that of Irish gardens. Scotland suffered from a combination of political insecurity, economic poverty and colonization as did Ireland. It has also been noted that utility and productivity were influential in how Scottish gardens evolved. See Charles McKean, 'The Scottish Renaissance country seat in its setting', *Garden History*, 31:2 (2003), pp 141–2.

36   'Dineley's journal', *JKSIAS*, 6:1 (1867), p. 75.

37   *Clarendon letters*, vol. 1, p. 237. Flower Hyde, née Blackhouse, countess of Clarendon (?–1700). Married Henry Hyde, 2nd earl of Clarendon, lord lieutenant of Ireland between September 1685 and February 1687. Henry Hyde's sister was married to James II.

38   Hardiman Atlas TCD MS 1209/2/82.

39   Charles E. Nelson, *Northern gardens* (Belfast, 1984), p. 5.

40   Now derelict, the building was dramatically altered and enlarged in neo-Gothic style in about 1812 with new wings and 4 slender towers to the front by Richard Morrison.

41   Arthur Vicars, 'Old Bawn, Co. Dublin', *JCKAS*, 5 (1906–8), pp 229–37, p. 229.

42   Bulkeley had a non-specified 'deformity' and was regarded as exceedingly accomplished. He was a fellow of Trinity College Dublin and contributed several papers to the Royal Society of which he was a fellow, giving a paper on one of his inventions, a self-propelling chariot. He was a friend and correspondent of John Evelyn and died in 1710. Vicars, 'Old Bawn', p. 230.

43   Journal of a tour to Dublin by James Verdon, 1699, BL, Add. MS 41769, fos. 29–43.

44   For a detailed account of the construction of Dromoland, see Finola O'Kane 'Leamaneh and Dromoland: the O'Brien ambition, parts I & II, *JIGS*, 7 (2004), pp 65–79 & 81–105. NLI, Inchiquin MS 14470, domestic and estate account of Donat O'Brien, 20 May 1714: A mason Dennis Flynn was paid to work 'in the new building on the south side [of] the new house and tower'.

45 Robert Molesworth (7 Sept. 1656–22 May 1725); his father had made a fortune supplying food and provisions to Cromwell's army in Ireland. He lived at Breckdenston House in Swords and was MP for Swords. He was created Viscount Molesworth of Swords in 1715.

46 The plan corresponds closely to the visible remnants of the garden and the early OSI maps. For a discussion see Finola O'Kane, 'Leamaneh and Dromoland: the O'Brien ambition, part I', *JIGS*, 7 (2004), pp 64–79, 70–4.

47 At Monivea in Galway, the ffrench family incorporated a tower house in to the new house. Borris House in Co. Carlow incorporated the original castle into an eighteenth-century house (rebuilt in 1820 to designs of Richard Morrison). An early tower house has been incorporated into the fabric of a later house at Rathcoffey, Co. Kildare. Another house tacked onto a tower house is Leamaneh in Clare.

48 'I amuse myself with the business of my estate and the diversions of my grounds and gardens. I dare aver that I have by much the finest canal near completed in the king's dominions, with regard to the situation, in respect to the house and gardens and to the sea and to all the prospects, 'tis not much less than that in St James's Park, but 'tis infinitely more beautiful and herein I do not exaggerate'. Robert Molesworth to Lord Coningsby, 26 May 1719, PRONI, De Ros MS D638/82/2.

CHAPTER 3
Improvement and the culture of improvement

1 'I sailed this morning with his Majesty [on] one of his yachts. Then he discoursed to me of the improvement of Gardens and buildings (now very rare in England, comparatively to other countries)', 1 Oct. 1661, de la Bédoyère (ed.), *Diary of John Evelyn*, p. 123.

2 In the mid-eighteenth century, Charles Smith observed that although Burton House in Cork had been destroyed by fire, the seventeenth-century 'improvements', orchards and a 'noble park' remained, which he described as 'very beautiful and extensive'. Charles Smith, *The ancient and present state of the city of Cork*, Book 2, vol. 1 (1750), p. 316.

3 'Dined next day at Moira Lord Rawdon's; his house pretty good, but his improvements not in the best taste'. John Loveday, *Diary of a tour in 1732* (London, 1890), p. 154.

4 Smith, *Cork*, vol. 1, p. 207.

5 Sir Robert Southwell to Sir Phillip Perceval, 21 Aug. 1679. Southwell advised his grandson Phillip Perceval to invest any money made in Ireland in the East India Company. *HMC Egmont*, 2, p. 84.

6 'Travels of Sir William Brereton in Ireland 1635' reprinted in C.L. Falkiner, *Illustrations of Irish history and topography* (London, 1904). Ormond Castle, Carrick-on-Suir, was rebuilt by the 10th earl of Ormond c.1532; Thomas Butler had the castle rebuilt again in the 1560s and 1570s.

7 25 Sept. 1686, Patrick Melvin (ed.), 'Sir Paul Rycaut's memoranda and letters from Ireland, 1686–1687', *AH*, 27 (1972), pp 120–82, at p. 134.

8 *The state letters of Henry Hyde, earl of Clarendon*, 2 vols (London, 1828), vol. 1, p. 7.

9 William Waring to William Layfield, undated, spring, 1675, PRONI, Waring MS D695 1. A cancelled draft letter on the other side of the paper read 'this country is so impoverished that unless God mend the times, as I hope he will, some of the tenants will not be able to pay any rent'. The town of Waringstown built up around the house, another new town formed post 1660.

10 See James Turner, *The politics of landscape: rural scenery and society in English poetry, 1630–1660* (Cambridge, MA, 1979).

11 BL, Add. MS 15950, fo. 153.

12 The full title is: *England's great interest in the well planting of Ireland with English people, discussed. Wherein is briefly stated the benefits that will arise thereby, viz. First, to England itself, secondly, to the English people in Ireland. Thirdly, to the Irish themselves. Fourthly, some rules proposed in order to the practicing of it. Fifthly, some objections against the work, answered* (1684).

13 William Brooke, TCD, Dub. Phil. Soc. MS 883/1 (I.1.2), fo. 223.

14 A later popular English book was the nurserymen London and Wise's *The retir'd gard'ner* (1706).

15 Dézallier d'Argenville, *Theory and practice of gardening*, pp 18–19.

16 See Douglas Chambers, *The planters of the English landscape garden* (New Haven, CT, 1993), p. 5.

17 E. Petty to Robert Southwell, 12 July 1684, BL, Add. MS 72855, fo. 21. William Petty himself wrote to Southwell on 9 Aug. That same year 'dear cousin Neddy can't lose his time in learning so much of the *Georgics* by heart, as contained the pure rules of husbandry'. BL, Add. MS 72850, fo. 23.

18 Virgil, *Georgics* book 1.

19 Ibid., book 2.

20 Chambers, *Planters of the English landscape garden*, p. 5.

21 John Worlidge, *Systema horticulturae* (London, 1677), p. 1.

22 Michael Leslie '"Bringing ingenuity into fashion": the reformation of husbandry' in Therese O'Malley and Joachim Wolschke-Bulmahn (eds), *John Evelyn's 'Elysium Britannicum' and European gardening* (New Haven, CT, 1998), p. 131.

23 Dennis E. Cosgrove, *Social formation and symbolic landscape* (Madison, WI, 1988), p. 7.

24 Mukerji, *Territorial ambitions and the gardens of Versailles*, p. 155.

25 Therese O'Malley, 'Introduction' in O'Malley et al. (eds), *John Evelyn's 'Elysium Britannicum'*, p. 19.

26 Cosgrove, *Social formation and symbolic landscape*, p. 196. In the context of gardens it was concluded by John Worlidge that man may 'without vanity conceive that a garden of pleasant avenues, walks, fruits, flowers, grots and other branches sprung from it, well composed is the only complete and permanent inanimate object of delight the world affords, ever complying with our various and mutable minds, feeding and supplying all fancies with daily novels'. Worlidge, *Systema horticulturae*, p. 1.

27 For example, the work by Newton, Descartes and the members of the Royal Society.

28 Rawdon was Conway's brother-in-law and also his land agent.

29 Edward, 1st Viscount Conway (*c.*1623–11 Aug. 1683). He was also 3rd Viscount Killultagh. Conway was a member of the Privy Council and the Royal Society and a friend of the duke of Ormond.

30 The contribution of women to the development of gardens and estate management has frequently been overlooked. Lettice Molesworth oversaw almost all of the garden work and landscape interventions at Breckdenston in her husband Robert's absence. Likewise, Elizabeth Ormond was entirely responsible for improvements at Dunmore and directed many of the municipal improvements to Kilkenny town. Ann Conway, née Finch, 1630–79, the wife of Edward Conway, 3rd Viscount Conway, was a highly educated and substantial person. She converted to Quakerism and was a regular correspondent with William Penn. Her philosophical work *Principia philosophiae* (Amsterdam, 1690) was posthumously published.

31 Blanche Henrey, *British botanical and horticultural literature before 1800*, 3 vols (London, 1975), vol. 2, p. 169.

32 Lawrence intended to write a chapter in part 2 of *The interest of Ireland* concerned with 'distilling, preserving and conserving, with the right ordering of cider, perry, metheglin, wines of plums, currants, strawberries, gooseberries etc.'. Anonymous, *The art of pruning fruit-trees, with an explanation of some words which gardeners make use of in speaking of trees, etc.* (London, 1685); *Fruit walls improved by inclining to the horizon* (1669) (no copies of this book survive). John Worlidge, *Vinetum Britannicum* (1676); William Ellis, *The compleat planter and ciderist or choice collections and observations for the propagating all manner of fruit trees* (1685); John Evelyn's translation of Jean de la Quintinye's *Instruction pur les jardins fruitiers et potagers*, published as *The compleat gard'ner; or directions for cultivating and right ordering of fruit-gardens and kitchen-gardens* (London, 1693).

33 Though producing little himself, Hartlib was instrumental in the commissioning and publishing of many works. After the Restoration his fortunes declined, perhaps in part to his close association with the Commonwealth, and also to the falling out of fashion of his canon. Few if any of his books were reprinted after 1660, although much of them was incorporated into later works by new authors such as his friend and close associate John Evelyn. For example, Evelyn borrowed liberally from Hartlib's *Reformed commonwealth of bees* (1655), *Legacy* (1655) and *Cornu-copia* (1652) in *Elysium Britannicum*, BL, Add. MS 78628 A-B.

34 Ralph Austen, *A treatise of fruit-trees* (London, 1653).

35 Anthony Wood, *Athenae oxonienses*, quoted in Henrey, *British botanical and horticultural literature*, pp 170–2.

36 Michael Leslie, 'Bringing ingenuity into fashion' in O'Malley et al. (eds), *John Evelyn's 'Elysium Britannicum'*, p. 144.

37 *Elysium Britannicum*, BL, Add. MS 78628 A-B.

38 Ibid.

39 Ibid.

40 Used for dye. 'Mather … grows naturally in Kerry' and can be bought 'for a trifle' which yielded 'as much as ten pounds an acre'. TCD, Dub. Phil. Soc. MS 883/1 (I.1.2), fo. 266.

41 Lawrence, *The interest of Ireland*, ch. 3.

42 Bligh, who 'beat his ploughshare into a sword', was a captain in the Roundhead army, and dedicated his introduction 'to the Rt. Hon the L General Cromwell', adding the legend 'Vive La Re Publick'. G.E. Fussell, *The old English farming books* (London, 1957), p. 52.

43 Publication of Irish almanacs appears to have been virtually suspended during the Commonwealth.

44 John D'Alton, *History of the county of Dublin* (Dublin, 1838), pp 328–9.

45 The entire library was sold c.1721. See Patrick Kelly, 'The improvement of Ireland', *AH*, 35 (1992), pp 45–84.

46 Ibid. The book was published almost coincidentally with founding of Dublin Society, later the Royal Dublin Society, in 1731. Although it is curious that Rye does not appear to have been a member.

47 Mukerji, *Territorial ambitions and the gardens of Versailles*, p. 29.

48 Evelyn himself pointed out that these topics had been covered extensively in his own translation of Nicolas de Bonnefon's *Le jardinier François* (1658). Mark Laird, 'Parterre, grove, and flower garden: European horticulture and planting design in John Evelyn's time' in O'Malley et al. (eds), *John Evelyn's 'Elysium Britannicum'*, p. 75.

49 6 Dec. 1658, de Beer (ed.), *John Evelyn's diary*, vol. 3, p. 106.

CHAPTER 4

Pleasure gardens

1 For an important account of Molesworth's improvements at Breckdenston, see Finola O'Kane, *Landscape design in eighteenth-century Ireland* (Cork, 2004), chapter 1, pp 10–45. Robert Molesworth to Lettice Molesworth, 7 Aug. 1704, Killadoon MS Q/1/1.

2 Contract, 27 Sept. 1670, for house at Burton, Co. Cork 'That the said William Kenn shall build at the place aforesaid a house, whose length outside shall be 76 feet, breadth outside shall be 57 feet, the height from the upper part of the hall floor to the wall place 30 feet and a half. The walls to be made with stone, lime and sand, the outside walls to be three feet and a half in thickness; the middle wall to be seven feet in thickness for the first storey and three foot for the outward walls for the second storey, and the same thickness for the middle wall, which must rise higher than the outer walls, six feet. In this wall there must be placed 12 chimneys, viz four in the hall story, four in the dining room storey, and four in the garret, and all the said chimneys to be made in proportion to the several rooms, and to rise by shafts of brick seven feet above the top of the roof, the shafts standing from each other ten inches', *HMC Egmont*, 2, p. 14. William Kenn died before the house was completed and his son Benjamin worked with Thomas Smith to finish the house.

3 24 Nov. 1683, *HMC Egmont*, 2, p. 137.

4 26 Apr. 1593, *Inchiquin papers*, p. 288.

5 James Turner, *The politics of landscape*, p. 1.

6 William Temple, *Upon the gardens of Epicurus* (London, 1690), p. 22.

7 'Olitory' meaning kitchen garden from holitory, *holitor* a market gardener in Latin.

8 William Montgomery, 1683, TCD, Dub. Phil. Soc. papers MS 883/1 (I.1.2).

9 Richard Bagwell, *Ireland under the Stuarts*, vol. 3 (London, 1963), p. 311.

10 The extent to which ideas and influences were transferred around Europe can be seen in the career of Salomon de Caus (1576–1626). De Caus, a Huguenot from Dieppe, was an architect who had made a tour of Italy between 1595 and 1598 where he visited the gardens of Pratolino. He then worked in Brussels for the Archduke Albert VII as an engineer. In 1610 he travelled to England to work for Henry, prince of Wales, where he was commissioned by the Elector Palatine Friedrich V, husband to Princess Elizabeth Stuart, to work on his gardens at Heidelberg Castle. Reinbard Zimmermann, '*Hortus palatinus* of Salomon de Caus' in Monique Mosser and George Teyssat (eds), *The history of garden design: the Western tradition from the Renaissance to the present day* (London, 1990), p. 157.

11 Temple, *Upon the gardens of Epicurus*, p. 23.

12 Claudia Lazzaro, 'Italy is a garden' in Mirka Beneš and Dianne Harris (eds), *Villas and gardens in early modern Italy and France* (Cambridge, 2001), p. 29.

13 See Christopher Thacker, *The history of gardens* (Oakland, CA, 1985), p. 139.

14 Pliny's influence on the Italian Renaissance garden was enormous. The reawakening of interest in classic texts led to gardeners trying to recreate Pliny's garden on their own estates. Examples of this can be seen in the series of famous paintings of the Medici villas depicted by Giusto Utens, which in turn were highly influential on European gardening in the following centuries. 'The design and beauty of the buildings are greatly surpassed by the riding-ground. The centre is quite open so that the whole extent of the course can be seen as one enters. It is planted round with ivy-clad plane trees, green with their own leaves above, and below with the ivy which climbs over trunk and branch and links tree to tree as it spreads across them. Box shrubs grow between the plane trees, and outside there is a ring of laurel bushes, which add their shade to that of the planes. Here the straight part of the

course ends, curves round in a semicircle, and changes its appearance, becoming darker and
more densely shaded by the cypress trees planted round to shelter it, whereas the inner
circuits – for there are several – are in open sunshine; roses grow there and the cool shadow
alternates with the pleasant warmth of the sun. At the end of the winding alleys of the
rounded end of the course you return to the straight path, or rather paths, for there are
several separated by intervening box hedges. Between the grass lawns here there are box
shrubs clipped into innumerable shapes, some being letters which spell the gardener's name
or his master's; small obelisks of box alternate with fruit trees, and then suddenly in the
midst of this ornamental scene is what looks like a piece of rural country planted there. The
open space in the middle is set off by low plane trees planted on each side; farther off are
acanthuses with their flexible glossy leaves, then more box figures and names'. *The letters of
the younger Pliny*, pp 142–3.

15 30 Jan. 1682, BL, Egmont, Add. MS 46960A, fos. 39b–40. Barbor appears to have
    completed the work satisfactorily as he was paid £33, 13s., 11 Dec. 1684. BL, Egmont, Add.
    MS 46961, fo. 168.

16 NLI, Inchiquin MS14,389, f. 30. See also O'Kane, 'Leamaneh and Dromoland, part II', p. 95.

17 25 Oct. 1720, *Kenmare MS*, p. 121.

18 Dineley's drawing of the Turrets in Carlow shows the house of 'Joseph Davis, Gardiner':
    'Dineley's journal', *JKSIAS*, 4:1 (1862), p. 44.

19 TCD, MS 1460/21.

20 La Quintinye implored gardeners managing jardins potagers to exercise restraint and
    benevolence by not selling excess produce to enrich themselves. At Versailles, Louis XIV
    ordered that a stand be set up in order to distribute excess produce to the poor of Versailles,
    which Mukerji suggests transformed the potential profit of gardens into means for a
    paternalistic exchange. Mukerji, *Territorial ambitions and the gardens of Versailles*, p. 170.

21 It was recorded that 'hucksters' selling fruit in Kinsale left their rotting detritus on the street
    outside Robert Southwell's house, with the result that the town scavenger had to be ordered
    to keep it clean. Grand jury presentments for Kinsale, 25 June 1658. Edward MacLysaght
    (ed.), 'Report on Old Mss of Kinsale', *AH*, 15 (1944), p. 163.

22 'I wish the rest has not been so to'. Edward Doyne to Thomas Flower, 4 Oct. 1690, NLI,
    Flower MS 11473 (1).

23 Lettice Molesworth to Robert Molesworth, 19 Apr. 1700, *HMC Various collections*, vol. 8
    (1913), p. 220

24 Countess of Orrery to Lionel Beecher, 13 Jan. 1682/3 MacLysaght, *Orrery papers*, p. 267.

25 Richard Bagg's book of payments on behalf of Burlington estates, NLI, Lismore MS 6300.

26 'I am very glad you have pieced up with Francis; My Lord Chesterfield give £10 a year
    standing wages, and 10d. a week board wages, and many other profits of his garden, to a
    worse gardener than Francis'. Edward Conway to George Rawdon, 20 June 1671, Sarah
    Hutton (ed.), *The Conway letters* (Oxford 1992), pp 249–51.

27 Walter FitzGerald, 'Carton', *JCKAS*, 4 (1903–5), pp 1–34, p. 11.

28 Roger Boyle, 1st earl of Orrery (1621–79), third son of the 1st earl of Cork. See T.C.
    Barnard, 'Gardening, diet and "improvement" in later seventeenth-century Ireland', *Garden
    History*, 10:1 (1990), pp 71–85, p. 79.

29 Ibid., p. 79.

30 BL, Egmont, Add. MS 46940, fos 39–40. Blandstone was gardener to Sir John Perceval. For
    Mr Phillips, see TCD, King MS 751/1 fo. 16.

31 Val Savage to John Perceval 2 Dec. 1653, *HMC Egmont* 1, p. 528

32 Richard Bulkeley to Martin Lister, Nov. 1694, Bodl., Lister MS 36, fo. 106.

33 Henshaw also worked for Lord Barrymore, where he staked out an area to 'take 8,460 elms', *Kenmare manuscripts*, pp 35–6.

34 Ibid.

35 George Rawdon to Edward Conway, *CSPI, 1663–5*, p. 441.

36 'I am very glad you have pieced up with Francis; My Lord Chesterfield give £10 a year standing wages, and 10d a week board wages, and many other profits of his garden, to a worse gardener than Francis'. Edward Conway to George Rawdon, 20 June 1671, Hutton, *Conway letters*, pp 249–51.

37 'I have taken a gardener at London one Thomas Harrison, who Mr Sherard has sent on to come over and have sent to bring me over some things, and I do desire of you yet you would recommend him to some of the merchants to draw a bill on me for what he shall have occasion for his journey and those things which I suppose will not be above 20l'. Rawdon to Sloane, 24 June 1691, BL, Sloane MS 4036 fo. 105.

38 Rawdon's Harrison was engaged in 1691, Bulkeley mentions his Mr Harrison in 1694, so there is a strong likelihood that they were one and the same.

39 '[A]t Killruddery, Co. Wicklow, the seat of the earls of Meath, there still exists intact the most complete late seventeenth or early eighteenth-century formal garden in the country'. Desmond FitzGerald, 'Irish gardens of the eighteenth century', *Apollo* (Sept. 1968), p. 186; Mark Bence-Jones, *Burke's guide to country houses*, vol. 1 (London, 1978), p. 172.

40 'Sir William Petty was complaining that Bonnet, his French gardener, who had been in his service for twelve years, had gone to live with the earl of Meath'. Keith Lamb and Patrick Bowe, *A history of gardening in Ireland* (1995), p. 22. 'It is known that a gardener called Bonet, thought to be French, entered the service of the 4th earl of Meath in 1684': *The Phaidon garden book* (London, 2008), p. 299. 'In 1684, the 4th earl employed a noted French gardener, Monsieur Bonet, who was inspired by King Louis XIV's garden designer, Andre Le Nôtre, at Versailles'; FitzGerald, *Irish gardens*, p. 162. According to Killruddery's own website, 'Bonnet' was both a 'landscape architect' and 'a pupil of [André] Le Nôtre'.

41 *The Dublin Intelligence*, 4 Apr. 1711.

42 James Brewer, *The beauties of Ireland*, vol. 1 (London, 1825), pp 284–5.

43 William Petty to Elizabeth Petty, 27 Mar. 1864, BL, Add. MS 72856, fo. 230.

44 This statement appears in Lamb and Bowe, *History of gardening in Ireland*, p. 102.

45 Marquis of Lansdowne, *Petty papers* (London, 1927), vol. 2, p. 103. Dance appears to have been acting as chief agent in Dublin for Petty's Irish estates. The letter is addressed to James Waller, Petty's brother-in-law (and sometime amanuenses), in England and is dated 28 Aug. 1686. Dance does not mention that Bonel was a gardener, or in the employ of Petty. The 'Bonel' in the letter of 1686 may have been a reference to James Bonnell, accountant general of Ireland. Bonnell was in the same circle as Petty; both were members of the Dublin Philosophical Society and Bonnell's 'chief friend' was Anthony Dopping, the bishop of Meath – or 'lord of Meath'.

46 Earl of Meath papers, Killruddery, J3/2.

47 Edward Brabazon succeeded to the title upon the death of his brother William Brabazon.

48 NAI, Minutes of the Royal Hospital of Charles II, 1 Apr. 1693.

49 The term Grand Tour was introduced by Richard Lassels in his book *The voyage of Italy, or a compleat journey through Italy* (Paris, 1670).

50 Ohlmeyer, *Making Ireland English*, p. 442.

51 Letter from earl of Burlington to Mary, dowager countess of Orrery, 3 Feb. 1685/6, Edward MacLysaght (ed.), *Orrery papers* (Dublin, 1941), p. 313.

52 Jane Ohlmeyer, *Making Ireland English*, p. 443.

53 This speculation is based on the fact that the 4th earl was a friend of Sir John, whose gardens were laid out in a similar style.

54 R. Molesworth to L. Molesworth, 3 May 1712, NLI, P3752. See also O'Kane, *Landscape design*, p. 11.

55 See letter from R. Molesworth to L. Molesworth dated 25 May 1714, NLI, P37532, in which he suggests that Jack act as 'supervisor' on the work on the canal at Breckdenston. Reference is also made approvingly to his son's work in the garden: 'Bysse is a rare young fellow in a garden, which he loves and works like any labourer', Same to same, 13 Oct. 1716, NLI, P1752.

56 Hugh May also worked for Arthur Capel, earl of Essex, at Cassiobury and for the King at Windsor. BL, Stowe MS, 211 fos. 3, 53.

57 The earl of Longford to duke of Ormond, 27 Dec. 1681, *HMC Ormond*, n.s. vol. 6, pp 38–9.

58 The building of his Conway's English seat, Ragley Hall in Warwickshire, did not commence until 1679 (illustration by Johannes Kipp and Leonard Knyff in *Britannia illustrata* (1707)). Lord Conway died in 1683 and the house was still unfinished. He assigned to his trustees the task of completing the house 'by as much annually as they thought fit'. (The house was designed by Dr Robert Hooke, Royal Academician and rival of Sir Isaac Newton.)

59 30 Jan. 1682, BL, Add. MS 46,960A, fos. 39b–40.

60 Mukerji, *Territorial ambitions and the gardens of Versailles*, pp 41–2, 149–50. Vauban used his fortress and canal engineering experiences to help with the reservoir system and a massive array of dams, canals and pipes at Versailles.

61 'The brick wall in the lower gardens is now finished; and the masons are now at work upon the utmost wall of the gardens which bounds it in along the highway from the great bridge'. George Rawdon to Edward Conway, 4 Aug. 1665, *CSPI, 1663–5*, p. 618.

62 For a discussion of walled gardens see Robert Williams, 'Fortified gardens' in Christopher Ridgway and Robert Williams (eds), *Sir John Vanbrugh and landscape architecture in baroque England, 1690–1730* (Stroud, Gloucestershire, 2000), p. 49. See also Petty's letter to his wife in which he discusses a stone and brick wall on which to grow fruit. W. Petty to E. Petty, 6 Oct. 1677, BL, Add. MS 72,856.

63 Robert Molesworth made several references to 'flankers' in his garden in his letters to his wife Lettice: 'I do really intend to bring up the water from the tuckmill wheel to a pretty large cistern on the top of the hill behind the south flanker'. 12 July 1709; 'and so round till it comes to the south flanker of the wall garden' undated; 'I mean ... the cherry orchard going down to the ponds and believe the bank near the flanker must be made up with strong and thick masons work ... as strong as a castle' 19 Jan. 1718/19, NLI, P3752. See O'Kane, *Landscape design*, pp 12 & 22.

64 Mukerji, *Territorial ambitions and the gardens of Versailles*, pp 43, 64.

65 The seventeenth-century gateway from Leamaneh was moved to Dromoland in the early eighteenth century and is in the walled garden there. Mark Bence-Jones, *Burke's guide to country houses*, vol. 1, p. 110.

66 King's Inns, The Black Book, 1607–1730, MS B1/1, fo. 64v. The Blackfriars monastery was closed following the suppression of religious houses in 1537. A grant of 1611 of Blackfriars referred to 'divers gardens and orchards enclosed with stone walls'.

67 Dézallier d'Argenville, *Theory and practice of gardening*, p. 41.

68 Ibid., pp 41–2.

69 Feb. 1700, TCD, King MS 751/2, fo. 209.

70 R. Molesworth to L. Molesworth, 7 Jan. 1720, NLI, P3752.

71 Temple wrote that 'the part of our garden next to our house (besides the walks that go round it) should be a parterre for flowers, or grass-plots bordered with flowers; or if, according to the newest mode, it be cast all into grass-plots and gravel walks, the dryness of these should be relieved with fountains, and the plainness of those with statues; otherwise, if large they have an ill effect upon the eye'. Temple, *Upon the gardens of Epicurus*, p. 24.

72 Ibid., p. 19.

73 A coronary garden was used to grow flowers that could be used for wreaths and garlands ('like a crown'). 'The catalogue of coronary plants is not large in Theophrastus, Pliny, Pollux, or Athenæus; but we may find a good enlargement in the accounts of modern botanists; and additions may still be made by successive acquists of fair and specious plants, not yet translated from foreign regions or little known unto our gardens', Thomas Brown, 'Of garlands and coronary or garland-plants' in *Browne's miscellany tracts* (London, 1684). In his 'plan of a royal garden, describing, and shewing the amplitude, and extent of that part of *Georgics*, which belongs to horticulture' Evelyn wrote 'of the coronary garden: flowers and rare plants, how they are to be raised, governed and improved'. John Evelyn, *Acetaria, a discourse on sallets* (London, 1699), p. 120.

74 Worlidge, *Systema horticulturae*, p. 19.

75 Dézallier d'Argenville, *Theory and practice of gardening*, p. 42.

76 24 Nov. 1683, BL, Egmont Add. MS 46960B, fo. 101.

77 R. Molesworth to L. Molesworth, 7 June 1704 NLI, P3752. See O'Kane, *Landscape design*, p. 17.

78 Among the flowering plants listed by Worlidge are roses, jasmine, ornamental cherries, laburnum, Spanish broom, honeysuckle, auriculas, anemones, peonies, cowslip, lily of the valley, primroses, columbines, larkspurs, poppies, hollyhocks, snapdragons, scabious and lupins. Worlidge, *Systema horticulturae*, pp 215–19.

79 Richard Bulkeley of Old Bawn wrote to a friend saying 'I would desire the favour of you to save me some of your seed of your perennial sunflower, the beauty of Versailles'. Richard Bulkeley to Martin Lister, 1 July 1693, Bodl. Lister MS. 36, fo. 55. Louis XIV commenced his programme to enlarge and create the *grand siècle* gardens at Versailles after 1663; work continued until his death in 1715.

80 For instance, acacia (*Acacia farrnesiana*), Jasmine (*Jasminum humile* and *J. sambac*), Lignum vitae (*Guaiacum officinale*), Mimosa or sensitive plant (*Mimosa sensitive*), Oleander (*Nerium oleander*), and passion flower (*Passiflora incarnata*).

81 *Elysium Britannicum*, insertion on p. 296. Cited in Mark Laird, 'Parterre, grove, and flower garden: European horticulture and planting design in John Evelyn's time' in O'Malley et al. (eds), *John Evelyn's 'Elysium Britannicum'*, p. 197.

82 John Skeffington, 2nd Viscount Massereene.

83 Richard Dobbs, 1683, TCD, Dub. Phil. Soc. MS 8267/2.

84 *Antrim Ordnance Survey memoir*, pp 26–7.

85 Worlidge, *Systema horticulturae*, p. 67.

86 For instance, the obelisk in Stillorgan Park was built in 1741. Samuel Lewis, *Topographical dictionary of Ireland* (1837), vol. 2, p. 574.

87 Temple, *Upon the gardens of Epicurus*, p. 28.

88 PRONI, De Ros MS D638/82/2.

89 Rolf Loeber, 'An introduction to the Dutch influence in seventeenth and eighteenth-century Ireland: an unexplored field', *QBIGS*, 13:2/3 (1970), pp 1–29, p. 18.

90 Bezemer Sellers, *Courtly gardens in Holland, 1600–1650*, pp 224–5.

91 John Molesworth to Robert Molesworth, 10 Dec. 1721, *HMC Various collections*, vol. 8, p. 328.

92 William Chetwood, *A tour through Ireland* (London, 1748), p. 208.

93 Worlidge, *Systema horticulturae*, p. 19.

94 This house was destroyed in the eighteenth century and replaced again in the nineteenth century on a new site west of the original house.

95 Smith, *Cork*, vol. 1, p. 55.

96 John Molesworth to Robert Molesworth, 10 Dec. 1721, *HMC Various collections*, vol. 8, p. 328. See O'Kane, *Landscape design*, p. 17.

97 Agreement dated 23 Dec. 1681. Under the agreement Bonnier was also to cast upon 'certain parts' of the figures 'drapery or other ornament in case the duke or duchess approve of it'. The agreement further provided for the casting of 16 smaller statues, two and a half feet tall 'with a due proportion for bigness'. The price for the large statues on plinths was £40 each and the smaller £5 each. *HMC Ormond*, n.s. vol. 4, p. 279.

98 Walker, 'The rise and progress of gardening in Ireland' *TRIA*, 4 (1790), p. 12.

99 Thomas Campbell, *A philosophical survey of the south of Ireland, 1778* (Dublin, 1778), pp 169–70.

100 George Rawdon to Edward Conway, 24 Dec. 1667, *CSPI, 1666–9*, p. 530.

101 Worlidge, *Systema horticulturae*, pp 67–8.

102 George Rawdon to Edward Conway, 24 Dec. 1667, *CSPI, 1666–9*, p. 530. Shipping goods by the packet boat was a hit and miss affair. Ships were frequently held up by bad weather, and on a number of occasions the boat went down altogether, sometimes with all hands perishing. Even if the packet arrived safely its freight had often been damaged in rough seas. 'Mr. Neale has received 11 dozen flower pots, but the other dozen were broken and spoiled'. George Rawdon to Edward Conway, 31 Aug. 1667, *CSPI, 1666–9*. An amusing series of letters survives chronicling the delivery of flowerpots to Lord Conway's gardens in Lisburn. George Rawdon apparently attached great importance to the flowerpots and became increasingly anxious about their whereabouts, which suggests that they may have been sent from the Continent and were rather valuable. On 26 Oct. 1667 Rawdon related that a number of flowerpots had been shipped six weeks earlier, but that they had not yet arrived in Belfast and more worryingly added, '[w]e do not know what has become of the vessel'. Two weeks later he wrote 'I fear the flower pots are lost, unless they be put into Scotland', 9 Nov. 1667. Ten days later he wrote that the ship had been diverted to Scotland in bad weather and then sailed to Carrickfergus via Beaumorris. Rawdon reported that the flowerpots were 'all broken and all the goods in the vessel spoiled', 19 Nov. 1667.

103 July 1695 Accounts, TCD, King MS 751/1, fo. 77.

104 Lord Shannon to Sir John Perceval, 13 Mar. 1682–3, *HMC Egmont* 2, p. 129.

105 *Elysium Britannicum*, BL, Add. MS 78628 A-B, p. 158.

106 Worlidge, *Systema horticulturae*, p. 67.

107 Pete Smith, 'The sundial garden and house-plan mount: two gardens at Wollaton Hall, Nottinghamshire, by Robert (*c*.1535–1614) and John (?–1634) Smythson', *Garden History*, 31:1 (2003), p. 6.

108 Dunton, *Dublin scuffle*.

109 Kenny, *King's Inns and the kingdom of Ireland: the Irish 'Inns of court', 1541–1800*, pp 113–14.

110 'Sir, I raised the dial sent by the Harp', John Hartnall to George Rawdon, 29 May 1665, *CSPI, 1663–5*, p. 586.

111 Earl of Clarendon to John Evelyn, 26 Dec. 1686, Douglas (ed.), *Clarendon letters*, vol. 1, p. 128.

112 In *The interest of Ireland* Richard Lawrence complained of those who contributed to Ireland's instability and poor economy, among whom were the 'labourers and mechanic gamblers that consume time and money in bowling alleys', p. 43.

113 The duke of Ormond and the earl of Antrim met and discussed State business at the bowling alley on College Green Dublin in 1661. *CSPI, 1660–2*, p. 208.

114 The Egerton papers feature a reference to MPs present at a dinner at the bowling green banqueting house to celebrate the 3rd duke of Ormond's birthday on 29 Apr. 1706, BL, Egerton MS 917, fo. 234.

115 Lord Caulfield 'who dined here yesterday and he and some Armagh gentlemen with him, bowled all the day'. 1 July 1665, George Rawdon to Edward Conway, *CSPI, 1663–5*, p. 602.

116 John Dunton, *The life and errors of John Dunton* (London, 1705), p. 595.

117 Duchess of Ormond to George Mathew, 11 Jan. 1669, NLI, Ormond MS 2503.

118 John Dunton, *The life and errors of John Dunton* (London, 1705), p. 595.

119 William Chetwood, *A tour through Ireland*, p. 179.

120 Prudence Leith-Ross, 'Fruit planted around a new bowling green at John Evelyn's Garden and Sayes Court, Deptford, Kent in 1684/5', *Garden History*, 31:1 (2003), p. 33.

121 Garret Fleming to Henry Boyle, 8 Mar. 1728, NLI, Shannon MS 13,296. The Revd Samuel Wilson, while renting Castleisland from Lord Herbert wrote that he intended 'to run two rows of Dutch willows, sycamore or other spreading trees of quick growth from the front of the house towards a bridge with a gate at the end'. See William James Smith, *The Herbert correspondence* (1963), p. 228.

122 Worlidge, *Systema horticulturae*, p. 30.

123 Ibid., p. 20.

124 William Petty to Elizabeth Petty, 6 Oct. 1677, BL, Add. MS 72856. In *The life of Sir William Petty* (London, 1895). Edmond Fitzmaurice erroneously states that this letter was written to Robert Southwell; it was in fact addressed to Elizabeth Petty, the author's wife. Petty lived in 'St George's Lane', which is where today's South Great George's street lies. The house was probably described as 'mean' because it was a town house in the centre of the city.

125 Colum Kenny, *King's Inns and the kingdom of Ireland*, p. 113.

126 Dézallier d'Argenville, *Theory and practice of gardening*, p. 51.

127 And also at Patshull in England, see Couch, 'The practice of avenue planting in the seventeenth and eighteenth centuries', p. 174.

128 Worlidge, *Systema horticulturae*, p. 20.

129 Dézallier d'Argenville, *Theory and practice of gardening*, p. 41.

130 Ibid., p. 51.

131 Countess of Clarendon to John Evelyn, 8 Feb. 1685–6, *Clarendon letters*, vol. 1, p. 237.

132 Lucius O'Brien to Catherine O'Brien, 8 Feb. 1712, NLI, Inchiquin MS 45,297/1. See O'Kane, 'Leamaneh and Dromoland, part II', p. 67.

133 Dézallier d'Argenville, *Theory and practice of gardening*, p. 63.

134 John Tichbourne to Robert Molesworth, 23 July 1710, NLI, P3753. See O'Kane, *Landscape design*, p. 14.

135 This was recommended by Worlidge in *Systema horticulturae*, p. 20.

136 Edward MacLysaght (ed.), 'Report on the Longford papers', *AH*, 13:15 (1944), p. 123.

137 Dézallier d'Argenville, *Theory and practice of gardening*, p. 51.

138 Michael Charlesworth, 'A plan by John Evelyn for Henry Howard's garden at Albury Park, Surrey' in O'Malley et al. (eds), *John Evelyn's 'Elysium Britannicum'*, p. 291.

139 John Loveday, *Diary of a tour in 1732* (London, 1890), p. 43.

140　Dr John Wesley June 1750, quoted in Clohosey, 'Dunmore House', *OKR*, 4 (1951), p. 48.

141　Thanks to Margaret Gowen, archaeologist, for allowing me to use her report into excavations at Blessington.

142　Countess of Clarendon to John Evelyn, 8 Feb. 1685–6. *Clarendon letters*, vol. 1, p. 237.

143　Worlidge, *Systema horticulturae*, pp 32–3.

144　Temple, *Upon the gardens of Epicurus*, p. 29.

145　Worlidge, *Systema horticulturae*, pp 32–5.

146　24 Nov. 1683, BL, Egmont Add. MS 46960B, fo. 101.

147　Adam Leathes to Conway, 23 Jan. 1666, *CSPI, 1666–9*, p. 16

148　'The gardener is still busy gravelling which, through the multiplicity and great breadth of his walks will, I doubt, prove a tedious work'. George Rawdon to Edward Conway, 4 Aug. 1665, *CSPI, 1663–5*, p. 618.

149　TCD, King MS 751/2, fo. 207v.

150　George Rawdon to Edward Conway, 19 Oct. 1667, *CSPI, 1666–9* (1908), p. 472.

151　Robert Molesworth to Lettice Molesworth, 18 Feb. 1720, NLI, P3752.

152　Worlidge, *Systema horticulturae*, pp 32–5.

153　Dézallier d'Argenville, *Theory and practice of gardening*, p. 43.

154　Journal of a tour to Dublin by James Verdon, 1699, BL, Add. MS 41769, fos. 29–43.

155　All traces of this early garden are absent on the first edition of the Ordnance Survey map for the area. On Leamaneh generally see O'Kane, 'Leamaneh and Dromoland, part I', pp 65–79. See, here, p. 67.

156　Donat O'Brien to Catherine O'Brien, 8 Mar. 1713/4, NLI, Inchiquin MS 45,295/3.

157　The house was sold a couple of years later to raise some money. The conveyance was described in a letter dated 16 Apr. 1670 where the duchess noted that the duke had agreed the sale of Moore Park to the duke of Monmouth 'good and all' for £13,200. The duke of Monmouth clearly struck a hard bargain as she later notes, on 11 June, that in fact only £11,500 was paid. *HMC Ormond*, n.s. vol. 4 (1906), p. 445. The gardens were replaced by a park designed by Lancelot Brown in the late eighteenth century and is now used as a golf course.

158　Temple, *Upon the gardens of Epicurus*, p. 30.

159　Earl of Anglesey to Ormond, 8 Sept. 1663, *HMC Ormond*, n.s. vol. 3 (London, 1904), p. 197.

160　John Worlidge, *Systema horticulturae*, p. 61.

161　*Elysium Britannicum*, BL, Add. MS 78628 A-B, p. 10.

162　Worlidge, *Systema horticulturae*, p. 17.

163　Ibid., pp 37–41. John Aubrey's description of the duke of Norfolk's garden at Albury designed by Evelyn notes 'a handsome banqueting house' surrounded with trees. John Aubrey, *The natural history and antiquities of the county of Surrey* (London, 1718), vol. 4, p. 67.

164　King's Inns Black Book, fo. 199 (16 Nov. 1664). A banqueting mound was the descendent of the mounds found in medieval gardens. The diners could eat in style, comfort and safety while appreciating the views beyond the walls of the garden.

165　Accounts, Oct. 1696, TCD, King MS 751/1, fo. 116.

166　*HMC Ormond*, n.s. vol. 5 (1908), p. 292.

167　Temple, *Upon the gardens of Epicurus*, p. 30.

168　NAI, Pembroke 2011/2/3.

169　Finola O'Kane, 'Leamaneh and Dromoland, part II', p. 93.

170　James Howley, *The follies and garden buildings of Ireland* (New Haven, CT, 1993), pp 134–5.

171　Worlidge, *Systema horticulturae*, p. 54.

172 Early examples of bee boles can be seen at Milford House in Tipperary North, Dromoland Castle and Kilcolgan House in Offaly.

173 Timothy Raylor, 'Samuel Hartlib and the commonwealth of bees' in Michael Leslie and Timothy Raylor (eds), *Culture and cultivation in early modern England* (Leicester, 1992), p. 95.

174 Ibid., p. 92.

175 Fifth chapter of heads of a treatise concerning trade in Ireland, 10 Sept. 1677, *HMC Ormond*, n.s. vol. 3 (London, 1904), p. 371.

176 Robert Molesworth wrote from Edlington: 'we have here four swarms of bees, so I shall take a couple of old stocks, which may perhaps finish the proportion of honey'. Robert Molesworth to Lettice Molesworth, 16 Nov. 1706, NLI, Killadoon MS Q/1/1.

177 *CSPI, 1663–5*, pp 319, 150.

178 TCD, Dub. Phil. Soc. MS 883/1 (I.1.2).

179 Sir Richard Cox (1650–1733), future lord chancellor of Ireland, TCD, Dub. Phil. Soc. MS 883/1 (I.1.2).

180 Pepys, Samuel, *Diary*, 5 May 1665, p. 1157

181 Richard Bulkeley to Martin Lister, 1 July 1693, Bodl., Lister MS 36, fo. 55.

182 R.G. Martin, 'Ice houses and the commercial ice trade in Brighton', *SIH*, 14 (1984/5), p. 11. John Evelyn, referring to a 'sweet place in Chelsea', which the earl of Ossory had declined to purchase, mentioned that it had an 'ice house etcetera'; Evelyn to Ossory, 14 Feb. 1679–80, *HMC Ormond*, n.s. vol. 5, p. 279.

183 Peter Brears et al. (eds), *A taste of history* (London, 1993), p. 193.

184 R.G. Martin, 'Petworth ice-house', *SIH*, 13 (1983), pp 15–21, p. 15.

185 'Dorothy Parsons her Booke of Choyce Receipts all written in her own hand in 1666'. Rosse MSS, A/17.

186 Martin, 'Petworth ice-house', p. 20.

187 Robert Molesworth to Lettice Molesworth, 8 Dec. 1698, *HMC Various collections*, vol. 8, p. 219.

188 Martin, 'Ice houses and the commercial ice trade', p. 12.

189 In Jan. 1669, the duchess of Ormond wrote from London that 'the weather here is cold unto so great a degree that I have not found the like of it in England, which gives my lord hopes that the frosts are in some proportion equalling it in Ireland, that so his snow houses may be filled'. Elizabeth Ormond to George Mathew, 28 Jan. 1668–9, *HMC Ormond*, n.s. vol. 1 (London, 1902), p. 440. And in 1674 Garret Roche was able to report that 'we have had great snow'. Roche to Burlington, 7 Mar. 1674, NLI, Lismore papers, MS 7177.

190 The Civil Survey of 1654 makes reference to a 'decayed dovehouse' at Old Carton. Arnold Horner, 'Carton, Co. Kildare, a case study of the making of an Irish demesne', *QBIGS*, 18:2/3 (1975), p. 50. In 1635 Brereton observed a dove house at Joymount, Sir Arthur Chichester's house in Carrickfergus. 'Travels of Sir William Brereton in Ireland 1635', Reprinted in Falkiner, *Illustrations of Irish history and topography* (London, 1904).

191 For instance, a lease in the Ormond papers grants the lessor 'liberty to make use ... of the pigeon house warren and gardens also'. NLI, Ormond MS 2503.

192 Fine of Easter 3 William and Mary between Thomas Newcome Kt and Hugh Galbraith a merchant plaintiffs and Alexander Fraser defendant 'the manor of Le Ward with a castle ... 200 gardens, 5 orchards ... a pigeon house'. NLI, Walker papers Report No. 33.

193 Robert Molesworth to Lettice Molesworth, 4 Aug. 1704, NLI, P3752. See also O'Kane, *Landscape design*, p. 19. 'The walls of the pigeon house are finished and will be very handsome when whitened'; same to same, 7 June 1703, NLI, P3752; 'Pray let the pigeon

house be roughcast whilst the hot weather lasts, that it may be white and dry before rain comes in. As soon as it is clean you may stock it with half a score pairs of young pigeons of the best sort, who must have meat and fresh water every day and a salt stone'; same to same, 7 Aug. 1704, NLI, Killadoon MS Q/1/1.

194   According to a survey of Breckdenston carried out in 1775 by Arthur Neville the great avenue was the approach avenue to the house on the east of the demesne and not the avenue running southwards towards Forrest House which O'Kane identified as the great avenue; which was the great avenue remains a mystery. NLI, MS 21F 52–72.

195   George Rawdon to Edward Conway, 30 April 1667: 'the pigeon house your lordship wishes to have made at Portmore will soon be made if £5 will do it. Your lordship must give Totnall full instructions as to the making of it. *CSPI, 1666–9*, p. 368.

196   Smith, 'the sundial garden', p. 16.

197   Horner, 'Carton', *QBIGS*, 28:2, 3 (1975), p. 54.

198   'Dineley's journal', *JKSIAS*, 4:1 (1862), p. 44.

199   John Worlidge, *Systema horticulturae*, p. 42.

200   A square tiered mount was at Wollaton Hall in Nottinghamshire, Pete Smith, 'The sundial garden', *Garden History* 31:1 (2003), p. 16.

201   For instance, at the seventeenth-century Powis Castle in Wales.

202   'The mount at the gate and the outlet to lengthen the walk to the orchard are newly done, and the stairs out of the garden. The millrace is arched and covered through the low garden plot. But rents come in slowly, not enough some weeks to pay the workmen. What help this peace may produce (if there be peace) I cannot tell yet, but am certain the country is in a sad condition now for want of money and trade'. George Rawdon to Edward Conway, 6 Apr. 1667, *CSPI, 1666–9*, p. 501.

203   George Rawdon to Edward Conway, 13 April 1667, *CSPI, 1666–9*, p. 506. Volary presumably stems from the word volar meaning relating to or employed in flying.

204   The works were carried out in the seventeenth century.

205   See Colum Kenny, *King's Inns and the kingdom of Ireland* (Dublin, 1992), appendix 4. In 1675 Sir John Temple requested a lease of the 'high green walk', promising to enclose the same with a brick wall. Lease from judges to Temple, 1699, PROI, MS D11847/1a, fo. 36.9.

206   'In some gardens where water is at your command the sinking of an aqueduct or piscary will afford you materials for your terrace-walk. Both of which are best and most proper to be made at the farthest distance from your house'. John Worlidge, *Systema horticulturae*, pp 36–7.

207   William Chetwood, *A tour through Ireland* (London, 1748), p. 89.

208   TCD, Dub. Phil. Soc. papers MS I.I.3.

209   24 Nov. 1683, BL, Egmont Add. MS 46960B, fo. 101.

210   Ibid.

211   The plan is published in William Upcott (ed.), *The miscellaneous writings of John Evelyn, Esq. F.R.S.* (London, 1825) and is reproduced in Charlesworth, 'A plan by John Evelyn for Henry Howard's garden', p. 290.

212   Aubrey, *The natural history and antiquities of the county of Surrey*, p. 67.

213   He also noted that since the house had been destroyed by fire in 1664, Sir Robert had completely rebuilt it. William Montgomery, 1683, TCD, Dub. Phil. Soc. MS 883/1 (I.1.2).

CHAPTER 5
Horticultural improvement

1 Chandra Mukerji, *Territorial ambitions and the gardens of Versailles*, p. 151.

2 George Holmes, *Sketches of some of the southern counties of Ireland during a tour in autumn 1797* (London, 1801).

3 T.C. Barnard, *A new anatomy of Ireland: the Irish Protestants, 1649–1770* (New Haven, CT, 2003), p. 300.

4 NLI, Lane MS 8645 (1) 1701–1713 (8).

5 TCD, Dub. Phil. Soc. papers MS 883/2 (I.1.2), fos. 259–60.

6 Thomas James Rawson, *Statistical survey of the county of Kildare* (1807), p. 9.

7 1683, TCD, Dub. Phil. Soc. papers MS 883/1 (I.1.2). Chapter 3 of George Rye's *Considerations on agriculture dealing with manures* was based on William King's writing on the subject. J.F. Collins, 'George Rye (1685–1735) his family and an appreciation of his book: *Considerations on agriculture*', *BHJ*, 17 (2001), p. 39.

8 TCD, Dub. Phil. Soc. papers MS 883/1 (I.1.2).

9 Ibid.

10 Walker, 'The rise and progress of gardening', p. 11.

11 Henry Bathurste to Orrery, 9 Sept. 1672, MacLysaght, *Orrery papers*, p. 108.

12 Colum Kenny, *King's Inns and the kingdom of Ireland*, at p. 113.

13 In *Systema horticulturae* John Worlidge referred to potatoes as 'the bread of the Irish'.

14 *The life and errors of John Dunton*, p. 606.

15 'Dineley's journal', *JKSIAS*, 1:1 (1856), p. 186.

16 Reprinted in Falkiner, *Illustrations of Irish history and topography* (London, 1904), p. 220.

17 John Evelyn, *Acetaria: a discourse on sallets* (London, 1699), p. 154.

18 Samuel Pepys, a close friend and correspondent of both Sir William Petty and Evelyn, was determined that his nephew and heir John should become as polished and rounded a gentleman as Evelyn. In his letters Pepys gave him tips on how to achieve this, for instance dusting off his letters with lettuce seed in order to impress Lord Clarendon 'who you know is a great saladist and curious'. Quoted in Stephen Coote, *Samuel Pepys: a life* (London, 2000), p. 354.

19 Clarendon to Evelyn, 25 May 1686, *Clarendon letters*, p. 407. Evelyn believed that Irish asparagus passed more quickly through the body and so had less time to leave traces. Evelyn to Lady Clarendon, 13 Mar. 1685, *Clarendon letters*, p. 407.

20 TCD Mun P/4F2/25/2.

21 *c.*1678, MacLysaght, *Orrery papers*, pp 213–17.

22 Bodl., Carte MS 229, fo. 67.

23 Erasmus D. Burrowes, 'The French settlers in Ireland, No. 5', *UJA*, 3 (1855), p. 55.

24 'The more particular products of this county are coleseed in the marshland, a commodity brought hither by Dutchmen'. Hugh Brigdall, TCD, Dub. Phil. Soc. papers MS 883/1 (I.1.2), fos. 234–9. Daniel Hignet also observed that rape and 'cole seed' were grown in Limerick: TCD, Dub. Phil. Soc. papers MS 883/1 (I.1.2), fo. 240.

25 Bulkeley stated that he had made good bread with a mixture of wheat and kidney bean which made 'the bread extremely white which will be of great service to the baker in sale to the vulgar people'. Bulkeley to Lister, 19 Mar. 1686, Bodl., Lister MS v.3, fo. 51. He also experimented with different types of grass: 'I am now deeply engaged in ploughing and sowing and all other agriculture, and I am ready and desirous to receive from you a letter upon any subject of that nature having sent over the knotgrass root which I sent for to

Yorkshire, I find whole fields of it here in divers parts of my estate and I suppose in other mans too in several counties and nonesuch also with in my meadows'. Richard Bulkeley to Martin Lister, undated May 1704, Bodl., Lister MS3, fo. 50.

26 Richard Bulkeley to Martin Lister, 1 July 1693, Bodl., Lister MS 36, fo. 55.

27 One of the perceived advantages of Rathfarnham Castle was its proximity to Dublin, excess fruit and herbs were sent there regularly. Journal of a tour to Dublin by James Verdon, 1699, BL, Add. MS 41769, fos. 29–43

28 Stephen Switzer, *The practical fruit gardener* (London, 1724), p. 2.

29 TCD, Dub. Phil. Soc. papers MS 8267/2.

30 The forfeited estates record of *c.*1700 mentions 'a very fine House, with all manner of convenient offices and fine gardens etc., being the Mansion-house of the late duke of Tyrconnell'. Horner, 'Carton', p. 50.

31 Ibid., p. 50.

32 Temple, *Upon the gardens of Epicurus*, p. 28.

33 From the mid-eighteenth century onwards, kitchen gardens began to be sited further away from the main house and pleasure gardens.

34 Worlidge, *Systema horticulturae*, p. 18.

35 John Loveday, *Diary of a tour in 1732*, p. 47.

36 Mukerji, *Terrotorial ambitions and the gardens of Versailles*, p. 159.

37 Worlidge stated the best form of fence was of brick as it held on to the sun's heat and was therefore good for growing fruit against. *Systema horticulturae*, p. 22.

38 'The masons think we have drawn stone enough for the finishing of the house and chapel wall, so that what truckles can be spared from drawing stone for the garden wall shall draw brick because both are to be used together.' William Cooper to the countess of Orrery, 18 July 1664, MacLysaght, *Orrery papers*, p. 38.

39 John Ainsworth, 'Sidelights on eighteenth-century Irish estate management', *JRSAI*, 90:2 (1963), pp 181–6.

40 Olivier de Serres recommended that all fields and orchards should be enclosed by banks of trees, stone walls or bushes to shelter plants from wind and inclement weather. Mukerji, *Territorial ambitions and the gardens of Versailles*, p. 159. On 8 April 1710 Robert Molesworth wrote to his wife Lettice that 'whenever we build our wall to enclose all the ground as we must do before we shall be able to preserve any fruit from thieves'. NLI, P3752.

41 For example, the late eighteenth-century-craze for the pineapple motif, as seen on many gateposts, and at its most extreme, at the Brighton Pavilion in 1805.

42 James Buck to Ormond, 5 Dec. 1665, *HMC Ormond*, n.s. vol. 3 (London, 1904), pp 197–8.

43 'The country hereabouts begins to be troubled much with thieves. Poverty is so great that many run away from their farms and betake themselves to stealing'. George Rawdon to Edward Conway, 24 Dec. 1667, *CSPI, 1666–9*, pp 530–1.

44 31 Aug. 1668, Dublin, George Rawdon to Edward Conway, *CSPI, 1666–9*, p. 587.

45 Bulkeley to Lister, 19 Mar. 1686, Bodl., Lister MS 35, fo. 116.

46 Paid 8s. 30 June 1688, Richard Bagg's book of payments on behalf of Burlington estates, NLI, MS 6300.

47 George Rawdon to Edward Conway, 3 Oct. 1667, *CSPI, 1666–9*, p. 530.

48 Erasmus D. Burrowes, 'The French settlers in Ireland, No. 6', *UJA* (1855), p. 213.

49 'White fig trees must be planted against the walls in vacant spaces ... pray order the quince trees'. Robert Molesworth to Lettice Molesworth, 7 Aug. 1704, NLI, P3752. 'The white figs also which were in the nursery ought to be transplanted to some good south wall in the room of some plum or cherry trees'. Robert Molesworth to Lettice Molesworth, 11 June 1707, NLI, P3752.

50 John Loveday, *Diary of a tour in 1732* (London, 1890), p. 28.

51 'Sir as for the garden I have had Derby here to prune and nail the wall trees and to sow some seeds, so that your wall trees are in good order'. Edmond Doyne to Col. Thomas Flower, 9 Jan. 1691, NLI, Flower MS 11,473 (2).

52 R. Molesworth to L. Molesworth 14 Mar. 1720/1, NLI, P3752.

53 John Temple to Robert Colville, 21 Jan. 1682, TCD, Temple MS 1178, fo. 11v.

54 Temple, *Upon the gardens of Epicurus*, p. 31.

55 'The stone and brick wall will be 1/5 part of a mile, the house you sufficiently know is very mean'. W. Petty to E. Petty, 6 Oct. 1677, BL, Add. MS 72856.

56 'I knew we had stocks enough of that sort in the cherry orchard to increase the sorts in the long walks and the black cherry at the lower end of the bowling green'. Robert Molesworth to Lettice Molesworth, 8 July 1710, NLI, P3752. He later wrote that he had some 'bergamot' pear trees against his walls, including 'some in the bowling green and some in the parterre'. Ibid., 14 Mar. 1721, NLI, P3752. See O'Kane, *Landscape design*, p. 17.

57 Journal of a tour to Dublin by James Verdon, 1699, BL, Add. MS 41769, fos. 29–43

58 'I think we shall have a good fruit year this year, and that the wall-fruit on the new walk will bear. The walks are closed, so I hope the fruit will be preserved'. George Rawdon to Edward Conway, 30 April 1667, *CSPI, 1666–9*, p. 499.

59 John Dunton's letters, quoted in MacLysaght, *Irish life in the seventeenth century*, pp 385–6.

60 Leith-Ross, 'Fruit planted around a new bowling green at John Evelyn's garden at Sayes Court', pp 30–1.

61 He incorporated this in his design for the duke of Norfolk's garden at Albury. Yew trees were grown along the walk 'just high enough to defend' the trees from winds 'without injuring it by its shade'. Cobbett, *Rural rides*, pp 98–100.

62 Killruddery, Earl of Meath papers, J3/2.

63 NAI, Minutes of the Royal Hospital of Charles II, 8 Feb. 1702.

64 *HMC Egmont*, vol. 2, p. 137.

65 Edward MacLysaght, 'Report on Connor papers', *AH*, 15 (1944), p. 157.

66 23 Jan. 1719, NLI, O'Hara MS 20,385.

67 William Chetwood, *A tour through Ireland*, pp 217–19

68 The late sixteenth- and early seventeenth-century Chancery Bills preserved in the National Archives of Ireland contain a number of cases where plaintiffs sought the recovery of orchards. See *Vicar's Choral of St Patrick's v. Thomas*, NAI Chancery Bills H/45, re an Orchard in Bride Street, Dublin; see also NAI Chancery Bill E/211.

69 He was appointed attorney general for Ireland in 1606, elected MP for Fermanagh in 1612 and speaker of the Irish parliament in 1613. Davis, *Historical tracts*, p. 286.

70 Henrey, *British botanical and horticultural literature before 1800*, p. 169.

71 Nelson, *Northern gardens*, p. 5.

72 In *Paradisi in sole paradisus terrestris* (London, 1629), John Parkinson referred to the choke pear which in his time applied to any wild, very astringent type of pear.

73 Bodl., Carte MS 229, fo. 65.

74 Worlidge, *Vinetum Britannicum*, p. 15.

75 George Rawdon to Edward Conway, 21 Oct. 1665, *CSPI, 1663–5*, p. 636.

76 Henrey, *British botanical and horticultural literature before 1800*, p. 172.

77 Lease 18 July 1681 to Major Lawrence Byrne: 'Tenant to plant an orchard of 2 acres to be enclosed with a ditch 5 [feet] high and two rows of quickset'. Land at Rosderagh leased by 'the brigadier' to Richard Archbold, 1695: 'Tenant within the first 7 years to enclose 100 acres in one or two closes with thorn quicksets, build a good stone house and plant an orchard'. 300 acres of land at Clonburran, leased 30 Sept. 1695 by Brigadier to Richard

Hutchinson: 'Tenant plant an orchard, within the first 7 years'. Lease of lands at Kilmulfoile and Clorandiff between Capt. Fitzpatrick and Carbery Keagan, 3 Sept. 1697: 'Tenant to enclose 40 acres in 4 closes with a ditch 5' wide and 4' deep with two rows of thorn quicksets, plant half with fruit trees'. Lease between 'the Brigadier' and Mortagh Griffin, 2 Jan. 1696: condition requiring tenant to 'plant an orchard'. Lease of 'lands at Ardmeallagh etc.' between Captain Fitzpatrick and Thos. Bellew, 25 Aug. 1697: Tenant 'to plant an orchard'. Lease of lands at Grangeville to Thomas Fitzpatrick, 7 Aug. 1678: 'Tenant to ditch an acre for an orchard and plant fruit trees in it, within a year to set 10 ash trees yearly'. Fitzpatrick papers, NLI Report on Private Collections No. 152 1412. See also, for example: lease of lands at Ballynetra, Co. Wexford, of land in Gorey, 10 Oct. 1693, between James Annesley, earl of Anglesey, and James White: Tenant required 'while within the first five years of tenancy to … plant a good orchard'. White papers, NLI Report on Private Collections No. 52. Lease between Richard Phillips of Finglas, Co. Dublin, and Philip Castleton of Dublin, 29 Aug. 1670, of 'all that small parcel of ground part of the Lords demesnes in Finglas … now planted as an orchard and garden, area 1.12.0', Kirkpatrick papers, NLI Report on Private Collections No. 131 1218. Conveyance of land and castle of Killadowen between Sir Joshua Allen of Dublin and Mathew Plunkett of Tallanstowne, 1597; 23 Jan. 1677 'with … arable, a wood, a garden, an orchard', for £440. Louth papers, NLI Report on Private Collections No. 165. Lease in 1665 by earl of Arran of land in Galway. Reserved the right of earl 'to hunt, hawk etc'; provision was also made for 'planning 100 fruit trees in a fenced orchard and 2000 oak, ash and elm'. Edward MacLysaght, 'Report on Dunsdale papers', *AH*, 15 (1944), p. 395.

78   Those include the 'gergonell' (now known as the Jargonelle), Catherine, winter, bon Chrétien, Windsor and the bergamot. Parkinson, *Paradisi in Sole Paradisus Terrestris*.

79   George Rawdon to Edward Conway, 21 Oct. 1665, *CSPI*, *1663–5*, p. 636.

80   George Rawdon to Edward Conway, 5 Oct. 1664, 'the object of the orchard is chiefly to make cider'; George Rawdon to Edward Conway, *CSPI*, *1663–5*, p. 441.

81   A hogshead is a unit of capacity of 54 imperial gallons in the case of beer and 52.5 gallons in the case of wine.

82   Edmond Doyne to Thomas Flower, 27 Oct. 1691, NLI, Flower MS 11473 (3).

83   Ibid., 14 May 1692, NLI, Flower MS 11,473 (4).

84   'Our cider here is much improved, but I doubt, is far short of satisfying your lordship's curiosity of palate. But if you were here I sent a butt of Canary from Dublin that I think would please your taste'. George Rawdon to Viscount Conway, 24 Dec. 1667, *CSPI*, *1666–9*, p. 531.

85   George Rawdon to Edward Conway, 19 Oct. 1667, *CSPI*, *1666–9*, p. 530.

86   Smith, *Down*, p. 205. He was similarly able to report on cider plantations at Lisnegar and Inshirahaill in Cork. He noted that Toonmore was so celebrated for its cider apples that one had been named the Toonmore apple.

87   Irvine, 'Richard Dobbs, notes for his description of Co. Antrim', p. 45.

88   An agricultural tract dating from sometime between 1701 and 1713 deals with 'beans, peas, melons, cowcumbers, asparagus, cabbages [and] the greater sort of garden beans'; NLI, Lane papers, MS 8645 (1). The Flower papers contain tree and seed accounts for 1717–41, reciting 'an account of what garden seed I want'; which includes 'orange carrots, onion, leeks, kidney beans, cauliflower, cowcumber', NLI, Flower papers MS 11,470 (3).

89   June 1699, TCD, King MS 751/1 fo. 206.

90   Barnard, 'Gardening, diet and "improvement"', p. 76.

91 NLI Lane papers, MS 8645 (1) 1701–1713 (8).

92 Worlidge, *Systema horticulturae*, p. 86.

93 'The moon herself has set certain days as auspicious for certain kinds of work'. Virgil, *Georgics*, book 1. The deeply religious Ralph Austen however was of the view that 'the moon hath no such influence upon fruit-trees. Men (we see by experience) graft in all seasons of the moon, and find no such difference in the bearing of the trees', *A treatise of fruit-trees* (1653). Evelyn disagreed in his *Elysium Britannicum* stating that the moon had a 'great operation' on vegetables. BL, Add. MS 78628 A-B.

94 *The compleat gard'ner … made English by John Evelyn* (London, 1693).

95 Robert Molesworth to Lettice Molesworth, 12 July 1707 (NLI 3752). See O'Kane, *Landscape design*, p. 44.

96 George Rawdon to Edward Conway, 26 Oct. 1667, *CSPI, 1666–9*, p. 395.

97 *The compleat vineyard, or a most excellent way for the planting of vines: not only according to the German and French way, but also along experimented in England etc.* (London, 1665).

98 Rose, *The English vineyard vindicated* (London, 1691). In 1677, John Beale published a further tract, which was included in *Nurseries, orchards, profitable gardens, and vineyards encouraged*. See Henrey, *British botanical and horticultural literature before 1800*, p. 175.

99 Temple recommended that 'grapes, peaches and winter-pears, to be good, must be planted upon full south, or south-east; figs are best upon south-east, but will do well upon east and south-west; the west are proper for cherries, plums, or apricots; but all of them are improved by a south wall both as to early and taste …' Temple, *Upon the gardens of Epicurus*, p. 30.

100 Richard Bulkeley to Martin Lister, 10 May 1694, Bodl., Lister MS 36, fo. 95.

101 Martin Lister (1638?–1712), physician and zoologist. He wrote extensively on medicine, anatomy, natural philosophy and botany. Richard Bulkeley to Martin Lister, 10 Aug. 1693, Bodl., Lister MS 36, fo. 61.

102 Ibid., 25 Aug. 1693, Bodl., Lister MS 36, fo. 63.

103 Ibid., Nov. 1694, Bodl., Lister MS 36, fo. 106.

104 Richard Molesworth to L. Molesworth, 18 Feb. 1710, *HMC Various collections*, vol. 8, p. 245.

105 Robert Molesworth to Lettice Molesworth, 18 Feb. 1720, NLI, P3752. See O'Kane, *Landscape design*, p. 38. The reference is to Richard Bradley and Edward Lawrence, both prolific garden writers.

106 Edward MacLysaght, 'Report on Conner papers', *AH*, 15 (1944), p. 157.

107 *London Quarterly Review*, 61–2 (1838), p. 183.

108 *Field guide to trees and shrubs of Britain*, p. 47.

109 Bodl., Carte MS 229 pp 1–61.

110 Published between 1600 and 1675.

111 Richard Bulkeley to Martin Lister, 25 Aug. 1693, Bodl., Lister MS 36, fo. 63.

112 Ibid., undated May 1704, Bodl., Lister MS. 3, fo. 50.

113 R. Molesworth to John Molesworth, 20 Oct. 1722, *HMC Various collections*, vol. 8, p. 349.

114 In 1579 William Crewtie of the city of Dublin memorialized the Lord High Admiral, complaining that one Gerald Fleming of Drogheda had defaulted in a contract for the freight of oranges and lemons from Spain. Petition of William Crewtie, Dec. 1579, TNA: PRO, HCA 14/19. See also *Council Book of Youghal Corporation*. When the earl of Cork spent Christmas 1662 in Dublin he ordered, among other things, 132 oranges and lemons. Barnard, 'Gardening, diet and "improvement"', p. 85.

115 Henrey, *British botanical and horticultural literature before 1800*, p. 182.

116 Tree and seed accounts 1717–41, NLI, Flower MS 11,470 (3).

117　Temple, *Upon the gardens of Epicurus*, p. 21.

118　1632–1705, politician, speaker of the Irish House of Commons and attorney general for Ireland.

119　Richard Bulkeley to Martin Lister, Nov. 1694, Bodl., Lister MS 36, fo. 106.

120　Robert Molesworth to Lettice Molesworth, 28 Dec. 1695, *HMC Various collections*, vol. 8; same to same, 7 June 1703, NLI, P3752.

121　'Elysium Britannicum', BL, Add. MS 78628 A-B, p. 19.

122　Smith, *Cork*, vol. 1 (1750), p. 87.

123　T.C. Barnard, *A new anatomy of Ireland; the Irish Protestants, 1649–1770* (New Haven, CT, 2003), p. 53.

CHAPTER 6

Trees, woodlands and plantations

1　For example, 'In the sixteenth and seventeenth centuries Ireland saw the wholesale destruction of its native forests'; Desmond FitzGerald and James Peill, *Irish furniture, woodwork and carving in Ireland* (New Haven, CT, 2007), p. 7.

2　Robert Molesworth to Lettice Molesworth, 25 Mar. 1690, NLI, P3752.

3　TCD, MS Dub. Phil. Soc. 883/1 (I.1.2), fo. 298.

4　NLI MS 412.

5　For example when the butchers' shambles in Cork in 1693 was pulled down, it was ordered 'the timber and other materials [be] safely kept, which will go a great way in the new building of same'. *Council book of Cork*, p. 186.

6　TCD, Dub. Phil. Soc. MS883/1 (I.1.2)

7　Singer, *Correspondence of Henry Hyde*, p. 46.

8　L.W. Dillwyn, Journal of a tour from Swansea to Killarney in 1809, TCD, MS 967, fo. 13.

9　Boate, *Ireland's natural history*, p. 119.

10　*CSPI, 1601*, p. 253.

11　'If you find the old silver fir tree in the parterre to be dead or quite despaired of, pray cut it down immediately and save the timber'. Robert Molesworth to Lettice Molesworth, 16 May 1721, NLI, Killadoon MS Q/1/1.

12　Aalen et al. (eds), *Atlas of the Irish rural landscape*, p. 122. Charles Smith commented on the well wooded appearance of several demesnes in his county guides. For example, Garretstown in Cork was described as being 'environed with good plantations of timber trees, among which is the French elm and silver fir', Smith, *Cork*, p. 214, while Rusheen in Kerry had plantations 'large and well grown, consisting of well enclosed orchards and gardens, with fine avenues and groves of timber trees, which were all raised and planted by that gentleman, forming several vistas, terminating in very agreeable points of perspective'. Charles Smith, *The antient and present state of the county of Kerry* (Dublin, 1756), p. 226.

13　Petty, *Political anatomy of Ireland*, p. 134.

14　An Act to prevent diverse misdemeanours in idle and lewd persons in barking of trees etc., 1634; 10 Chas. I sess. 2 c. 23. The penalty for such offences was a whipping.

15　Parliament further ordered that the ancient woodland at Shillelagh was not to be felled. A year later wood reeves were appointed by parliament for selling, felling and preserving woods in Wexford. Goats and other destructive livestock were banned from woodland, and wood from Commonwealth land was only to be cut for use in making barrel staves for cask building, small boats and 'barkes' and for supply of farriers. Orders also survive relating to the general management of woodland and providing for the felling and taking out of decayed and diseased trees. NLI, MS 11,959, fo. 353, 16 Mar. 1651, fo. 57, 11 Sept. 1652, fo. 80, 2 Apr. 1653, fos. 230–1.

16 Charles II to Ormond, 20 Aug. 1661 Bodl., Carte MS 42, fo. 374. Massereene to Sir Robert Clayton, 27 May 1696, PRONI, MS T2825/B/71/7.

17 The King to the Lords Justice of Ireland, 28 Aug. 1661, Bodl., Carte MS 42, fo. 374.

18 Order given to one Captain Pennefather and others concerned, 'to forbear to fell any more wood or timber upon the townlands of Watercastle and Kilballan-Tallagh, or either of them'. The King to the Lords Justice of Ireland, 19 Jan. 1661, Bodl., Carte MS 41, fo. 518.

19 Charles II to Marcus Trevor, 20 Aug. 1661, Bodl., Carte MS vol. 42, fo. 374.

20 Lease in 1665 by earl of Arran of land in Galway with provision made for planting 100 fruit trees in a fenced orchard and 2000 oak, ash and elm. MacLysaght (ed.), 'Report on Dunsdale papers', p. 401.

21 Lease of 18 July 1681, lease of 1695; NLI Fitzpatrick, MS 1412.

22 For example, see an agreement between the earl of Kildare and Thady Quinn, 26 Apr. 1683, TCD MS9827/10.

23 Primate Michael Boyle to his son Murrough, Viscount Blessington, 15 Nov. 1690, Edward MacLysaght (ed.), 'Report on the Rawlinson papers', *AH*, 1:2 (1930), p. 37.

24 Journal of a tour to Dublin by James Verdon, 1699, Add. MS 41769, fos. 29–43.

25 Bodl., Carte MS 229.

26 An Act for preserving timber trees and woods, 1698, 10 William III, c.12.

27 Ibid., Sections 1, 2, 3.

28 An Act for encouraging importation of iron and staves, timber for casks etc., 1703 (2 Anne c. 2). A further act was passed in 1705, An Act for planting and preserving timber-trees and woods, 1705 (4 Anne c. 9).

29 William Chetwood, *A tour through Ireland*, p. 208.

30 14 February 1699, John Hely to Lord Coningsby, PRONI, De Ros D638 (24); 23 Jan. 1700 (26).

31 Same to same, 7 May 1700, PRONI, De Ros D638 (27).

32 Donat O'Brien to Lord Inchiquin, 14 Aug. 1714, *Inchiquin papers*, pp 120–1.

33 NLI Bethan Transcripts, MS 11,959 fo. 353, 16 Mar. 1651, fo. 57, 11 Sept. 1652, fo. 80, 2 Apr. 1653, fos. 230, 231.

34 8 Aug. 1677, NLI, Lismore MS 7177.

35 NLI Bayly papers no. 95, 929: 6 Apr. 1681 lease of lands at Ballyarthur between Phillip Craddock of Dublin and Richard Edwards of Knockandufe, Co. Wicklow.

36 (1654–28 Aug. 1710), Irish politician from Meath and privy councillor.

37 Thomas Bligh to Peter Westenra, 26 Mar. 1691, PRONI, MS T2929/1/29.

38 Marchioness of Ormond to John Burden, 9 Oct. 1660, *HMC Ormond*, n.s. vol. 3, p. 6.

39 Ormond to Edward Cooke, 15 June 1667, 19 Aug. 1667, Bodl. Carte MS vol. 215, fo. 363.

40 NLI, Lismore MS 13,227.

41 Aalen et al. (eds), *Atlas of the Irish rural landscape*, p. 123.

42 Eileen McCracken, 'The Irish timber trade in the seventeenth century', *Irish Forestry*, 21:1 (1964), pp 7–18.

43 Rackham, *The history of the countryside*, p. 116.

44 Civil Survey vol. 10, in Aidan Clarke, 'The Irish economy, 1600–1660' in Moody et al. (eds), *Early modern Ireland*, p. 181.

45 Boate wrote 'it is incredible what quantity of charcoal is consumed by one iron-work in a year'. Boate, *Ireland's natural history*, p. 652.

46 *CSPD, 1670*, pp 510–11.

47 10 William III. c.12 The remedies prescribed by this Act were threefold: 1. All resident freeholders, having estates to the value of £10 yearly and upwards, and all tenants for years at a rent exceeding that sum, having an unexpired term of ten years, were required, under a penalty from and after March 25, 1703, to plant every year, for thirty-one years, ten plants of five years' growth of oak, fir, elm, ash, or other timber. Owners of iron-works were required to plant five hundred such trees annually, so long as the iron-works were going. 2. Every occupier of above five hundred Irish acres was required to plant and enclose, within seven years of the passing of the Act, one acre thereof, and to preserve the same as a plantation for at least twenty years. 3. All persons and corporations seized of lands of inheritance were charged with the planting of their respective proportions of 260,600 trees yearly of oak, elm, or fir for a period of thirty-one years. The proportions in which these trees were to be planted in each county is set out in a list in the fourth section of the Act, and the proportion in which each county should be planted was to be apportioned by the grand juries, by baronies, and parishes at each summer assizes.

48 An Act for preserving timber trees and woods, 1698, 10 William III, c. 12.

49 William Congreve (1637–1708). Congreve was the father of the playwright and poet of the same name (1670–1729).

50 Burlington to Congreve, 1698 NLI MS 13227 (2).

51 For example, Lewis described the approach to Castlemartyr from Middleton as being 'a magnificent avenue of lofty elms, one mile in length'. Lewis, *Topographical dictionary of Ireland*, vol. 2, p. 161.

52 *CSPD, March 1677–Feb. 1678*, p. 445.

53 Loveday, *Diary of a tour in 1732*, p. 131.

54 *A tour through Ireland* (London, 1748), p. 195.

55 R. Molesworth to L. Molesworth, 13 Oct. 1716, NLI, P3,752.

56 A. Jacques and D. van der Horst, *The gardens of William and Mary*, p. 106.

57 *OED*, 2nd edition (Oxford, 1989) dates this to a diary entry of 25 Aug. 1654: 'I went to see Kirby a very noble house of my lord Hatton's in Northamptonshire: built a la modern: Garden and stables agreeable, but the avenue ungraceful, and the seat naked'. In *Silva*, published in 1664, Evelyn wrote: 'let them read for avenue, the principal walk to the front of the house'. de Beer, *Diary of John Evelyn*, pp 133–4.

58 Holmes, *Sketches of some of the southern counties of Ireland during a tour in autumn 1797*, p. 185.

59 'Dineley's journal', *JKSIAS*, 4:1 (1862), p. 44.

60 John Loveday, *Diary of a tour in 1732*, p. 28.

61 TCD, Dub. Phil. Soc. 883/2 (I.1.2).

62 William Chetwood, *A tour through Ireland*, p. 208.

63 James Fraser, *Guide thro' Ireland* (Dublin, 1838), p. 55.

64 Duchess of Ormond to George Mathew, 1 Oct. 1670, NLI, Ormond MS 1056/3.

65 Earl of Anglesey to Ormond, 8 Sept. 1663, *HMC Ormond*, n.s., vol. 3, p. 197.

66 Sarah M. Couch, 'The practice of avenue planting in the seventeenth and eighteenth centuries', *Garden History*, 20 (1992), pp 173–200, p. 187.

67 Hardiman Atlas, Survey of the Manor of Castle Waterhouse, Co. Fermanagh by George Black, TCD, MS 1209/2/82.

68 'Dineley's journal', *JKSIAS*, 6:1 (1867), p. 47.

69 Stephen Switzer, *The nobleman, gentleman and gardener's recreation* (London, 1715), p. 55.

70 John Phibbs, 'Groves and belts', *Garden History*, 19:2 (1991), pp 175–86, p. 181.

71 Robert Molesworth to Lettice Molesworth, 8 Apr. 1710, NLI, P 3752, and 19 Nov. 1709, NLI, P3752.

72 John Bryan to duchess of Ormond, 18 Dec. 1667, *HMC Ormond*, n.s. vol. 3, p. 282.

73 8 Mar. 1728, PRONI, Chatsworth, D2707/A1/1/11A.

74 Anon., *An account of the life, character and parliamentary conduct of the Right Honourable Henry Boyle Esq.* (Dublin, 1754), p. 13.

75 *Antrim Ordnance Survey memoir, 1835–1840*, pp 26–7.

76 As required under lease of 1695, Fitzpatrick papers, NLI Report no. 152, no. 1412.

77 'According to your directions I now enclose you an ounce of Scotch fir seed, which cost 5s'. Philip Maddox to John Perceval, 10 Apr. 1683, *HMC Egmont* 2, p. 137.

78 *Antrim Ordnance Survey memoir, 1835–1840*, p. 27.

79 For a description of Sayes Court see Prudence Leith-Ross, 'The garden of John Evelyn at Deptford', *Garden History*, 25:2 (1997), pp 138–52.

80 Greens are used to refer to evergreen shrubs.

81 *An account of the life … of Henry Boyle Esq.*, p. 13.

82 Charles Smith, *Down*, p. 102.

83 Couch, 'The practice of avenue planting in the seventeenth and eighteenth centuries', p. 187.

84 Batty Langley, *A sure method of improving estates* (1728), p. 20.

85 Robert Molesworth to Lettice Molesworth, 12 July 1709, *HMC Various collections*, vol. 8, p. 242. On Molesworth's plantings see also O'Kane, *Landscape design*, p. 16.

86 Robert Molesworth to Lettice Molesworth, 19 Jan. 1718/19, NLI, P3752. This reference is possibly to the hornbeam borders which he was 'a raising and a dunging', referred to in a letter of 7 June 1703, NLI, P3752.

87 'Nothing in Antrim giving any account of, an ugly old town. Lady Massereene lives there in a very old house, the garden reckoned a fine one forty years ago – high hedges and long narrow walks'. John Loveday, *Diary of a tour in 1732*, p. 149.

88 *Antrim Ordnance Survey memoir, 1835–1840*, pp 26–7.

89 'I would have the tops of the high hornbeam hedge in the gravel walk cut as near ever as the growth of the hornbeam will admit, so as in a little time to bring it all to an equal height, which must be 20 foot or more, according as it will bear. I have seen some of above 30 foot, and very even on the sides and tops. Nick must also open and cut even (slantwise) the openings of the hornbeam hedges to the diagonal walks, in order to have a full prospect of those walks', Robert Molesworth to Lettice Molesworth, 16 May 1721, NLI, Killadoon MS Q/1/1.

90 Moses Cook, *The manner of raising, ordering, and improving forest-trees* (London, 1676), p. 137.

91 Ibid., p. 71.

92 Evelyn, *Silva* (1664) p. 30, lime; p. 18, elm; p. 25, sweet chestnut; p. 26, walnut.

93 Ibid., p. 303.

94 Switzer, *Ichnographia rustica*, vol. 2, p. 216.

95 Ibid., p. 187.

96 Thomas Milton, *Seats and demesnes of the nobility and gentry of Ireland* (1779).

97 Journal of a tour to Dublin by James Verdon, 1699, BL, Add. MS 41769, fos. 29–43.

98 Natives include *Quercus petrea* (the sessile oak), *Quercus robur* (the pedunculate oak), *Fraxinus excelsior* (ash), *Sorbus aucuparia* (rowan), *Ulmus glabra* (wych elm), *Pinus sylvestres* (Scot's pine), *Juniperus communis* (juniper), *Taxus baccata* (yew), *Arbutus unedo* (the strawberry tree), *Ilex aquifolium* (holly).

99 Robert Molesworth to Lettice Molesworth, 16 May 1721, NLI, P3752.

100 E. Charles Nelson, '"This garden to adorn all varietie" – the garden plants of Ireland in the centuries before 1700', *Moorea*, 9 (1991), pp 37–54, p. 47.

101 M.J.P. Scannell and D.M. Synnott, *Census catalogue of the flora of Ireland* (Dublin, 1987), pp 36, 39.

102 Feb. 1697, TCD, King MS751/1 fo. 162 and Mar. 1697, TCD, King MS751/1 fo. 164.

103 Rackham, *The history of the countryside*, pp 54–5.

104 William Cooper to countess of Orrery, 4 Oct. 1669; same to same, 12 Nov. 1669, MacLysaght, *Orrery papers*, pp 67–70.

105 R. Molesworth to L. Molesworth, 13 Oct. 1716, NLI, P3752. On Breckdenston's plantings generally see O'Kane, *Landscape design*, pp 13–15.

106 R. Molesworth to L. Molesworth, 12 Apr. 1707, NLI, P3752.

107 R. Molesworth to L. Molesworth, 10 Nov. 1695, NLI, P3752.

108 Sir Robert Southwell to Sir John Perceval, 8 Jan. 1684–5, *HMC Egmont* 2, p. 143.

109 John Evelyn, *Silva* (London, 1664), pp 3–4.

110 Robert Molesworth to Lettice Molesworth, 10 Nov. 1695, NLI, P3752, Smith, *Kerry*, p. 205.

111 Smith, *Kerry*, p. 164.

112 'I send you a parcel of young elms, I think about 70 or 71, nor have I forgot my lady's pippins'. Robert Henley to Sir John Perceval; 5 Dec. 1683.

113 Neville Wilkinson, 'Mount Merrion, the Old', *Irish Times*, 11 Sept. 1925.

114 Francis Elrington Ball, *A history of the county of Dublin*, part 1 (Dublin, 1902), p. 115.

115 Smith, *Kerry*, p. 205.

116 Brewer, *The beauties of Ireland*, vol. 1, pp 284–5.

117 Lewis, *Topographical dictionary of Ireland*, vol. 1, p. 305.

118 Jacques and van der Horst, *The gardens of William and Mary*, pp 116–18, 205–6.

119 Robert Molesworth to Lettice Molesworth, 23 Mar. 1720/21, NLI, P3752.

120 Molesworth wrote of how he would refuse payment to a 'gardener' 'till he makes good the 60 Dutch Elms which you say we wanted of our parcel'. R. Molesworth to L. Molesworth 28 Dec. 1695, NLI, P3752.

121 *CARD*, vol. 4, p. 469.

122 *HMC Egmont* 2, p. 137.

123 Robert Henley to John Perceval, 26 Nov. 1685, *HMC Egmont* 2, p. 137.

124 NAI, Minutes of the Committee of the Royal Hospital of Charles II, 18 Feb. 1692, ordered that £20 be paid to Mr Miller gardener for 200 lime trees to be planted about the hospital, according to the appointment of lord chief justice Pyne, and that money be also allowed for the necessary charge of planting them. 24 Dec. 1699 £10 4s. to be paid for '102 lime trees and for the charge of planting them in a sweep at the front of the hospital'. Minutes, 8 Feb. 1702 show that the following trees were ordered '150 elm trees for the west walk, 150 abeal trees for the same walk, 72 abeal trees to be planted with the walls'.

125 R. Molesworth to L. Molesworth, 5 Feb. 1714, NLI, P3752.

126 Petty recommended restocking Irish woodland with Norwegian imports (1673). *Kenmare MS*, p. 390, Lansdowne, *Petty papers*, vol. 2, p. 126.

127 John Kelly (ed.), *The Hillier gardener's guide to trees and shrubs* (Winchester, 1995), pp 436–7.

128 John Ainsworth, 'Sidelights on eighteenth-century Irish estate management', *JRSAI*, 90:2 (1963), pp 181–6.

129 W.G. Hiscock, *John Evelyn and his family circle* (London, 1950), p. 171.

130 Smith, *Kerry*, p. 217.

131 8 Mar. 1728, PRONI, Chatsworth, D2707/A1/1/11A.

132 Worlidge, *Systema horticulturae*, p. 76.

133 Robert Molesworth to Lettice Molesworth, 16 May 1721, NLI, P3752.

134 R. Molesworth to L. Molesworth, 12 Apr. 1707, NLI, P3752.

135 *Antrim Ordnance Survey memoir, 1835–1840.*

136 'According to your directions I now enclose you an ounce of Scotch fir seed, which cost 5s'. Philip Maddox to John Perceval, 10 Apr. 1683, *HMC Egmont* 2, p. 137.

137 Sir Thomas Hamar recorded that 'of late [he] had some few plants raised from seed, which are yet very small'. Nelson, '"This garden to adorn all variete"', p. 48.

138 Seen at Castle Forbes in Longford in 1680s: TCD, Dub. Phil. Soc. MS 883/2 (I.1.2), fos. 259–60.

139 Garret Fleming to Henry Boyle, 8 Mar. 1728, PRONI, Chatsworth D2707/A1/1/11A.

140 *The Hillier gardener's guide to trees and shrubs*, p. 452, and *Field guide to the trees and shrubs of Britain*, p. 138.

141 TCD, Dub. Phil. Soc. 883/2 (I.1.2), fos. 259–60. A reference to 'platanus' also appears in the Molesworth correspondence including one to 'layers', probably cuttings, of platanus in a nursery. Robert Molesworth to Lettice Molesworth, 7 Aug. 1704, NLI, P3752.

142 'The chestnut walk is finished and the grass appears in it very fine'. 8 Mar. 1728, Chatsworth, PRONI, D2707/A1/1/11A.

143 A survey by Arthur Neville, NLI MS21F, fos 52–72.

144 Worlidge suggested 'variegated or gilded leafed plants' such as holly, laurel, 'philerea and alaturnus'. Worlidge, *Systema horticulturae*, p. 79.

145 Ibid., p. 71.

146 John Evelyn, *Silva* (London, 1664), p. 67.

147 John Evelyn the younger to his father, John Evelyn: '[T]heir cypress and phyllerea were all killed last winter ...', quoted in Hiscock, *John Evelyn and his family circle*, p. 171.

148 *Elysium Britannicum*, BL, Add. MS 78628 A-B, fo. 70.

149 Smith, *Cork*, vol. 1, p. 87.

150 John Aubrey, *The natural history and antiquities of the county of Surrey* (London, 1718), vol. 4, p. 67. Cited in Michael Charlesworth, 'A plan by John Evelyn for Henry Howard's garden at Albury Park, Surrey' in O'Malley et al. (eds), *John Evelyn's 'Elysium Britannicum'*, p. 290.

151 *Antrim Ordnance Survey memoir, 1835–1840*, pp 26–7.

152 15 Apr. 1689, Richard Caulfield (ed.), *Journal of the Very Rev. Rowland Davies, LL.D.* (London, 1857), p. 8.

153 '[A]t Killruddery, the noble seat of lord Meath, in the county of Wicklow, there is a situation for private theatrical exhibitions in the open air, planted out with evergreens which arise there in most luxurious magnificence. It has a wild and romantic effect ...' Walter Scott, *St Ronan's Well* (London, 1832), p. 259.

154 John Worlidge, *Systema horticulturae*, p. 73.

155 John Evelyn, *Silva* (London, 1664), p. 107.

156 See Leith-Ross, 'The garden of John Evelyn at Deptford', pp 138–52.

157 TCD, King MS 751/2, fo. 262.

158 Hiscock, *John Evelyn and his family circle*, p. 171.

CHAPTER 7

Botanical developments and the physic garden

1 The Molesworths sent tulips and 'other roots' from their Edlington estate to Breckdenston. R. Molesworth to L. Molesworth, 16 Mar. 1696, NLI, P3752. Their gardener, Nick, also brought plants from Edlington to Ireland: 'Nick the gardener shall go over to you again in

Oct. and carry over some vines, yews and other trees'. R. Molesworth to L. Molesworth, 8 Aug. 1709, NLI, P3752.

2   George Rawdon to Edward Conway, 16 Mar. 1667, *CSPI, 1666–9*, p. 488.

3   'Bobart gave me at my being initiated into his garden [to call nothing a weed]', Richard Bulkeley to Martin Lister, 1 July 1693, Bodl., Lister MS 36, fo. 55.

4   Henry Capel was the younger brother of Arthur Capel (1631–83), earl of Essex, a former lord lieutenant of Ireland (1672–7). Capel was himself lord deputy of Ireland from 1695 until his death in 1696. John Evelyn was a regular visitor to Kew Park, and his diaries contain several entries relating what he had seen there. He noted in 1678: 'hence I went to my worthy friend Sir Henry Capel ... his garden certainly has the choicest fruit of any plantation in England, as he is the most industrious and understanding in it'. In 1683 he commented on the 'cupola made with pole work between two elms at the end of a walk, which being covered by plashing the trees to them ... very pretty'. In 1688 he recorded that Capel's 'orangerie and myretum are most beautiful and perfectly well kept. He is contriving very high palisades of reeds to shade his oranges during the summer and painting those reeds in oil'. In 1680s the gardens of Arthur Capel earl of Essex at Cassiobury were tended by Moses Cooke. Henrey, *British botanical and horticultural literature before 1800*, p. 177.

5   Richard Bulkeley to Martin Lister, 2 Nov. 1694, Bodl., Lister MS 36, fo. 105.

6   'As soon as I get Hunter's note [I] will take a journey to Kew to my Lord. Capel's gardener for whom I have a letter'. Robert Molesworth to Lettice Molesworth, 28 Dec. 1695, NLI, P3752.

7   Smith, *Cork*, vol. 1, p. 87. Probably *Staphylea*.

8   James Harlow was first noted as a collector in Virginia where James Watt, curator of Chelsea physic garden had sent him. Sometime in 1689 Arthur Rawdon commissioned Harlow to go to Jamaica to collect plants for him after observing Sloane's collection of plants on his return from Jamaica in May 1689.

9   Smith, *Down* (1754), p. 102.

10 Brompton Park Nursery was founded in 1681 by four gardeners, Roger Looker, 'gardener to her Majesty', Moses Cooke, John Field and George London. Cooke disposed of his share to Henry Wise in 1689 and the following year he and London went into partnership. Henrey, *British botanical and horticultural literature before 1800*, p. 181. The Molesworths obtained several trees from the London and Wise nursery at Brompton Park. Robert Molesworth to Lettice Molesworth, 14 Mar. 1720/1, NLI, P3752.

11 Andrew Bridges to Lord Kenmare 17 June 1727, *Kenmare manuscripts*, p. 35.

12 Stephen Switzer, *Ichnographia rustica*, vol. 2 (London, 1718), p. 216.

13 John Bryan to duchess of Ormond, 18 Dec. 1667, *HMC Ormond*, n.s. vol. 3, p. 282

14 Robert Molesworth to Lettice Molesworth, 7 June 1704, NLI, P3752. 'I long to know how your acorn and willow plantations do thrive'. Robert Molesworth to Lettice Molesworth, 11 June 1707, NLI, P3752.

15 R. Molesworth to J. Molesworth, 20 Oct. 1722, *HMC Various collections*, vol. 8, p. 349. See O'Kane, *Landscape design*, p. 38.

16 Ibid., 25 Feb. 1714, NLI 3752.

17 John Baxter to duchess of Ormond, 20 Mar. 1679–80, *HMC Ormond*, n.s. vol. 5, p. 292

18 Usually the black mulberry, *Morus nigra*.

19 8 Mar. 1728, PRONI, Chatsworth, D2707/A1/1/11A.

20 On 10 Mar. 1666 Conway wrote: 'Francis says all the apple trees are well set. But he fears they may fail through dryness of the roots. They were neglected on the way over'. On 24 Dec. 1667 he wrote: 'I have to say, with regret that of the trees Garrett brought very many

are dead, but if you send sciences, here are stocks to make good all defects'. On 25 Mar. 1668 he wrote: 'the sciences have been sent by sea from Dublin, but have not yet arrived at Belfast. The greens it seems are not yet landed'. On 4 Apr. 1668 he wrote: 'the grafts have arrived and are, most of them, grafted already. But the greens have not yet come'. *CSPI, 1666–9*, pp 531, 554, 586, 588.

21 Massereene to Newdigate, Antrim, 6 June 1688, Warwickshire Co. Registry Office: Warwick CR 136/B.288 (a), quoted in Anne Emily Newdigate-Newdegate, *Cavalier and puritan in the days of the Stuarts*, p. 241.

22 T.C. Barnard, 'Gardening, diet and "improvement"', p. 71.

23 William Boyle to Henry Boyle, PRONI, Chatsworth D2707/A1/1/11A.

24 Nicholas Plunkett was a younger son of the earl of Fingall and cousin of the martyr St Oliver Plunkett.

25 Plunkett to Flower, 8 Oct. 1691, NLI, Flower MS 11,472 (1).

26 Ibid., undated, 1682, NLI, Flower MS 11,472 (1).

27 Ibid., NLI, Flower MS 11,472 (1).

28 William Flower was the son of Thomas Flower and Anne Temple (daughter of Sir John Temple and niece of Sir William). He was made Baron Castle Durrow in 1733. NLI, Flower MS 11,470 (3).

29 Robert Molesworth to Lettice Molesworth, 7 June 1707, NLI, Killadoon MS Q/1/1.

30 'And whereas divers persons do hire themselves to work in noblemen's, gentlemen's, or nurserymen's gardens, with design to steal from thence trees, plants, greens, or flower roots'. S.16, of an Act for preserving timber trees and woods, 1698 (10 Will. III, c. 10).

31 Elizabeth Ormond to George Mathew, 6 July 1670, NLI, Ormond MS 2503. It was not just the Irish poor who were driven to theft. The English writer Timothy Nourse noted that the need for firewood was so acute among the city poor in his country that they would grub out hedgerows. Timothy Nourse, *Campania foelix or a discourse of the benefits and improvements of husbandry* (London, 1700), p. 59. Nourse suggested that rather than planting fences on land close to the city that it was better to create banks of earth as "'tis impossible almost to raise a quick-hedge, by reason of the great numbers of poor who inhabit the outskirts, who upon all occasions, and especially in cold weather will make plunder of whatsoever is combustible'.

32 Warwickshire Co. Registry Office: Warwick CR 136/B.288 (a), quoted in Newdigate-Newdegate, *Cavalier and puritan in the days of the Stuarts*, p. 241.

33 Ibid. 20 Feb. 1687/8, Warwickshire Co. Registry Office: Warwick CR 136/B.289 (b), quoted in Newdigate-Newdegate, *Cavalier and puritan in the days of the Stuarts*, p. 241.

34 George Rawdon to Edward Conway, 3 Mar. 1669, *CSPI, 1666–9*.

35 'I hope you have received safely the box of seeds … and the gardener shall soon, I hope, have the trees. You say not a word of your bedding etc … which went by long sea. If you cannot procure any beech trees for love at Santry (though' my cousin Forster is trustee to the young lord) let my gardener buy from the gardener there as much as will make good the avenue'. Robert Molesworth to Lettice Molesworth, 10 Nov. 1695, NLI, P3752.

36 Robert Molesworth to Lettice Molesworth, 10 Oct. 1716, NLI, P3753.

37 James Johnston, 1643–1737 was secretary of state for Scotland.

38 Molesworth wrote regarding the making of walks at Breckdenston 'when we come to accomplish Mr Secretary Johnston's project of carrying forward two long diagonal walks from the middle of the high walk towards Tom Cullen's' and Jerry Hand's …' Robert Molesworth to Lettice Molesworth, 13 Oct. 1716, NLI, P3753. For a discussion of the relationship between Molesworth and Johnston see Hugh Mayo, 'Robert Molesworth's account of Denmark: its roots and its impact' (PhD, Odense, 2000).

39 Richard Bulkeley to Martin Lister, 25 Aug. 1693; Bodl., Lister MS v.36, fo. 63. 'Yesterday I received the book and the seeds from Mr Lovet, I give you my hearty thanks for them'. Richard Bulkeley to Martin Lister, 2 Nov. 1694; Bodl., Lister MS 36, fo. 105.

40 Accounts among the Flower papers include a bill from Mr Cosgrave for 'garden seeds trees etc.' for the year 1735. NLI, Flower MS 11,470 (3).

41 For example, in Feb. 1719, TCD, King MS 751/3 fo. 19.

42 R. Molesworth to L. Molesworth, 1 Sept. 1701, NLI, P3752. A few days later he wrote 'I hope you have received safely the box of seeds ... and the gardener shall soon I hope have the trees'. Robert Molesworth to Lettice Molesworth, 15 Sept. 1701, NLI, P3752.

43 Frederick James Routledge (ed.), *Calendar of the Clarendon State Papers: vol. 5, 1660–1726* (Oxford, 1876), p. 540.

44 'Take the berries when they are ripe and put them in a box close covered for fear of mice and when they have lain till the beginning of March you wash them and take all and dry them at the sun, winnow them that the light stuff be cleansed, then pick the little bowls that you will find and in my lees, the seeds which you must save in the fattest earth you can get, put the earth in a case or box and keep it in a shady place and the seeds will come up'. Dated 1687, in MacLysaght, *Irish life in the seventeenth century*, p. 109.

45 PRONI, De Ros D638 (15), 29 Dec. 1699.

46 Edward Cooke to Ormond, 19 Aug. 1667, Bodl., Carte MS 215, fo. 363.

47 Ibid., 24 Aug. 1667, MS, 215, fo. 367.

48 'The westerly winds make me lose the season for grafting a great many cuttings of fruit trees from Surrenden which are still detained in the river Thames'. John Perceval to Robert Southwell, 3 Apr. 1683, *HMC Egmont* 2, p. 128.

49 *Platanus orientalis*, or oriental plane, very rare in Britain and Ireland today.

50 TCD, Dub. Phil. Soc. MS 883/2 (I.1.2), fos. 259–60.

51 W.H. von Hohberg, *Georgica Curiosa* (Nürnburg, 1682).

52 William Wotton, *Reflections upon ancient and modern learning* (2nd ed., London, 1697), p. 303.

53 TCD, Dub. Phil. Soc. papers MS 883/2 (I.1.2), fo. 86.

54 Worlidge, *Systema horticulturae*, pp 41, 70.

55 E. Charles Nelson, 'Some records (c.1690–1830) of green houses in Irish gardens', *Moorea*, 2 (1983), pp 2–28, 21.

56 Ibid.

57 BL, Add. MS 15950, fos. 142–73.

58 10 Sept. 1677, Guy de la Bédoyère (ed.), *Diary of John Evelyn* (Suffolk, 1995), pp 214–15.

59 Worlidge, *Systema horticulturae*, p. 41.

60 Captain Bellingham 'walked in the afternoon to Moyra, saw Sir Arthur Rawdon's house, and walk ... to the conservatory', 2 June 1690, A. Hewitson (ed.), *Diary of Thomas Bellingham, an officer under William III* (Preston, 1908), p. 123.

61 Sloane was born 16 Apr. 1660 at Killyleagh, Co. Down. He studied medicine in London, and at the University of Orange in France where he obtained his doctorate in 1683, retuning to London the following year. Brilliana Rawdon to Sloane, 26 Sept. 1705, BL, Sloane MS 4039.

62 While staying at Viscount Fitzwilliam's house at Mount Merrion, Archbishop William King wrote: 'I find it a very healthy place ... I have had out of your gardens melons, peach, apricots, ripe almonds as only in France' (indicating that the fruit was grown against walls or in conservatories). Undated, 1714, TCD, King MS 8191, fo. 54.

63 *HMC Egmont*, 2, p. 130.

64 In November (undated) 1683, Sir John Perceval received a letter from Robert Henley informing him 'I send you a parcel of young elms, I think about 70 or 71, nor have I forgot my Lady's pippins'. *HMC Egmont*, 2, p. 137.

65 George Rawdon to Edward Conway, 31 Mar. 1668, *CSPI, 1666–9*, p. 587.

66 Accounts for June 1719, TCD, King MS 751/3 fo. 99.

67 'The trees came down from Dublin on Saturday last, and tomorrow Garret intends to go along with the gardener to Tunny orchard to see them planted'. 23 Jan. 1666, Adam Leathes to Conway, *CSPI, 1666–9*, p. 16.

68 'I read out your letter to our gardener, and he assures me you have all the summer pears you wrote for; and that you made no mention of a nutmeg peach, whereupon I searched for that letter and found my gardener was in the right, if you will be at the cost of the lime'. Plunkett to Flower, 8 Oct. 1691, NLI, Flower MS 11,472 (1).

69 Ibid.

70 Temple, *Upon the gardens of Epicurus*, p. 49.

71 Ibid.

72 'Some of the fruit trees are doing well, though some of Garrett's are dead that made some little show last year', George Rawdon to Edward Conway, 30 Apr. 1667, *CSPI, 1666–9*, p. 354.

73 Edmond Doyne to Flower, 15 Mar. 1691, NLI, Flower MS 11,472 (1). One of the meanings of the word 'blast' is a sudden pernicious influence or effect, e.g. the blast of a huge epidemic or a disease of plants that causes the foliage or flowers to wither.

74 'P.S. Sir I had almost forgot to let your hon know that we have had a great blast this year so that you have not much fruit, but as for your wall-fruit is pretty well and hopes your hon will be here before they are ripe', Doyne to Flower, 2 July 1692, NLI, Flower MS 11,473 (4). Doyne to Flower, 25 July 1691, MS 11743 (2).

75 B. Bourchier to Frances Keightley, *c.*24 Apr. 1696, 'Mrs Bourchier's rag orders for trees', NLI MS45,722/2.

76 George Rawdon to Edward Conway, 19 Oct. 1667, *CSPI, 1666–9*, p. 473.

77 Bulkeley clearly mistook a common pest such as apple scab disease for the blatta, which are insects of the cockroach family; it is unlikely that the trees were infested with cockroaches.

78 Richard Bulkeley to Martin Lister, 19 Mar. 1686, Bodl., Lister MS 35, fo. 116.

79 Ibid., 24 June 1686, MS 35, fo. 119.

80 William Lawson, *The country house-wifes garden* (London, 1618), p. 44.

81 George Rawdon to Edward Conway, 3 Sept. 1665, *CSPI, 1663–5*, p. 636.

82 Temple, *Upon the gardens of Epicurus*, p. 234.

83 In 1681 one of the earl of Orrery's agents was pleased to report of Charleville that he 'never saw the great house, orchard and gardens in such good repair as now'. John Love to dowager countess of Orrery, 20 May 1681, *Orrery papers* (1941), pp 244–5.

84 Lettice Molesworth to Robert Molesworth, 20 July 1699, *HMC Various collections*, vol. 8, p. 220.

85 Richard Bulkeley to Martin Lister, 19 Mar. 1686, MS 35, fo. 116.

86 'Pray my dear make your gardener inoculate for us some of his best fruit this year peaches and nectarines that we may preserve and increase the kinds'. Robert Molesworth to Lettice Molesworth, 11 June 1707, NLI, P3752.

87 Garret Roche, 28 Oct. 1674, NLI Lismore, MS 7177.

88 'The news sent to you about removing of trees at Portmore House is a mistake. I was lately there myself examining the orchards and find none missing'. George Rawdon to Edward Conway, 31 Aug. *CSPI, 1666–9*, p. 246.

89 Lucius O'Brien to Catherine O'Brien at Corofin, 8 Jan. 1712, NLI MS 45,297/1. O'Kane, 'Leamaneh and Dromoland, part I', p. 67. For Lucius's debt problems see the entry for 2 Dec. 1706 at p. 269, a letter from Catherine's father Thomas Keightley to Donat O'Brien in which he mentions that Lucius was in great debt again. He proposed the debt be satisfied by Donat, Lucius should make over all his present estate, as life tenant to his father, and 'live cheerfully at Leamaneh' and when once out of debt, live 'with such remaining pension out of his own, as you shall be pleased to allow him, or ever by way of farmer, if you will set him a farm'.

90 Donat O'Brien was a francophone. Lord Inchiquin wrote that he relied on Donat to assist a Mr Bordier/Boydemay: 'I have also written to my uncle O'Brien about them, because he speaks the language', 29 June 1694 in John Ainsworth (ed.), *Inchiquin papers* (Dublin, 1961), p. 57.

91 Rawdon to Sloane, 10 May 1688, BL, Sloane MS 4036, fo. 35.

92 'I shall be much obliged if you will send me any seeds, which if sent soon to Mrs. Burton at the French King's Head in the Old Exchange, to be sent to me by Mrs Butterfield, who is coming down they will come safe, or else given to my cousin Dunbar who is coming down and is to be found at the Roe Duck in Haymarket'. Rawdon to Sloane, 31 Mar. 1689/90, BL, Sloane MS 4036, fo. 73.

93 Sloane to Rawdon, 29 Apr. 1689, E. Berwick (ed.), *The Rawdon papers consisting of letters on various subjects* (London, 1819), pp 391–2.

94 Rawdon to Sloane, 4 May 1692, BL, Sloane MS 4036, fo. 121.

95 Sloane arranged for William Sherrard to come to Ireland to research its flora. Sherrard was friends with Jacob Bobart at Oxford and the plantsman John Ray. Sherard came to regret his time in Ireland, writing to Sloane on 7 Mar. 1714/15 that 'I lost three years and a half of my life … which would have been much better spent elsewhere', quoted in Nelson, 'Sir Arthur Rawdon', p. 37.

96 Sherrard to Sloane, 3 May 1692, BL, Sloane MS 4036, fos. 119–20.

97 The Wardian case was an early type of glazed protective container for plants akin to a miniature greenhouse. It was often used in the nineteenth century to protect plants stored on the decks of ships during importation from overseas, which previously often died from exposure during long sea journeys, frustrating the many scientific and amateur botanists of the time. The Wardian case was named after its inventor, Dr Nathaniel Bagshaw Ward (1791–1868), of London, in about 1829.

98 Nelson, 'Sir Arthur Rawdon', pp 30, 43.

99 'I have taken a gardener at London one Thomas Harrison, who Mr Sherrard has sent on to come over and have sent to bring me over some things, and I do desire of you yet you would recommend him to some of the merchants to draw a bill on me for what he shall have occasion for his journey and those things which I suppose will not be above 20l'. Rawdon to Sloane, 24 June 1691, BL, Sloane MS 4036 fo. 105.

100 Rawdon's Harrison was engaged in 1691, Bulkeley mentions his Mr. Harrison in 1694, so there is a strong likelihood that they were one and the same.

101 John Rawdon to Sloane, 30 Oct. 1711, BL, Sloane MS 4054, fo. 331.

CHAPTER 8
Use and control of water in the seventeenth-century garden

1 George London and Henry Wise, *The complete gardener abridged by London and Wise from the original by M de la Quintinye* (London, 1704), p. 21.

2 Stephen Switzer, *An introduction to a general system of hydrostaticks and hydraulics, philosophical and practical* (1729), p. 301.

3 For examples, see Vaux le Vicomte, Versailles, Chateau de Courances, Killruddery and Antrim Castle. See also Christopher K. Currie, 'Fishponds as garden features', *Garden History*, 18:1 (1990), pp 22–46, p. 28.

4 Plot discusses the use of lock gates in shallow natural rivers for managing water for use in garden features. Robert Plot, *The natural history of Oxfordshire* (Oxford, 1677), p. 233.

5 Smith, *Cork*, vol. 1, p. 337.

6 For a detailed account of the works at Breckdenston see generally O'Kane, *Landscape design in eighteenth-century Ireland*, chapter 1. Robert Molesworth to Lettice Molesworth, 19 Jan. 1719, NLI, P3752.

7 Oliver Rackham, *The history of the countryside* (London, 1986), p. 366.

8 'Leat' a trench or ditch that conveys water to a mill wheel: *OED*.

9 Rackham, *History of the countryside*, p. 366.

10 Belan, inaccurately recorded as being 'three miles from Bray', had 'several ponds also well stocked with fish'. John Loveday, *Diary of a tour in 1732*, p. 28; Thomastown, Co. Tipperary, the home of the honourable George Mathew, brother-in-law to the duke of Ormond, had a long fish pond, sleeping under 'a green mantle' between 'two rectilineous banks, appears in the midst'. Walker, 'The rise and progress of gardening in Ireland', p. 12.

11 For a detailed discussion of fishponds, see Currie, 'Fishponds', pp 22–46.

12 Sir John Temple was solicitor general. (The Temple family subsequently acquired the title Palmerston.) In 1675 he petitioned the King's Inns stating that he was in treaty for the corner house next to the Inns garden. He claimed that 'the high green walk next to the said house is of very little use to the society', and asked for permission to build on the forepart and to make 'a little walk of the residue thereof'. Temple requested a lease of the walk and promised to enclose the same with a brick wall, undertaking to surrender the enclosed part if ever the four courts should come to be built in the Inns garden. In 1699 Sir John returned successfully to seek a new lease for 99 years, claiming to have 'improved very considerably on the premises'. Kenny, *King's Inns and the kingdom of Ireland*, p. 113.

13 Hiscock, *John Evelyn and his family circle*, p. 171.

14 Francis, earl of Longford, to Patrick Kenny, Dublin, 29 Mar. 1690; Edward MacLysaght (ed.), 'Report on the Connor papers', *AH*, 15 (1944), p. 15.

15 Izaak Walton, *The compleat angler, or the contemplative man's recreation* (London, 1868); part 1 is 'a discourse of rivers, fish-ponds, fish and fishing'.

16 Ibid.; carp, bream and tench being at chapters 9, 10, 11.

17 Francis Aungier (*c*.1632–1700). Aungier was the 3rd Baron and 1st Viscount Longford. TCD, Dub. Phil. Soc. papers MS 883/2 (I.1.2), fo. 266.

18 Charles Smith, *A history of the present and antient state of the county of Waterford* (Dublin, 1756), p. 89.

19 Robert Molesworth to Lettice Molesworth, 17 June 1704, *HMC Various collections*, vol. 8, p. 230.

20 For instance, 'Carpes to stew', 'to collar [fillet] ells', 'carp to dress', 'dressed cod's head', 'frigasee rabbets': Dorothy Parsons Booke of Choyce Receipts, 1666, Birr Castle, Rosse MS A/17.

21 Gervase Markham, *Country contentments*, John Worlidge, *Systema agriculturae*, John Balgrave, *The epitome of the art of husbandry* (London, 1685), John Mortimer, *The whole art of husbandry* (London, 1707).

22 John Norden, *The surveyor's dialogue* (London, 1607), p. 172.

23 William Lawson, *The English husbandman* (London, 1613), p. 10.

24 John Taverner, *Certain experiments concerning fish and fruit* (London, 1600), p. 1.

25 Janus Dubravius, *A new book of good husbandry* (London, 1599), p. 18.

26 Markham, *The English husbandman*, p. 185.

27 Roger North, *A discourse on fish and fishponds* (London, 1713), p. 7.

28 The town was established in 1605, so the plan must date from some time later than this. The King's Castle may, of course, have been sited on an earlier settlement such as a monastery, so the garden layout could date from an earlier period.

29 TCD, MS 1209/32/2.

30 North, *Discourse on fish and fishponds*, pp 24–6.

31 The early house at Belan was demolished and a new one built in 1743.

32 TCD, Dub. Phil. Soc. papers MS 883/2 (I.1.2). A lady who wished to remain anonymous recounted her memories of Belan during her childhood in 'Recollections of visits to Belan House, Co. Kildare in the early Victorian period', *JCKAS*, 5:5 (1908), pp 298–310: 'the grounds of Belan were very beautiful, and of considerable extent. On one side, though not seen from the house, were the celebrated fish ponds (not that in my time there were fish in them), large and deep, the trees around giving them a secluded and fascinating look'.

33 Gervase Markham recommended that the mixture of orchard walks with fishponds combined leisure with profit. William Lawson, *A new orchard and garden* (1638).

34 George Rawdon to Edward Conway, 2 Sept. 1665, *CSPI, 1665*, p. 636.

35 John Loveday, *Diary of a tour in 1732* (London, 1890), p. 28.

36 Smith, *Cork*, vol. 1, p. 337.

37 23 June 1677, *Orrery papers*, p. 179.

38 Tom Williamson, *Suffolk's gardens and parks* (East Anglia, 2000), p. 38.

39 Timothy Mowl, *Gentlemen and players* (Stroud, Gloustershire, 2000), p. 36.

40 Map Room, Killruddery.

41 1719, reproduced in frontispiece to Tom Williamson, *Polite landscapes* (Stroud, Gloustershire, 1995). See also Linda Cabe Halpern, 'Wrest Park, 1686–1730s: exploring Dutch influence', *Garden History*, 30:2 (2002), pp 131–52.

42 In his autobiography Pole Cosby makes several references to improvements he and his father, Dudley, carried out in the garden at Stradbally. Dudley Cosby built the 'big house' in 1699. The waterworks appear to have been in existence prior to 1714 when Cosby took up residence. At this date 'he made the avenue that is, planted the trees, he built the bridges going to it'. 'Autobiography of Pole Cosby', p. 84.

43 Lewis, *Topographical dictionary of Ireland*, vol. 1, p. 578.

44 'Dineley's journal', *JKSIAS*, 6:1 (1867), p. 75.

45 North, *A discourse on fish*, p. 33.

46 Undated, 1707/8, *Council book of Cork*, p. 108.

47 3rd earl of Burlington and 4th earl of Cork. He came of age in 1716, so the work would have been carried out under the instructions of his guardian Henry Boyle, later Lord Carleton, 1698–1710, younger brother of Charles Boyle, and the 2nd earl of Burlington. Burlington to Roche, 28 Aug. 1707, NLI Lismore, MS 13231.

48 Robert Molesworth to Lettice Molesworth, 29 Nov. 1712, NLI, P3752. See O'Kane, *Landscape design*, p. 240.

49 10 Sept. 1677, de la Bédoyère (ed.), *Diary of John Evelyn*, pp 214–15.

50 Robert Molesworth to Lettice Molesworth, undated, NLI, P3752.

51 Robert Molesworth to Lettice Molesworth, 29 Nov. 1712, NLI, P3752, the Ward river ran through Breckdenston. See O'Kane, *Landscape design*, pp 21, 26.

52 Robert Molesworth to Lettice Molesworth, 17 Apr. 1720, NLI, P3752.

53 NLI, MS 21F 52–72.

54 Worlidge, *Systema horticulturae*, p. 49.

55 Switzer, *Ichnographia rustica*, quoted in Currie, 'Fishponds as garden features', p. 26.

56 James P. Farrell, *History of the county of Longford* (Dublin, 1891), p. 333.

57 Robert Molesworth to Lettice Molesworth, 12 June 1709, NLI, P3753.

58 Worlidge, *Systema horticulturae*, p. 44.

59 Henry Boyle, 1st earl of Shannon, 1684–1764, second son of Col. Henry Boyle, and grandson of Roger, earl of Orrery.

60 John McVeagh (ed.), *Richard Pococke's Irish tours* (Dublin, 1995), p. 184.

61 In *Landscape design in eighteenth-century Ireland*, O'Kane suggests that the summerhouse that housed the cistern also contained a mill wheel with which to power further water interventions at upper levels of the garden. See pp 22–3 here.

62 Robert Molesworth to Lettice Molesworth, 12 June 1709, NLI, P3752.

63 Worlidge, *Systema horticulturae*, p. 54.

64 Robert Molesworth to Lettice Molesworth, 18 Nov. 1710, NLI, P3732. This analysis is from O'Kane, *Landscape design in eighteenth-century Ireland*, p. 22.

65 11 Oct. 1660, Samuel Pepys, *Diary of Samuel Pepys* (Raleigh, NC, 1983), p. 217.

66 Stephen Switzer, *An introduction to a general system of hydrostaticks and hydraulics, philosophical and practical* (1729), p. 323. Chapter entitled 'Of crank work, vibrating lever, and complicated or treble wheel engine for raising water', p. 319.

67 In 1697, two years after his death, Morland's tract *Hydrostatics, or instructions concerning water works* was published by his son. This work was probably highly influential on Switzer's later work. Anon., *A brief account of the life, writings and inventions of Sir Samuel Morland, master of mechanics to Charles the Second* (1838), pp 11–15.

68 'An engine of curious artifice by the help of one horse furnisheth all the offices of the castle with that necessary element': 'Dineley's journal', *JKSIAS*, 4:1 (1862), pp 105–6.

69 Earl of Longford to Ormond, 27 Dec. 1681. NLI, Ormond MS 2367–363. John Evelyn described another interesting work by Morland; a sort of drawbridge at Viscount Hereford's. Sir Samuel Morland invented a 'skrew bridge, which being turned with a key lands you 50 foot distance, at entrance of an ascending walk of trees for a mile in length'. 10 Sept. 1677, de la Bédoyère (ed.), *Diary of John Evelyn*, pp 214–15.

70 Plot, *The natural history of Oxfordshire*, p. 235.

71 Robert Molesworth to Lettice Molesworth, 18 May 1717, NLI, P3752.

72 'Dineley's journal', *JKSIAS*, 4:1 (1862), pp 105–6.

73 Robert Molesworth to Lettice Molesworth, 18 May 1717, NLI, P3752.

74 Ibid.

75 See O'Kane, *Landscape design*, p. 22.

76 At Listerne, Co Waterford, 'there was a large and beautiful canal, at the further end of which is a jet d'eau that cast up water to a considerable height'. Walker, 'The rise and progress of gardening in Ireland', p. 11.

77 Currie, 'Fishponds as garden features', p. 25.

78 Temple was of the opinion that because those in northern climes suffered less from heat, they made 'little provision against it, and are careless of shade, and seldom curious in fountains'. Temple, *Upon the gardens of Epicurus*, p. 230.

79 Hiscock, *John Evelyn and his family circle*, p. 171.

80 Worlidge, *Systema horticulturae*, p. 50.

81 Ibid.

82 Ibid., p. 57.

83 Plot, *The natural history of Oxfordshire*, p. 237. Plot (1640–96) was a naturalist, the first professor of chemistry at the University of Oxford and first keeper of the Ashmolean Museum.

84 *Systema horticulturae*, p. 58.

85 Plot, *The natural history of Oxfordshire*, p. 235.

86 Ossory to Ormond, 2 July 1664, Bodl., Carte MS, vol. 220, fo. 151.

87 Longford to Ormond, 24 Dec. 1681 *HMC Ormond*, n.s. vol. 6, p. 220. The letter encloses an agreement between John Bonnier and the earl of Longford for the work.

88 Longford to Ormond, 24 Dec. 1681, NLI, Ormond MS 2367–363.

89 Ibid.

90 William Robinson to Ormond, 30 Sept. 1682, Bodl., Carte MS 54, fo. 74.

91 The waterworks at Castle Durrow were eventually improved. Household accounts disclose that £1.3s. 6d. was paid to a carpenter in Mar. 1714 for 'making 3 sluices for the canals' and that in Feb. 1716 he was paid 'for making two gate posts going to the canals'. NLI, Flower MS 11,469 (2) (Carpenter's work done for William Flower Esq. by Jon Owens since 29 July 1712). The Irish Treasury Accounts for Jan. 1703/4 include an estimate of the charge for enclosing the wood in the Phoenix Park with a stone wall of six foot high, draining the said wood and making a fishpond. The cost of 'digging the canal or fishpond' and 'for 150 perch of mason work on the sluices' and 'for carpenters work and stuff in making three sluices' was £64 10s. TCD, Southwell MS 1180, fo. 179.

92 North, quoted in Currie, 'Fishponds as garden features', p. 35.

93 Stephen Switzer, *A universal system of water and water-works, philosophical and practical* (London, 1734), p. 117.

94 George Cartwright to Robert Molesworth, 27 Feb. 1722, NLI, P3753: 'I spoke to Mr Adair again about the Alder from Powerscourt and he has promised to take care to get them'. See O'Kane, *Landscape design*, p. 23.

95 Shannon to John Perceval, *HMC Egmont*, 2, p. 129.

96 Robert Molesworth to Lettice Molesworth, 16 May 1721, NLI, P3752.

97 North, *A discourse on fish*, p. 12, quoted in Currie, 'Fishponds as garden features', p. 35.

98 Robert Molesworth to Lettice Molesworth, 2 Feb. 1712, NLI, P3752.

99 Ibid., 18 Nov. 1710.

100 Ibid., 13 Oct. 1716.

101 Ibid., 27 Dec. 1720. For an interpretation and analysis of the waterworks at Breckdenston see O'Kane, *Landscape design*, pp 21–9.

102 Plot, *The natural history of Oxfordshire*, p. 234.

103 Worlidge, *Systema horticulturae*, p. 51.

104 Dézallier d'Argenville, *Theory and practice of gardening*, p. 82.

105 Robert Molesworth to Lettice Molesworth, 27 Dec. 1720, NLI, P3752.

106 North, *A discourse on fish*, quoted in Currie, 'Fishponds as garden features', p. 32.

107 Ibid.

108 Switzer, *A universal system of water and water-works*, quoted in Currie, 'Fishponds as garden features', p. 33.

109 Robert Molesworth to Lettice Molesworth, 25 May 1714, NLI, P3752.

110 Ibid., 27 Dec. 1720, NLI, P3752.

111 Taverner, *Certaine experiments concerning fish and fruit*, p. 2.

112 Markham, *The English husbandman*, p. 185.

113 Dézallier d'Argenville, *Theory and practice of gardening*, p. 283.

114 Possibly Bishop Anthony Dopping of Ossory, d. 1728.

115 Gaulstown was owned by George Rochfort. His son Robert Rochfort, 1st earl of Belvedere, 'the wicked earl' (1708–74), built Belvedere House. On the death of his first wife in 1731 he married Mary Molesworth, aged sixteen, the daughter of the 3rd Viscount Molesworth, in 1736.

116 TCD, Dub. Phil. Soc. papers MS 883/2 (I.1.2), fo. 103.

117 Samuel Johnson, *The works of the English poets* (London, 1810), vol. 42, p. 226. *A supplement to Dr Swift's works: containing miscellanies in prose and verse, by the Dean; Dr Delany, Dr Sheridan, Mrs Johnson, and others* (London, 1779), vol. 3, p. 289.

118 Rolf Loeber, 'Irish country houses and castles of the late Caroline period; an unremembered past recaptured', *QBIGS*, 16:1 (1973), p. 2.

119 John Loveday, *Diary of a tour in 1732*, p. 131.

120 *Antrim Ordnance Survey memoir, 1835–1840*, pp 26–7.

121 Edward MacLysaght (ed.), 'Report on the Longford papers', *AH*, 13:15 (1944), p. 123.

122 See Currie, 'Fishponds as garden features', p. 29. This argument is further undermined by the acknowledgment that the Blenheim and Hampton Court canals (46m x 150m), considered 'too large', being the largest formal water features of their kind in England, were used for fishing.

123 John Evelyn recorded a visit to the earl and countess of Clarendon at Swallowfield in Berkshire in October 1685: 'but above all, the canal and fish ponds ... so well and plentifully stocked with fish, that for pike, carp, bream, and tench, I never saw anything approaching it. We had at every meal carp and pike of a size fit for the table of a prince'. de Beer, *John Evelyn's diary*, vol. 1, p. 226.

124 See, for example, the painting of Stradbally Hall.

125 Robert Molesworth to Lettice Molesworth, 23 June 1713, NLI, P3752

126 *Account of the life of ... Henry Boyle*, p. 13. Henry Boyle, 1st earl of Shannon (1682–28 Dec. 1764).

127 Smith, *Cork*, vol. 1, p. 136.

128 'Redoubt' in this context means refuge, presumably for wildfowl. Other examples of this could be seen at Somerleyton in Suffolk,

129 Accounts, March 1714, Flower MS 11,469 (1).

130 Dézallier d'Argenville, *Theory and practice of gardening*, p. 282.

131 The removal of kitchen gardens to a place distant from the main house was a late eighteenth-century phenomenon. Up until the mid-eighteenth century they were generally sited close to the house and incorporated into the general decorative scheme. See Worlidge, *Systema horticulturae*, p. 18.

132 Nicholas Plunkett to Thomas Flower, NLI, Flower MS 11,469 (2), 1 July 1682.

133 Lewis, *Topographical dictionary of Ireland*, vol. 2, p. 622.

134 Thomastown, undated, 1732, John Loveday, *Diary of a tour in 1732*, p. 43.

135 Robert Molesworth to Lettice Molesworth, 29 Nov. 1712, NLI, P3752.

136 William Kenn of Cahermary in Co. Limerick worked for the Perceval family and for the earl of Orrery at Charleville.

137 3 Aug. 1665, 'I was the second instant at Churchtown, where I was honoured with the company of lieutenant Beare, and what I did there concerning the river and fish ponds he was pleased to take recognizance of ...' *HMC Egmont*, 2, p. 14.

138 Robert Molesworth to Lettice Molesworth, 3 June 1715, NLI, P3752.

139 Later 1st earl of Shannon, 1756.

140 Undated, 1728, William Boyle to Henry Boyle, PRONI, Chatsworth, D.2707/A1/1/3.

141 Holmes, *Sketches of some of the southern counties of Ireland during a tour in autumn 1797*, p. 124.

142 Rawdon to Conway, 31 Aug. 1670, *CSPI, 1669–70*, p. 246.

143 Lettice Molesworth to Robert Molesworth, 12 June 1714, NLI, P3753. See O'Kane, *Landscape design*, pp 23–8.

144 Ibid.

145 Ibid.

146 Robert Molesworth to Lettice Molesworth, 25 May 1714, NLI, P3752.

147 Same to same, 28 Mar. 1719, NLI, P3752: 'begin again your canal, the small leaks in the head or bank do not disturb me … I think more of that plug leak'.

148 George Cartwright to R. Molesworth, 19 Feb. 1722, NLI, P3753.

149 Same to same, 8 July 1710, NLI, P3752.

150 Dézallier d'Argenville, *Theory and practice of gardening*, p. 64.

151 Robert Molesworth to Lettice Molesworth, 12 July 1709, *HMC Various collections*, vol. 8, p. 242.

152 Campbell, *A philosophical survey of the South of Ireland, 1778*, pp 169–70.

153 Robert Molesworth to Lettice Molesworth, 27 Dec. 1720, NLI, P3752. See O'Kane, *Landscape design*, pp 25–6.

154 Same to same, 25 May 1714, NLI, P3752. Molesworth's gardener Nick was confident 'that he had elms enough in his own nurseries fit for that canal', Molesworth was not impressed with these specimens as he sent for 'seventeen bundles of elms (wherein are 212 trees)' from England because Nick's elms were not 'of equal size', Robert Molesworth to Lettice Molesworth, 13 Oct. 1716, NLI, P3752.

155 *Antrim Ordnance Survey memoir, 1835–1840*, pp 26–7.

156 Robert Molesworth to Lettice Molesworth, 27 Dec. 1720, NLI, P3752.

157 Smith, *Cork*, vol. 1, p. 337.

158 Ibid.

CHAPTER 9

Field sports and hunting

1   Journal of a tour to Dublin by James Verdon, 1699, BL, Add. MS 41769, fos. 29–43

2   Chitty, *A treatise on the law of the prerogatives of the Crown*, p. 141.

3   George Rawdon to Edward Conway, 13 Apr. 1667, *CSPI, 1666–9*, p. 345

4   Killruddery, earl of Meath papers, J3/2.

5   Oliver Cheney, agent to the earl of Meath, wrote that the earl was planning to 'make a treble ditch without the south wall and quickset the fen to the end that the deer may not get to the fruit and that the park may be completed'. Killruddery, Meath papers, J3/2.

6   Richard Dobbs, 1683, TCD, Dub. Phil. Soc. MS 8267/2.

7   TCD, Dub. Phil. Soc. 883/1 (I.1.2).

8   Ibid.

9   Earl of Anglesey to Ormond, 8 Sept. 1663, *HMC Ormond*, n.s. vol. 3, p. 197.

10 John Chetwood, *A tour through Ireland*, pp 142–3.

11 Journal of a tour to Dublin by James Verdon, 1699, BL, Add. MS 41769, fos. 29–43

12 George Rawdon to Edward Conway, 24 Dec. 1667, *CSPI, 1666–9*, p. 531.

13 John McVeagh (ed.), *Richard Pococke's Irish tours* (Dublin, 1995), p. 184.

14 Also Evelyn, *Silva*, p. 279; Claude Mollet, *Théâtre des Plans et Jardinages* (Paris, 1652).

15 Clohosey, 'Dunmore House', *OKR*, 4 (1951), p. 44.

16 Undated and part missing, early seventeenth century 'for the duke of Ormond': 'I writ last unto you I went to Carrick where I had a view of a very ruinous house, in the outward appearance of it ... the orchard is not fine but well planted with good fruit; but the park is I think the finest one of the bigness that can been seen anywhere, and the dry wall the best of any that ever I saw and all finished, and the ground fully stocked with fine large fat deer'; Bodl., Carte MS, vol. 243, fo. 18.

17 George Rawdon to Edward Conway, 24 Dec. 1667, *CSPI, 1666–9*, p. 531.

18 Accounts of Arthur, earl of Anglesey, vice treasurer of Ireland, 1660–6, TCD, MS 808 (26).

19 These open pastures were called 'lannes', 'launes', 'launds' or 'lawnds', meaning a smooth open space of grassland, or pasture between woods; from this comes the modern word lawn. See reference to a 'lanne' in the deer park; W. Harbord to earl of Rochester, undated, 1685. *Clarendon letters*, vol. 1, p. 176.

20 These were the *jura coronae* or rights of the Crown; so long as they were attached to the monarch, they were called prerogatives. But when such prerogatives were delegated to a subject they were known as franchises.

21 The King was the ultimate owner of all land in the kingdom. 'The right of the Sovereign to reserve to himself and to confer on his subjects, certain peculiar and exclusive privileges respecting game was part of the policy of the feudal constitution, for the purposes of keeping people in a state of subordination, and preserving, for the exclusive enjoyment of the higher classes, a sport suited to the martial genius of the age ...' Joseph Chitty, *Treatise on the law of the prerogatives of the Crown* (London, 1820), p. 134.

22 Limerick, by Daniel Hignet, TCD, Dub. Phil. Soc. 883/1 (I.1.2), fos. 239–43.

23 7 Aug. 1677, NLI Lismore, MS 7177.

24 John Manwood, *Treatise of the forest laws* (1717), p. 42. Forests referred to both ancient existing forests and new creations such as the New Forest in Hampshire. The owner of a forest chase or warren was entitled to kill game within his franchise, though if he strayed out of the limits of his district he was liable to penalties imposed by the various court and offices incidental to a forest. A chase was defined as 'an unenclosed place'; a chase could encroach onto another's land and the owner of the chase had the right to game as opposed to the owner of the land. Such chases came into existence when a landowner sold land but reserved the right to the chase for him or herself. A free chase referred to a right to hunt and kill game over a certain district. If a subject owned a forest, he could grant a licence to another to make and enclose a park within the forest. The law relating to warrens was similar to that of chases except that rather than being stocked with deer, warrens were 'a place privileged for the keeping of beasts and fowls of warren'. Chitty, *A treatise on the law of the prerogatives of the Crown*, p. 141.

25 Chitty, *A treatise on the law of the prerogatives of the Crown*, p. 140.

26 MacLysaght, 'Report on Dunsdale papers', p. 400.

27 For example, lease by Arthur Chichester, Lord Chichester, baron of Belfast etc.; Sir Maurice Eustace, Kt. Sergeant at Law, and Sir Robert Dixon of Dublin Kt. to William Dobbin of Carrickfergus, gent. of 'the territory or circuit of land situate in ... Antrim ... called Ballinaboyle ... excepting warren and chase'. 20 July 1652, Grove papers, NLI Report No. 276.

28 Fine of Easter 3 William and Mary between Thomas Newcome Kt and Hugh Galbraith a merchant, plaintiffs and Alexander Fraser defendant, 'the manor of Le Ward' with a castle, 200 gardens, five orchards and a pigeon house. NLI, Walker papers, Report no. 33.

29 Ormond wrote that when Lord Rochester is in Ireland to reside at Kilkenny 'my parks are at his service', 28 Dec. 1684, Bodl., Carte MS, vol. 220, fo. 74.

30 Duchess of Ormond to George Mathew, 6 July 1670, NLI, Ormond, MS 2503.

31 Henry Boyle, 1st earl of Shannon, 1684–1764, second son and heir of Hon. Col. Henry
    Boyle, son of Roger, earl of Orrery, and grandson of Richard, 1st earl of Cork. Henry Boyle
    looked after Boyle and Burlington estates in Cork and Waterford for his brother-in-law
    Richard Boyle, 3rd earl of Burlington and 4th earl of Cork.

32 NLI, Lismore, MS 13227.

33 Ibid.

34 Williamson, *Polite landscapes*, p. 23.

35 Section 2 of the Act provided that persons not having a freehold of £40 per year or personal
    estate of £1000 were not to keep any hounds or spaniels, except whelps for persons qualified;
    'hounds' were said to include beagles, greyhounds or land-spaniels. Section 3 prohibited
    persons of small estates from keeping hounds. Section 4 outlawed the employment by
    Protestants of 'papists or reputed papists' as fowlers – this qualification ensured that Roman
    Catholic landowners such as George Mathew of Thomastown in Tipperary could employ
    Catholics if they so wished. The Act further provided that no person to shoot deer except
    on his own ground or (being a Protestant) the ground of his master (s.4,) or take pigeon 'save
    belonging to his own Dove house' (ss.7 and 8). A shooting 'season' was enshrined in law by
    s. 6 of the Act: stalking of male deer began on the 14 June, and finished at Michaelmas. The
    season for taking hares, grouse and game birds began on 14 June, and ended on 2 February.
    An Act for the Preservation of the Game and the more easy conviction of such as shall
    destroy the same, 1698, 10 William III c.13.

36 Williamson, *Polite landscapes*, p. 24.

37 A note of food eaten at Castlemartyr on Thursday 3 July 1679 includes '1 haunch of
    venison': *Orrery papers*, p. 222. In fact, venison was so highly regarded that attempts were
    made to produce 'mock' venison dishes such as a beef pastry, baked like venison with
    instructions on how to 'make red deer' using 'a leg of beef', Thomas Dawson, *The good
    huswifes jewel*, pt 1 (Amsterdam, 1696), pp 14, 20.

38 Henry O'Brien, 7th earl of Thomond, to Sir Donough O'Brien, Ainsworth, *Inchiquin papers*
    (1961), p. 31.

39 6 Aug. 1708, Ainsworth, *Inchiquin papers*, p. 118.

40 Burlington to his commissioners, 28 Oct. 1690, NLI Lismore, MS 13226 (1).

41 'The deer in the Spring park here do well. Mr Philips has made a park at Limavady and begs
    me for a brace ...' and 'Dr Colville wants eight or ten brace of deer to stock his park'. George
    Rawdon to Edward Conway, Oct. 1667, *CSPI, 1666–9*, p. 531.

42 'I was last week to new Moore Park, which I find to be still the same sweet and pleasant seat
    I knew it before, and had a taste of the goodness of your grace's venison... the gardens are
    extraordinary, full of delightful walks and fountains and terraces with covered walks for rainy
    weather ... the park is set out into walks shaded with trees set in rows, and there is a fair
    brick lodge, that hath the prospect of most of the park and country, and may be seen at the
    end of a long walk out of your dining room window.' *HMC Ormond*, n.s. vol. 3, p. 197.

43 James Buck to Ormond, 5 Dec. 1665, *HMC Ormond*, n.s. vol. 3, pp 197–8.

44 A 'deer house' is marked on the first edition Ordnance Survey map of Howth Castle.

45 'Paid labourer for building the deer house in the park'. 2 Mar. 1686, Richard Bagg's book of
    payments on behalf of Burlington estates, NLI, Lismore, MS 6300. 'Paid two men for two
    days work cleaning the deer house in the park', 7 Sept. 1687, Richard Bagg's book of
    payments on behalf of Burlington estates, NLI Lismore, MS 6300.

46 NLI, Lane, MS 8645 (1).

47 27 Mar. 1685/6. Richard Bagg's book of payments on behalf of Burlington estates, NLI, Lismore, MS 6300.

48 '£4 6s. 2d. paid to mowers for mowing the great meadow park and for weeding the meadow'. 31 July 1683, Richard Bagg's book of payments on behalf of Burlington estates. NLI, Lismore, MS 6300. Labourers paid for spreading dung on the park meadow. 23 Feb. 1687, Richard Bagg's book of payments on behalf of Burlington estates. NLI, Lismore, MS 6300.

49 James Coleman paid for glassing at the lodges in the park. 28 May 1688, NLI, Lismore, MS 6300.

50 TCD, MS 1460/21.

51 27 Sept. 1687, NLI, Lismore, MS 6300. The sergeant of Burlington's park in Waterford, a Dennis Dawley, was paid a mere £3 per year. 28 May 1688, NLI, Lismore, MS 6300.

52 Henry Boyle to dowager countess of Orrery, 12 Dec. 1684, *Orrery papers*, pp 303–4.

53 Richard Dobbs, TCD, Dub. Phil. Soc. MS 8267/2.

54 11 Dec. 1665, Warrant by duke of Ormond, Bodl., Carte MS, vol. 154, fo. 273.

55 'The park wall is well built', 20 July 1672, NLI Lismore, MS 7177. There are frequent mentions of the park and management of both Lismore and Youghal parks. They appear to have been worked on at around the same time.

56 George Rawdon to Edward Conway, *CSPI, 1663–5*, p. 636; see also Adam Leathes to Conway, 30 Sept. 1665, pp 646–7: 'Paid out £6 to John Totnell [for] mending the pales about Castle Robin park, making two ponds, etc.'.

57 'John Totnell is here and tells me of red deer come into the Tunny Park. There are nine of them now in all, and many brave old bucks. That keeper pleases him well and hath made three couple of excellent buck-hounds that will not change. There is a strong covey of partridge in the park, but I hear not of any pheasants there'. George Rawdon to Edward Conway, 19 Oct. 1667, *CSPI, 1666–9*, p. 531.

58 Burlington ordered that no dogs were to be allowed to hunt in the park unless his keeper approved them first. NLI Lismore, MS 13,227.

59 When John Dunton spent a night in Co. Galway, he was 'strangely surprised to hear the cows and sheep all coming into my bed-chamber. I enquired the meaning and was told it was to preserve them from the wolf, which every night was rambling about for pray'. MacLysaght, *Irish life in the seventeenth century*, p. 333. 'The keeper and all our gun men are watching the wolves that haunt the Tunny park almost every night … The wolf haunts that park of late and hath killed three or four of a few muttons'. George Rawdon to Edward Conway, 7 Oct. 1665, *CSPI, 1663–5*, pp 637–49. Christopher Crofts to John Perceval, 22 Jan. 1662–3 'we are much troubled with wolves … lost three sheep in one night', also four sheep lost in one night at Ballyadam'. *HMC Egmont*, 2, p. 5; MacLysaght notes that Irish wolfhounds were much prized abroad. Cardinal Richelieu, the Shah of Persia and the Great Mogul were all said to have owned Irish wolfhounds; *Irish life in the seventeenth century*, p. 140; the earl of Orrery sent Secretary Bennet three wolfhounds as a gift in 1663, Orrery to Bennet, *CSPI, 1663–5*, p. 291.

60 27 Apr. 1652 and 31 Nov. 1652, NLI Bethan Transcripts of papers relating to Ireland during the Commonwealth, MS 11,959, pp 61–2, 135.

61 HMC Egmont, 2, Diary of Sir John Perceval, 20 Feb. 1685/6, p. 369.

62 The Territory of West Connaught, 13 Feb. 1683/4, in the diocese of Tuam and county of Galway by Roderick O'Flaherty, TCD, Dub. Phil. Soc. MS 883/1 (I.1.2).

63 The English *Boke of St Albans* indicated that falcons were flown mainly to provide spectacular flights for the aristocracy, whereas a goshawk 'for a yeoman' could be expected to keep the larder stocked with common small-game; Juliana Berners, *Bake of St Albans* (London, 1901), p. 6.

64 Quoted in Bagwell, *Ireland under the Stuarts*, vol. 3, p. 311.

65 The 'lord lieutenant, or Chief Governor when his majesty's important affairs will admit leisure to unbend and slacken from trying cares' went to the Curragh for recreation, TCD, Dub. Phil. Soc. MS 883/1 (I.1.2).

66 NLI Ormond, Bodl., Carte MS, vol. 49, fo. 645.

67 TCD, Dub. Phil. Soc. MS 883/1 (I.1.2). It is recorded that Sir Donat O'Brien raced his horses at the Curragh. Henry O'Brien to Sir Donat O'Brien, 6 Mar. 1714/15, *Inchiquin papers*, p. 125. Only the very rich could afford to keep good horses. In 1676 the earl of Orrery estimated that it cost '£24 a year' to maintain his stable and coach and his hounds and huntsmen. Orrery to Lady Broghill, 19 Oct. 1676, *Orrery papers*, p. 157.

68 Bagwell, *Ireland under the Stuarts*, vol. 3, p. 311.

69 MacLysaght, *Irish life in the seventeenth century*, p. 133.

70 TCD, King MS 751/1. fo. 24.

71 An Act to refrain the carrying of hawks out of this kingdom, 1480 20 Ed. IV c.9.

72 A messuage was a house and its associated outbuildings and land or a small farm.

73 NLI Report no. 133, 1242, Michaelmas 26 Chas. 1674; Lease dated Michaelmas 22 Chas. II in consideration of a sparrowhawk. Fine between Thomas Lord Windsor and James Barry Lord Santry and others: NLI Report no. 33. Papers belonging to the Mansfield family contain a deed the consideration of which was 'a sparrow hawk'. NLI Report no. 11.

74 George Rawdon informed Lord Conway that he feared he 'must disappoint you about the hawks, either they have not bred this year or else they have, as I fear, been stolen'. George Rawdon to Edward Conway, 31 May 1665, *CSPI, 1663–5*, p. 587.

75 O'Donovan papers, NLI Report no. 153.

76 Accounts for Feb. 1699, TCD, King MS 751/1 fo. 14.

77 'I have your lordship's letter in Lord Aungier's hand about a cast or a goshawk for the duke of Albermarle. If your lordship can, when you go to London, with conveniency provide plate for the next year's race and get it sent over by Mr Viner'. George Rawdon to Edward Conway, 31 May 1665, *CSPI, 1663–5*, p. 587.

78 See, generally, James Kelly, *Sport in Ireland, 1600–1840* (Dublin, 2014).

79 Mr Kennington's remarks on Co. Kerry, TCD, Dub. Phil. Soc. MS 883/1 (I.1.2).

80 Richard Dobbs, TCD, Dub. Phil. Soc. MS 8267/2.

81 30 Aug. 1683, Richard Bagg's book of payments on behalf of Burlington estates. NLI Lismore, MS 6300.

82 'I desire when you come over into England as I expect you will be shortly that you will bring over with you two or three of my young horses or mares such as you shall conceive fit.' Ormond to Captain John Baxter, 14 June 1672, Bodl., Carte MS 160, fo. 62.

83 TCD, Dub. Phil. Soc. MS 883/1 (I.1.2).

84 Cooke to Ormond, Moore Park, July 1664, Bodl., Carte MS 215, fo. 376.

85 Quoted in Bagwell, *Ireland under the Stuarts*, vol. 3, p. 311.

86 See letter disputing petition for payment of £50 'for keeping my dogs at the Phoenix Park'. Ormond to John Baxter, 14 Mar. 1669, Bodl., Carte MS 160, fo. 52.

87 Quoted in Bagwell, *Ireland under the Stuarts*, vol. 3, p. 311.

88 'I shall first return to London and fully finish my begun charge at Moore Park' he added that he 'had been in forest I have great hopes to provide a suitable kennel of beagles to your grace's liking, for … speed and hunting, size and colour'. Cooke to Ormond, 12 Aug. 1667, Bodl., Carte MS 215, fo. 363.

89 18 Aug. 1677, NLI, Lismore, MS 7177.

90 'The lurcher and the greyhound were sent me by sire Richard Hastings ... both proved good'. Ossory to Ormond, 2 July 1664, Bodl., Carte MS 220, fo. 151. '[I] have a fine bitch well-bred for your lordship. I will bring her you next April, if these acts permits me to stay in the kingdom so long ... I breed only good hounds of all sorts, good beagles, and a double sort of wolf dog'. Undated, 1697, Revd John ? to Lord Howth (Thomas St Lawrence, 13th Baron Howth), St Lawrence papers, NLI Report no. 140 1311.

91 4 Aug. 1683, PRONI, De Ros, T1135 2.(4).

92 'He is to have the running of a hare or two in my park. Also a buck and a doe in their season when he calls for them. He is a very worthy gentleman my old acquaintance and therefore I desire all civility may be shown to him'. Ormond to George Mathew, 2 July 1670, Bodl., Carte MS 160, fo. 52.

93 J.G. Kohl, *Travels in Ireland* (London, 1844), p. 260.

94 In some circumstances when other meat was scarce rabbit was in great demand. During the Rebellion in Ireland Robert Bysse (grandfather to Robert Molesworth), who was then high sheriff of Dublin, wrote to his brother who had fled to England with tales of the hardship suffered in Ireland, stating that rabbits were four shillings a pair. February 1642, Ball, *History of Dublin*, vol. 6, p. 330.

95 The strict definition of warrens did not confine them to rabbits: 'beasts and fowls of warren are hares, conies, and roes; fowls are either campestres, [such] as partridges, rails and quails, or sylvestres, [such] as wood cocks and pheasants; or aquatiles, as mallards and herons'. Chitty, *A treatise on the law of the prerogatives*, p. 141. A warren was defined by the *Carta foresta* or Forest charter in 1217 as a 'place privileged by prescription or grant of the Queen for the preservation of hares, conies, partridges and pheasants'; Richard Burn, *The justice of the peace, and parish officer*, vol. 2 (London, 1793), p. 321.

96 George Rawdon to Edward Conway, 24 Dec. 1667, *CSPI, 1666–9*, p. 531.

97 Oliver Rackham, *The history of the countryside*, p. 292.

98 Worlidge, *Systema agriculturae*, pp 162–3.

99 On 6 Dec. 1687 a mason was paid £8 for 11 days work 'about the warren'. On 15 May 1688, 8d. was paid for mending the 'warrener's' gun. On 7 July 1688, a labourer was paid to clear nettles in the warren. On 25 Nov. 1685 money was paid to Cornelius Lyne for repairs to the park wall, paddock and warren. On 2 Jan. 1686 a labourer was paid for attending the mason about the park and warren. Richard Bagg's book of payments on behalf of Burlington estates, NLI, Lismore, MS 6300.

100 George T. Stokes (ed.), *Pococke's tour in Ireland in 1752* (Dublin, 1891), p. 121.

101 TCD, MS 1460/21.

102 14 Aug. 1688, Richard Bagg's book of payments on behalf of Burlington estates, NLI, Lismore, MS 6300.

103 Ibid., 27 Sept. 1687.

104 'John Olliver says if you will have two or three burrows made near the place you used to eat at, it is a good place for rabbits by the lough side'. George Rawdon to Edward Conway, 19 Oct. 1667, *CSPI, 1666–9*, p. 531.

105 Magillegan, Co. Londonderry by Thomas Beck as told to Mr Parnwell, 17 Oct (year unknown, possibly 1688). TCD, Dub. Phil. Soc. MS 883/1 (I.1.2).

106 The duchess of Ormond wrote to her brother-in-law, George Mathew: 'I understand that the new warren at Kilkenny does not thrive, which the reason is I know not but do think it very requisite if that place be not fit that some other near [in] the town should be had for that use, which I pray advise with Mr Bryane and Baxter', 27 Jan. 1670, NLI, Ormond, MS 2503. George Mathew replied to the duchess of Ormond: 'I have partly fixed upon a piece

of ground near Kilkenny for a warren, but suspended the storing of it until the comptroller or Mr Bryan be able to inform me [of] their judgments of it'. 9 May 1671, NLI, Ormond MS 2503.

107 G. Roche to Burlington, 15 Oct. 1673, NLI, Lismore, MS 7177.

108 Burlington to Congreve, 1698, NLI, Lismore, MS 13227 (2).

109 Rackham, *The history of the countryside*, p. 125. The fruit of timber trees such as oak and chestnut were used as food for the deer.

110 Garret Roche to Richard, 1st earl of Burlington, 24 Sept. 1672, wrote to agree with his lordship that 'no cattle shall be kept in the parks'. NLI, Lismore MS 7177; Burlington to William Congreve; wrote that he wants cattle removed from the park and informed him that he intends to live at Lismore. 4 Oct. 1690, NLI, Lismore MS 13226 (1).

111 Williamson, *Polite landscapes*, pp 33–4.

112 Dr Thomas Molyneux, younger brother of William Molyneux, wrote in 1709 that 'tis a well sheltered park, with firs, good land, and well divided with pretty small paddocks, here is a good pheasantry kept, which stocks the whole country about'. Clohosey, 'Dunmore House', *OKR*, 4 (1951), p. 44.

113 Ossory to Ormond, 26 Feb. 1664, Bodl., Carte MS, vol. 220, fos. 212, 213.

114 See, generally, Vandra Costello, 'Dutch influences in seventeenth-century Ireland: the duck decoy', *Garden History*, 30:2 (2002), pp 177–90.

115 A.W. Brian Simpson, *Leading cases in the common law* (Oxford, 1995), p. 47.

116 Other methods of catching fowl were described in F. Willughby, *The ornithology of Francis Willughby of Middleton in the county of Warwick esquire* (London, 1678). See also Richard Blome, *The gentleman's recreation* (London, 1705). Techniques included shooting with bows and arrows, which necessitated a skill in marksmanship. Another means of catching wildfowl was 'punt gunning', which involved the use of a miniature cannon built into a shallow boat or punt. By this rather hit and miss method the punt was paddled or poled within range of flock of ducks or geese, whereupon the cannon discharged up to a pound or more of lead shot, killing or maiming a considerable number of birds in the process, which were then retrieved by a gamekeeper and water dogs. J. Wentworth-Day, *A history of the fens* (London, 1954), chaps. 12 and 13.

117 The anglicized spelling 'ende-kooy' is used in much of the literature.

118 Ralph Payne-Gallwey, *The book of duck decoys their construction, management, and history* (London, 1886), p. 7.

119 T. Southwell, 'On some early Dutch and English Decoys', *TNNNS*, 7 (1904), pp 606–17.

120 de Beer (ed.), *John Evelyn's diary*.

121 Payne-Gallwey quotes Sir Henry Spelman (who died in 1641): 'Sir W. Wodehouse (who lived in the reign of James I, 1603–25) made among us the first device for catching ducks, known by the foreign name of a koye'. Payne-Gallwey, *The book of duck decoys*, p. 2.

122 Brereton was a parliamentary general during the Civil War. He was the author of *Travels in Holland and the United Provinces, England, Scotland and Ireland, describing a tour in 1634 and 1635* (London, 1904), p. 394.

123 R.N. Dore, 'Letter books of Sir William Brereton', *RSLC*, 12 (1984), p. 88.

124 Withy refers to the willow, usually osier or *Salix viminalis*.

125 29 Mar. 1665, in de Beer (ed.), *John Evelyn's diary*, vol. 3, p. 404.

126 Ibid.

127 Peter Cunningham, *Hand-nook of London* (London, 1850), p. 259. I would like to thank Guy de la Bédoyère for this reference.

128 Travels of Sir William Brereton in Ireland 1635, reprinted in Falkiner, *Illustrations of Irish history and topography*, p. 394.

129 'I hear the earl of Arran began a decoy last year, but have not heard if he finished it or how it prospers'. George Rawdon to Edward Conway, 12 Apr. 1665, *CSPI, 1663–5*, pp 568–9. There followed: 'Lord Arran's decoy is not ready yet', George Rawdon to Edward Conway, 26 Apr. 1665, p. 574. Robert Molesworth to Lettice Molesworth, 8 Dec. 1698, referred to a proposed ice house 'on the hill side over the tuckmill and to a decoy'. *HMC Various collections*, vol. 8, p. 219.

130 A map shows 'a description of Thomastown deer park and decoy and part of Rosnegrally belonging to the honourable George Mathew'; John Cooley drew in deer in 1682; Campbell, *A philosophical survey of the South of Ireland*, pp 169–70.

131 'Dineley's journal', *JKSIAS*, 6:1 (1867), p. 201.

132 Smith, *Cork*, vol. 1, p. 337.

133 Journal of a tour to Dublin by James Verdon, 1699, BL, Add. MS 41769, fos. 29–43.

134 On 5 Aug. 1665, Adam Leathes, one of Lord Conway's agents, wrote that he had paid 'to John Totnell, on the decoy account, £83 4s. 3d.' and to a Dutch decoy designer, Martin Johnson, 'in full of a quarter's wage £2'. On 30 Sept. 1665, Leathes wrote that £27 was spent on the decoy account. *CSPI, 1663–5*, pp 617, 647.

135 Letter dated 22 Apr. 1665, from George Rawdon to Edward Conway, *CSPI, 1663–5*, p. 574: 'I was at Antrim to visit Lord Massereene. He is very anxious to have Johnson's advice on a decoy at the grange. He has promised young decoy ducks, he having the right breed'. The grange lies to the east of the demesne about 1.5 miles from the walls of the castle.

136 For a fuller description of the gardens at Moira see Smith, *Down*, p. 103.

137 George Rawdon to Edward Conway, 20 May 1665, *CSPI, 1663–5*, p. 582.

138 'An account of Lincolnshire', *Universal Magazine*, 10 (1752), pp 153–5.

139 *The ornithology of Francis Willughby*, p. 39.

140 Payne-Gallwey, *The book of duck decoys*, p. 192. The Thomastown decoy is depicted in a map dated 1682 by John Cooley, 'A description of Thomastown deere park and decoy and part of Rosnegrally belonging to the honourable George Mathew', J.H. Andrews, *Plantation acres: an historical study of the Irish land surveys* (Dublin, 1985), p. 72.

141 Martin Jansen van Heyninge to Conway, 12 Apr. 1665, *CSPI, 1663–5*, p. 369.

142 12 Apr. 1665, *CSPI, 1663–5*, p. 568

143 John Hartnall (Totnall?) to Rawdon, 29 May 1665, *CSPI, 1663–5*, p. 585.

144 3 Oct. 1674, NLI Lismore, MS 7177.

145 R. Molesworth to L Molesworth, 16 May 1721, NLI, P 3752.

146 Journal of a tour to Dublin by James Verdon, 1699, BL, Add. MS 41769, fos. 29–43.

147 George Rawdon to Edward Conway, 12 Apr. 1665, *CSPI, 1663–5*, pp 568–9.

148 Ibid., 22 Apr. 1665, *CSPI, 1663–5*, p. 573.

149 The decoy at Killruddery appears to have had only one pipe.

150 Payne-Gallwey, *The book of duck decoys*, p. 192.

151 Cheney to Meath, 12 Feb. 1682/3, Killruddery, earl of Meath papers, J3/2. The remains of this decoy lie just outside of the walled garden to the south west of the house and are overgrown with trees and shrubs today.

152 Ralph Payne-Gallwey, *The fowler in Ireland* (London, 1882), p. 76.

153 Janet Kear, 'Duck decoys, with particular reference to the history of bird ringing', *ANH*, 20 (1993), pp 229–39.

154 Joseph Stroude to Lord Conway, 27 Aug. 1665, *CSPI, 1663–5*, p. 143.

155 Ibid.

156 George Rawdon to Edward Conway, 21 Oct. 1665, *CSPI, 1663–5*, p. 653.

157 Lettice Molesworth to Robert Molesworth, 20 July 1699, *HMC Various collections*, vol. 8, p. 220.

158 'He is very anxious to have Johnson's advice on a decoy at the Grange. He has promised young decoy ducks, he having the right breed'. George Rawdon to Edward Conway, 22 Apr. 1665, *CSPI, 1663–5*, p. 574.

159 Ibid., 21 Oct. 1665, p. 637.

160 Ibid.

161 Christopher H. Davis, *Norfolk broads and rivers* (London, 1884), p. 167.

162 The letters of the duke of Ormond contain many discussions on the import of hemp and flax from the Low Countries to Ireland; for instance 'his majesty may be invited to expend money employed to purchase eastland hempseed and flaxseed to send into Ireland to stock that country therewith, and [to send] artificers for this trade from Flanders and Germany and other parts, with their engines and loom and tools …' Ormond to earl of Danby, 5 Aug. 1678, *HMC Ormond*, n.s. vol. 4, p. 175.

163 George Rawdon to Edward Conway, 2 Sept. 1665, *CSPI, 1663–5*, p. 636.

164 Ibid., 21 Oct. 1665, p. 654.

165 Robert Molesworth to Lettice Molesworth, 16 May 1721, NLI, Killadoon MS Q/1/1.

166 Payne-Gallwey, *The book of duck decoys*, p. 193.

EPILOGUE

1 Aalen et al. (eds), *Atlas of the Irish rural landscape*, p. 197.

2 TCD, Dub. Phil. Soc. MS 883/1 (I.1.3).

3 William Chetwood, *A tour through Ireland*, p. 211.

4 John D'Alton, *History of the county of Dublin*, p. 759.

5 George Bennet, *The history of Bandon* (Cork, 1865), p. 561.

6 Terence Reeves-Smyth, 'Demesnes' in Aalen et al. (eds), *Atlas of the Irish rural landscape*, p. 197.

7 Anon., 'Recollections of visits to Belan House, Co. Kildare in the early Victorian period', *JCKAS*, 5:5 (1908), p. 310.

Select bibliography

MANUSCRIPT SOURCES

The National Archives: Public Record Office, Kew, London
N.A., H.C.A. 14/19

Trinity College Dublin
MS 1178 Temple
MS 1180 (179) Papers of Sir Robert Southwell and Edward Southwell, principal secretaries of
  state in Ireland
MS 1209/32/2 Maps from Hardiman Collection
MS 1460/21
MS 2671 Dineley
MS 751 William King, bishop of Derry archbishop of Dublin, accounts
MS 8191 William King's letter book
MS 8267/2 Richard Dobbs' account of Carrickfergus
MS 883/1 Dublin Philosophical Society papers
MS 883/2 Dublin Philosophical Society papers
MS 967 Lewis Dillwyn's journal of a tour to Killarney
MS 9827 Deeds from the collection of the Duke of Leinster, Earl of Kildare.
Muniments: Bursar's vouchers P/4F2/25

King's Inns Library, Dublin
King's Inns' Records, The Black Book, 1607–1730 MS B1/1

National Archives of Ireland
NAI Chancery Bill E/211   NAI Pembroke 2011/2/3
NAI Chancery Bill E/211   NAI Minutes of the Royal Hospital of Charles II, 1 Apr. 1693
NAI Chancery Bills H/45   NAI MS D11847
NAI Chancery Bills H/45

Birr Castle Archives
Parsons family, earls of Rosse: family and estate papers

British Library
Journal of a tour by James Verdon, 1699 Add MS 41769
Egerton MS 917   Egmont, Add MS 46961
Egmont Add MS 46960   Evelyn Add. MS 15950
Egmont Add MS 46940   Evelyn, Add MS 78628 A-B

Petty Add MS 72850	Sloane MS 4036	Stowe MS 211
Petty Add MS 72855	Sloane MS 4039	
Petty Add. MS 72856	Sloane MS 4054	

Bodleian Library, Oxford

Carte papers: original papers of James Butler (1610–88), 1st duke of Ormond, lord lieutenant of Ireland

Lister papers: manuscripts of Dr Martin Lister (1638–1712)

Public Record Office of Northern Ireland

D638 De Ros	D2707 Chatsworth
T2825 Connolly	MS D695 Waring
T2929 Rossmore	

Killruddery Archives

Killruddery, earl of Meath papers, J3/2

PAPERS IN PRIVATE OWNERSHIP

Killadoon papers, private ownership, ref. Q/1/1

National Library of Ireland

MS 1056 Ormond papers	MS 13,227 Lismore papers
MS 2367 Ormond papers	MS 13,226 Lismore papers
MS 2376 Ormond papers	MS 13,227 Lismore papers
MS 11,469 Flower papers	MS 13,231 Lismore papers
MS 11,470 Flower papers	MS 20,385 O'Hara papers
MS 11,472 Flower papers	MS 34 Lane papers
MS 11,473 Flower papers	MS 42,094 Inchiquin papers
MS 11,959 Bethan transcripts of papers relating to Ireland during the Commonwealth	MS 8645 Lane papers
	MS21F 52–72 Map collection
MS 6300 Lismore papers	P3752 Molesworth papers
MS 7177 Lismore papers	P3753 Molesworth papers

NATIONAL LIBRARY OF IRELAND REPORTS ON PRIVATE COLLECTIONS

Bayly papers No. 95	O'Donovan papers No.153
Fitzpatrick papers No. 152	Private Collections No. 11
Grove papers No. 276	Walker papers No. 33
Kirkpatrick papers No. 131	Walker papers No. 33
Louth papers No. 165	White papers No. 52
Montgomery papers No. 133	

PRINTED SOURCES

Aalen, F.H.A., K. Whelan and M. Stout (eds), *Atlas of the Irish rural landscape* (Cork, 1997)

Ainsworth, John (ed.), *Inchiquin papers* (Irish Manuscript Commission, Dublin, 1961)

Andrews, J.H. and Anngret Simms (eds), *Irish historic towns atlas, 2: Carrickfergus* (Dublin, 1986)

Andrews, J.H., *Plantation acres, an historical study of the Irish land surveys* (Dublin, 1985)

Anon., 'An account of Lincolnshire', *Universal Magazine*, 10:4 (1752)

Anon., 'Recollections of visits to Belan House, County Kildare in the early Victorian period', *JCKAS*, 5:5 (1908), pp 298–310

Anon., *A brief account of the life, writings and inventions of Sir Samuel Morland, master of mechanics to Charles the second* (Cambridge, 1838)

Anon., *An account of the life, character and parliamentary conduct of the Right Honourable Henry Boyle Esq.* (Dublin, 1754)

Anon., *The art of pruning fruit-trees, with an explanation of some words which gardeners make use of in speaking of trees, etc.* (London, 1685)

Aubrey, John, *The natural history and antiquities of the county of Surrey* (London, 1718)

Austen, Jane, *Persuasion* (1818)

Austen, Ralph, *A treatise of fruit-trees* (1653)

Bagwell, Richard, *Ireland under the Stuarts*, vol. 3 (London, 1963)

Balgrave, John, *The epitome of the art of husbandry* (London, 1685)

Ball, Francis Elrington, *A history of the county of Dublin*, part 1 (Dublin, 1902)

Barnard, T., 'Gardening, diet and "improvement" in later seventeenth-century Ireland', *Garden History*, 10:1 (1990), pp 71–85

— *Cromwellian Ireland: English government and reform in Ireland, 1649–1660* (Oxford, 2000)

— *A new anatomy of Ireland: the Irish Protestants, 1649–1770*, (New Haven, CT, 2003)

Beaufort, Daniel Augustus, *Memoir of a map of Ireland* (Dublin, 1792)

Bence-Jones, Mark, *Burke's guide to country houses*, vol. 1 (London, 1978)

Beneš, Mirka and Dianne Harris (eds), *Villas and gardens in early modern Italy and France* (Cambridge, 2001)

Bennet, George, *The history of Bandon* (Cork, 1865)

Berwick, E. (ed.), *The Rawdon papers consisting of letters on various subjects* (London, 1819)

Bezemer Sellers, Vanessa, *Courtly gardens in Holland, 1600–1650* (Amsterdam, 2001)

Blome, Richard, *The gentleman's recreation* (London, 1705)

Boate, Gerard, *Ireland's natural history* (Dublin, 1726)

Bowden, Charles Topham, *Tour through Ireland* (Dublin, 1791)

Bowe, Patrick, *The gardens of Ireland* (London, 1986)

Boyceau, Jacques, *Traité du jardinage selon les raisons de la Nature et de l'Art* (Paris, 1631)

Boyle, James, *Antrim Ordnance Survey Memoir, 1835–1840* (PRONI, Belfast, 1969)

Brears, Peter, *A taste of history* (London, 1993)

Brereton, William, 'Travels of Sir William Brereton in Ireland 1635' reprinted in C. Litton Falkiner, *Illustrations of Irish history* (London, 1904)

Brewer, James, *The beauties of Ireland*, 3 vols, vol. 1 (London, 1825)

Brown, Thomas, 'Of garlands and coronary or garland-plants' in *Browne's miscellany tracts* (London, 1684)

Burrowes, Erasmus D., 'The French settlers in Ireland, No. 5', *UJA*, 3 (1855), pp 56–67

— 'The French settlers in Ireland, No. 6', *UJA* (1855), pp 213–31

Bush, J., *Hibernia curiosa – a letter from a gentleman in Dublin in 1764* (Dublin, 1769)

Butler, W.F.T., *Confiscation in Irish history* (Dublin, 1917)

Cabe Halpern, Linda, 'Wrest Park, 1686–1730s: exploring Dutch influence', *Garden History*, 30:2 (2002), pp 131–52

Calendar of Egmont papers, 2 vols (HMC, London, 1905, 1909)

Calendar of Kinsale documents, vol. 6 (HMC, London, 1998)

Calendar of Ormond papers, n.s. 6 vols (HMC, London, 1902–6)

Calendar of patent rolls (1597–8) (HMC, London, 2009)

Calendar of patent rolls, 40 Elizabeth I (1597–1598) (HMC, London, 2009)

Calendar of state papers: domestic series: 18 May–30 September, 1672 (HMC, London, 1899)

Calendar of the state papers, relating to Ireland preserved in the Public Record Office, 1660–70 (London, 1905)

Campbell, Thomas, *A philosophical survey of the south of Ireland* (Dublin, 1778)

Carty, James, *Henry Pierse in Ireland from the Flight of the Earls to Grattan's Parliament* (Dublin, 1951)

Cauldfield, Richard (ed.), *Council book of the Corporation of Youghal* (1878)

— *The council book of the Corporation of the city of Cork: from 1609 to 1643, and from 1690 to 1800* (1876)

— *Journal of the Very Rev. Rowland Davies, LL.D.* (London, 1857)

Chalmers, George (ed.), *Historical tracts by Sir John Davies* (London, 1786)

Chambers, Douglas, *The planters of the English landscape garden* (New Haven, CT, 1993)

Chandra, Mukerji, *Territorial ambitions and the gardens of Versailles* (Cambridge, 1997)

Chetwood, William R., *A tour through Ireland* (London, 1748)

Chitty, Joseph, *A treatise on the law of the prerogatives of the Crown* (London, 1820)

Clohosey, T.J., 'Dunmore House', *OKR*, 4 (1951), pp 44–58

Cobbett, William, *Rural rides* (1822)

Collins, J.F., 'George Rye (1685–1735): his family and an appreciation of his book: "Considerations on agriculture"', *Bandon Historical Journal*, 17 (2001), pp 39–56

Connolly, S.J. (ed.), *The Oxford companion to Irish history* (Oxford, 1998)

Cook, Moses, *The manner of raising, ordering, and improving forest-trees* (London, 1676)

Coote, Stephen, *Samuel Pepys; a life* (London, 2000)

Cosby, Pole, 'Autobiography of Pole Cosby, of Stradbally, Queen's County, 1703–1737(?)', *JCKAS*, 5 (1906–8), pp 79–99

Cosgrove, Denis E., *Social formation and symbolic landscape* (Wisconsin, 1998)

Costello, Vandra, 'Dutch influences in seventeenth-century Ireland: the duck decoy', *Garden History*, 30:2 (2002), pp 177–90

Couch, Sarah M., 'The practice of avenue planting in the seventeenth and eighteenth centuries', *Garden History*, 20:2 (1992), pp 173–200

Cunningham, Peter, *Hand-book of London* (London, 1850)

Currie, Christopher K., 'Fishponds as garden features', *Garden History*, 18:1 (1990), pp 22–46

d'Alton, John, *History of the county of Dublin* (Dublin, 1838)

Davis, Christopher H., *Norfolk broads and rivers* (1884)

Davis, G.C., *The handbook to the rivers and broads of Norfolk and Suffolk* (Norfolk, 1884)

Davis, Sir John, *Historical tracts* (Dublin, 1787)

Davison, Michael W. (ed.), *Field guide to the trees and shrubs of Britain* (London, 1981)

Dawson, Thomas, *The good huswifes jewell*, pt 1 (Amsterdam, 1596)

de Beer, E.S. (ed.), *John Evelyn's diary*, vol. 3 (Oxford, 2000)

de Caus, Salomon, *Raisons des forces mouvantes* (1615)

de Ganay, Valentine and Laurent Le Bon, *Courances* (Paris, 2002)

de la Bédoyère, Guy (ed.), *Diary of John Evelyn* (Suffolk, 1995) de la Cherois Purdon, Charles Nicholas, 'The French settlers in Ireland. No. 1: "The Huguenot Colony at Lisburn, county of Antrim"', *UJA*, 1 (1853), pp 209–20

de Serres, Olivier, *Théâtre d'Agriculture* (1600)

Desmond, R., *Dictionary of British and Irish botanists and horticulturalists* (London, 1994)

Dézallier d'Argenville, A.-J., *The theory and practice of gardening, translated by John James* (London, 1728)

Dictionary of national biography (London, 1908)

Digges la Touche, J.J. (ed.), *Registers of the French conformed churches of St Patrick and St Mary* (Dublin, 1893)

Dore, R.N., 'Letter books of Sir William Brereton', *RSLC*, 12 (1984)

Doubleday and De Walden (eds), *The complete peerage*, vol. 8 (London, 1932)

Dubravius, Janus, *A new book of good husbandry* (London, 1599)

Dudley, Rowena, 'The Cheney letters, 1682–85', *IESH*, 323 (1996), pp 97–112

Dunton, John, *Dublin scuffle* (Dublin, 1699)

— *The life and errors of John Dunton, citizen of London*, vol. 2 (London, 1818)

Evelyn, Philip Shirley & James Graves (eds), 'The journal of Thomas Dineley', *JKSIAS*, 1:1 (1856), pp 143–6, 170–88; 2:1 (1858), pp 22–32, 55–6; 4:1 (1862), pp 38–52, 103–9; 4:2 (1863), pp 320–38; 5:1 (1864), pp 40–8; 5:2 (1865), pp 268–90; 5:3 (1866), pp 425–46; 6:1 (1867), pp 73–91, 176–204

Evelyn, John, *Acetaria; a discourse on sallets* (London, 1699)

— *Silva; a discourse on forest trees* (London, 1664)

— *The compleat gard'ner* (London, 1693)

Everett, Nigel, *The Tory view of landscape* (New Haven, CT, 1994)

Falkiner, C. Litton, *Illustrations of Irish history and topography, mainly of the seventeenth century* (London, 1904)

Farrell, James, P., *History of the county of Longford* (Dublin, 1891)

Félibien, André, *Description sommaire de chasteau de Versailles* (Paris, 1674)

FitzGerald, D. and E. Malins, *Lost demesnes, Irish landscape gardening, 1660–1845* (Dublin, 1976)

FitzGerald, Olda, *Irish gardens* (London, 1999)

FitzGerald, Walter, 'Carton', *JCKAS*, 4:1 (1903), pp 2–34

— 'The deer park at Maynooth Castle', *JCKAS*, 2:4 (1897), p. 270

— 'The Dongan family in the county of Kildare at the commencement of the seventeenth century', *JCKAS*, 4:1 (1903), pp 67–70

Fitzmaurice, Edmond, *The life of Sir William Petty* (London, 1895)

Forbes, A.C., 'Some legendary and historical references to Irish woods, and their significance', *PRIA*, 41 (1933–4), pp 15–36

Foster, R.F. (ed.), *The Oxford history of Ireland* (Oxford, 1989)

Fraser, James, *Guide thro' Ireland* (Dublin, 1838)

Fry, Carole, 'Spanning the political divide: neo-Palladianism and the early eighteenth-century landscape', *Garden History*, 31:2 (2003), pp 180–92

Fussell, G.E., *The Old English farming books from Fitzherbert to Tull 1523 to 1730* (London, 1947)

Gilbert, J.T. (ed.), *Calendar of Ancient Records of Dublin*, vol. 4 (Dublin, 1894)

Gilbert, J.T., *A history of the City of Dublin*, vol. 1 (Dublin, 1861)

Gimlette, Thomas, 'The settlement in Waterford, the French settlers in Ireland, No. 7', *UJA* (1856), pp 198–221

Grafton, Gillian, *Pears and perry in the UK* (1996)

Hadfield, Miles, *British gardening* (Feltham, 1969)

— *Topiary and ornamental hedges* (London, 1971)

Hall, Augusta (ed.), *Autobiography and correspondence of Mary Granville, Mrs Delany*, vol. 1 (London, 1861)

Hardinge, W.H., *A memoir of manuscript mapped and other townland surveys in Ireland, 1688–1864* (Dublin, 1865)

Harris, Walter, *The history and antiquities of the city of Dublin* (London, 1766)

Hartlib, Samuel, *Cornu-Copia* (London, 1652)

— *Legacy* (London, 1655)

— *The reformed commonwealth of bees* (London, 1655)

Haverschmidt, F., 'Vandstcijfers van eenige Nederlandsche eendenkooien', *Ardea*, 20 (1931), pp 152–69

Hayton, David, *Ruling Ireland, 1685–1742* (Martlesham, Suffolk, 2004)

Henrey, Blanche, *British botanical and horticultural literature before 1800* (London, 1975)

Henrey, Blanche, *British botanical and horticultural literature before 1800*, vol. 1 (London, 1975)

Hewitson, A. (ed.), *Diary of Thomas Bellingham, an officer under William III* (Preston, 1908)

Hiscock, W.G., *John Evelyn and his family circle* (London, 1950)

HMC Cal. Egmont, 2 vols (HMC, London, 1905, 1909)

HMC Cal. Ormond, n.s., 6 vols (HMC, London, 1902–6)

HMC Various Collections, vol. 8 (HMC, London, 1913)

Holmes, George, *Sketches of some of the southern counties of Ireland during a tour in autumn 1797* (London, 1801)

Holt Marl, Samuel (ed.), *Five miscellaneous essays by Sir William Temple* (Ann Arbour, MI, 1963)

Hoppen, K. Theodore, *The common scientist in the seventeenth century: a study of the Dublin Philosophical Society, 1683–1708* (Virginia, 1970)

Hore, J.P., *The History of the royal buckhounds* (Newmarket, 1895)

Horner, Arnold, 'Carton, Co. Kildare, a case study of the making of an Irish Demesne', *QBIGS*, 18:2/3 (1975), pp 45–104

Hughes, William, *The Compleat vineyard: or, a most excellent way for the planting of vines* (London, 1665)

Hughes, William, *The flower garden and compleat vineyard* (London, 1670)

Hull, C.H. (ed.), *The economic writings of Sir William Petty* (Cambridge, 1899)

Hutton, Sarah (ed.), *The Conway letters* (Oxford, 1992)

Irvine, Jimmy, 'Richard Dobbs, notes for his description of county Antrim written in 1683', *Glynns*, 7 (1979), pp 35–49

Jacob, Giles (ed.), *Jacob's law dictionary* (London, 1797)

Jacques, D. and A. van der Horst, *The gardens of William and Mary* (London, 1988)

Johnson, Samuel, *The works of the English poets* (London, 1810)

Kear, Janet, 'Duck decoys, with particular reference to the history of bird ringing', *ANH*, 20 (1993), pp 229–40

Kelly, John (ed.), *The Hillier gardener's guide to trees and shrubs* (Winchester, 1995)

Kelly, P., 'The improvement of Ireland', *AH*, 35 (1992), pp 45–84

Kenny, Colum, *King's Inns and the kingdom of Ireland: the Irish 'inns of court' 1541–1800* (Dublin, 1992)

Kohl, J.G., *Travels in Ireland* (London, 1844)

Lamb, Keith and Patrick Bowe, *A history of gardening in Ireland* (Dublin, 1995)

Langley, Batty, *A sure method of improving estates* (1728)

Lansdowne, Marquis of, *Petty papers*, vol. 2 (London, 1927)

Lawrence, Richard, *The interest of Ireland in its trade and wealth stated* (1682)

Lawson, William (ed.) *The country house-wifes garden by Gervase Markham* (London, 1635)

Leatherbarrow, David, 'Character, geometry and perspective: the third earl of Shaftesbury's principles of garden design', *Garden History*, 4:4 (1984), pp 332–58

Leith-Ross, Prudence, 'Fruit planted around a new bowling green at John Evelyn's garden at Sayes Court, Deptford, Kent, in 1684/5', *Garden History*, 31:1 (1997), pp 29–33

— 'The garden of John Evelyn at Deptford', *Garden History*, 25:2 (1997), pp 138–52

Leslie, Michael and Timothy Raylor (eds), *Culture and cultivation in early modern England* (Leicester, 1992)

Lewis, Samuel, *Topographical dictionary of Ireland* (1837)

Loeber, Rolf, 'An introduction to the Dutch influence in seventeenth- and eighteenth-century Ireland: an unexplored field', *QBIGS*, 13:2 (1970)

— 'Irish country houses and castles of the late Caroline period; an unremembered past recaptured', *QBIGS*, 14:1 (1973)

— *The geography and practice of English colonization in Ireland from 1534 to 1609* (Dublin, 1991)

London, George and Henry Wise, *The compleat gardener* (London, 1704)

Loveday, John, *Diary of a tour in 1732* (London, 1890)

Lubbock, Jules, *The tyranny of taste, the politics of architecture and design in Britain, 1550–1960* (New Haven, CT, 1995)

MacLysaght, Edward, *Irish life in the seventeenth century* (Cork, 1950)

— (ed.), *Calendar of the Orrery papers* (Dublin, 1941)

— (ed.), 'Report on Connor papers', *AH*, 15 (1944), pp 153–60

— (ed.), 'Report on the Dillon papers', *AH*, 20 (1958), pp 17–54

— (ed.), 'Report on Dunsdale papers', *AH*, 15 (1944), pp 392–406

— (ed.), 'Report on MAA of Old Corporation of Kinsale', *AH*, 15 (1944), pp 161–226

— (ed.), 'Report on the Longford papers', *AH*, 13:15 (1944), pp 109–28

— (ed.), 'Report on the Rawlinson papers', *AH*, 1:2 (1930), p. 37

Malcomson, A.P.W., *The pursuit of the heiress: aristocratic marriage in Ireland, 1740–1840* (Belfast, 2006)

Malins, E. and D. FitzGerald, *Lost demesnes: Irish landscape gardening, 1660–1845* (London, 1976)

Manwood, John, (ed.), *Treatise of the forest laws* (1717)

Markham, Gervase, *A new orchard and garden* (1638)

— *Country contentments* (London, 1633)

— *The English husbandman* (London, 1613)

Martin, R.G., 'Ice houses and the commercial ice trade in Brighton', *SIH*, 14 (1984/5), 18–24

— 'Petworth ice-house', *SIH*, 13 (1983), pp 15–21

McKean, Charles 'The Scottish Renaissance country seat in its setting', *Garden History*, 31:2 (2003), pp 141–2

McNeill, Charles (ed.), *Tanner letters* (Dublin, 1943)

McVeagh, John (ed.), *Richard Pococke's Irish tours* (Dublin, 1995)

Melvin, Patrick, 'Sir Paul Rycaut's memoranda and letters from Ireland, 1686–1687', *AH*, 27 (1972), pp 125–82

Milton, Thomas, *The seats and demesnes of the nobility and gentry of Ireland* (Dublin, 1779)

Mollet, Claude, *Théâtre des Plans et Jardinages* (1652)

Mortimer, John, *The whole art of husbandry* (London, 1707)

Moryson, Fynes, 'The itinerary of Fynes Moryson', *AH*, 37 (1998)

Mosser, Monique and George Teyssat (eds), *The history of garden design* (London, 1990)

Mowl, Timothy, *Gentlemen and players* (Stroud, Gloustershire, 2000)

Mukerji, Chandra, *Territorial ambitions and the gardens of Versailles* (Cambridge, 1997)

Nelson, E. Charles, 'Some records (*c.*1690–1830) of green houses in Irish gardens', *Moorea*, 2 (1983), pp 2–28

— '"This garden to adorn all varietie" – the garden plants of Ireland plants of Ireland in the centuries before 1700', *Moorea*, 9 (1991), pp 37–54

— 'Sir Arthur Rawdon (1662–1695) of Moira: his life and letters, family and friends, and his Jamaican plants', *Moorea*, 10:2 (1981), pp 30–52

— *Northern gardens* (Belfast, 1984)

Newdigate-Newdegate, Anne Emily, *Cavalier and puritan in the days of the Stuarts* (London, 1901)

Nicholson, M.H., *Conway letters* (1930)

Norden, John, *The surveyor's dialogue* (London, 1607)

North, Roger, *A discourse on fish and fishponds* (London, 1713)

Nourse, Timothy, *Campania foelix or a discourse of the benefits and improvements of husbandry* (London, 1700)

O'Donovan, John, *Letters containing information relating to the antiquities of the County of Dublin collected during the progress of the ordnance survey in 1837* (Dublin, 2001)

O'Hart, John, *Irish pedigrees*, vol. 2 (Dublin, 1892)

O'Kane, Finola, *Landscape design in eighteenth-century Ireland* (Cork, 2004)

— 'Leamaneh and Dromoland: the O'Brien ambition, parts I and II', *JIGS*, 7 (2004), pp 80–105

O'Malley, Therese and J. Wolschke-Bulmahn (eds), *John Evelyn's 'Elysium Britannicum' and European gardening* (Washington, DC, 1998)

Ohlmeyer, Jane, *Making Ireland English* (New Haven, CT, 2012)

Ordnance Survey memoir for parish of Antrim, 1830–40 (PRONI, Belfast, 1969)

Oxford English dictionary, 2nd ed. (Oxford, 1989)

Parkinson, John, *Paradisi in sole paradisus terrestris* (London, 1629)

Payne-Gallwey, Ralph, *The book of duck decoys their construction, management, and history* (London, 1886)

— *The fowler in Ireland* (1882)

Pepys, Samuel, *Diary of Samuel Pepys* (Raleigh, NC, 1983)

Phibbs, John, 'Groves and belts', *Garden History*, 19:2 (1991), pp 175–86

Plot, Robert, *The natural history of Oxfordshire* (Oxford, 1677)

Prim, John G.A., 'Ancient Flemish colony in Kilkenny', *JSRAI*, 1:1 (1849–51), pp 87–40

Quinn, D.B., *The Elizabethans and the Irish* (Ithaca, NY, 1966)

Rackham, Oliver, *The history of the countryside* (London, 1986)

— *Trees and woodland in the British landscape* (London, 1990)

Radice, Betty (ed.), *The letters of the Younger Pliny* (London, 1963)

Rawson, Thomas James, *Statistical survey of the county of Kildare* (1807)

Reinbard Zimmermann, 'Hortus Palatinus of Salomon de Caus' in Monique Mosser and George Teyssat (eds), *The history of garden design: the Western tradition from the Renaissance to the present day* (London, 1990)

Ridgway, Christopher and Robert Williams, *Sir John Vanbrugh and landscape architecture in Baroque England, 1690–1730* (Stroud, Gloucester, 2000)

Ritchie, Robert C., *The duke's province: a study of New York politics and society, 1664–91* (Chapel Hill, NC, 1977)

Robertson, J.G., 'Architectural notes on Kilkenny Castle', *JRSAI*, 2:1 (1852–3), pp 115–19

Rose, J., *The English vineyard vindicated* (London, 1691)

Routledge, Frederick James, (ed.), *Calendar of the Clarendon State Papers, vol. 5, 1660–1726* (Oxford, 1876)

Scannell, M.J.P. and D.M. Synnott, *Census catalogue of the flora of Ireland* (Dublin, 1987)

Scott, Sir Walter, *St Ronan's Well* (London, 1823)

Simpson, A.W. Brian, *Leading cases in the common law* (Oxford, 1995)

Singer, S.W. (ed.), *Correspondence of Henry Hyde, earl of Clarendon* (London, 1828)

Sloan, Hans, *Voyage to Jamaica* (London, 1707)

Smith, Charles, *The ancient and present state of the city of Cork*, Book 2, vol. 1 (1750)

— *The antient and present state of the county Dublin* (Dublin, 1756)

— *The antient and present state of the county of Down* (Dublin, 1754)

— *The antient and present state of the county of Kerry* (Dublin, 1756)

— *The antient and present state of the county of Waterford* (Dublin, 1756)

Smith, Pete, 'The sundial garden and house-plan mount: two gardens at Wollaton Hall, Nottinghamshire, by Robert (*c.*1535–1614) and John (–1634) Smythson', *Garden History*, 31:1 (2003), pp 1–28

Smith, William James, *The Herbert correspondence* (1963)

Southwell, T., 'On some early Dutch and English Decoys', *TNNS*, 7 (1904), pp 160–70

Stokes, George T. (ed.), *Pococke's tour in Ireland in 1752* (Dublin, 1891)

Swift, Jonathan, *A supplement to Dr Swift's works: containing miscellanies in prose and verse, by the Dean; Dr Delany, Dr Sheridan, Mrs Johnson, and others*, vol. 3 (London, 1779)

Switzer, Stephen, *A universal system of water and water-works, philosophical and practical* (London, 1734)

— *An introduction to a general system of hydrostaticks and hydraulics, philosophical and practical* (1729)

— *Ichnographia rustica*, vol. 2 (London, 1718)

— *The nobleman, gentleman and gardener's recreation* (London, 1715)

— *The practical fruit gardener* (London, 1724)

Taverner, John, *Certaine experiments concerning fish and fruite* (London, 1600)

Taylor, Patrick, *Period gardens* (London, 1991)

Temple, William, *Upon the gardens of Epicurus* (London, 1690)

Thacker, Christopher, *The history of gardens* (Oakland, CA, 1985)

The State letters of Henry Hyde, Earl of Clarendon, vol. 1 (London, 1828)

Thomas, Avril, *The walled towns of Ireland*, vol. 1 (Dublin, 1992)

Thomas, James, *Statistical survey of Kildare* (1807)

Thomas, Keith, *Man and the natural world* (Oxford, 1983)

Turner, James, *The politics of landscape: rural scenery and society in English poetry, 1630–1660* (Cambridge, MA, 1979)

Turpin, John, 'Continental influence in eighteenth-century Ireland', *Irish Arts Review*, 4:4 (1987), pp 51–7

Twiss, Richard, *A tour in Ireland in 1775* (London, 1776)

Upcott, William (ed.), *The miscellaneous writings of John Evelyn, Esq. F.R.S.* (London, 1825)

Van der Horst, A.J. and David Jacques, *The gardens of William and Mary* (London, 1988)

Vicars, Arthur, 'Old Bawn, County Dublin', *JCKAS*, 5 (1906–8), pp 229–37

Virgil, *Georgics* (Oxford, 1990)

von Hohberg, W.H., *Georgica Curiosa* (Nürnburg, 1682)

Walker, Joseph Cooper, 'Essay on the rise and progress of gardening in Ireland', *TRIA*, 4 (1790), pp 3–19

Walton, Izaak, *The compleat angler, or, the contemplative man's recreation* (London, 1868)

Wentworth-Day, J., *A history of the fens* (London, 1954)

Wilkinson, Neville R., 'Mount Merrion, the old', *Irish Times*, 11 Sept. 1925

Williamson, Tom, *Polite landscapes* (Stroud, Gloustershire, 1995)
— *Suffolk's gardens and parks* (East Anglia, 2000)
Willughby, F., *The ornithology of Francis Willughby of Middleton in the county of Warwick, esquire* (London, 1678)
Wilson, William, *The post chaise companion, or, traveller's directory through Ireland* (Dublin, 1815)
Wood, Anthony, *Athenae oxonienses* (London, 1820)
Woodcock, George (ed.), *William Cobbett's rural rides* (London, 1967)
Worlidge, John, *Systema agriculturae, the mystery of husbandry discovered* (London, 1668)
— *Systema horticulturae, or the art of gardening* (London, 1677)
— *Vinetum Britannicum* (London, 1691)
Wotton, William, *Reflections upon ancient and modern learning* (London, 1697)
Wright, G.N., *An historical guide to ancient and modern Dublin* (Dublin, 1821)
Young, Arthur, *A tour in Ireland; with general observations on the present state of that kingdom, made in the years 1776, 1777, and 1778 and brought down to the end of 1779* (Dublin, 1780)

STATUTES

An Act for encouraging importation of iron and staves, timber for casks etc., 1703 Anne c. 2
An Act for planting and preserving timber-trees and woods, 1705 4 Anne c.9
An Act for preserving timber trees and woods, 1698 10 William III, c.12
An Act for the advancement of the trade of linnen manufacture, 1665 Chas. II 17and18 c. 9
An Act for the preservation of the game and the more easy conviction of such as shall destroy the same, 1698, 10 William c. 13
An Act to prevent diverse misdemeanours in idle and lewd persons in barking of trees etc., 1634 10 Chas. I sess. 2, c. 23
An Act to refrain the carrying of hawkes out of this kingdom, 1480 20 Ed. 4

Index